CORE TRANSFORMATION

Reaching the Wellspring Within

CONNIRAE ANDREAS
With
TAMARA ANDREAS

Real People Press

To our parents,
Lois Jean and William Andreas

Library of Congress Cataloging-in-Publication Data

Andreas, Connirae.
Core transformation : reaching the wellspring within / Connirae Andreas with Tamara Andreas.
p. cm.
Includes bibilographical references and index.
ISBN 0-911226-32-X ; $21.50
1. Behavior modification. 2. Behavior modification—Case studies.
3. Change (Psychology) 4. Self-actualization (Psychology)
5. Neurolinguistic programming. 6. Andreas, Connirae. 7. Andreas, Tamara. 1961- . I. Andreas, Tamara, 1961- . II. Title.
BF637.B4A54 1994
158'.1—dc20 93-41068
CIP

—About the Core Transformation Process—

This book gives therapeutic technique a new breakthrough. It provides deep and meaningful transformations in the lives of all who seek the CORE of living. Congratulations for an admirable achievement.

—Chungliang Al Huang, President and Founder, The Living Tao Foundation, author, Embrace Tiger, Return to Mountain

Connirae and Tamara Andreas have written a breakthrough book in the field of personal evolution. I highly recommend it to all those who want greater wholeness and fulfillment in their lives. This incredible depth of change is what we need as we move into the 21st century.

—Susan M. Lark, M.D., author, The PMS Self-Help Book

This book will help you make changes that lead directly to increased personal effectiveness. I recommend Core Transformation to anyone in business who wants to improve results.

—Dan Thomas, Ph.D., former Professor, Harvard and Stanford Business Schools, author, Business Sense

We come into the world knowing who we really are. Through life experience, things get distorted, and we forget who we really are. These processes are a way to clear away the blocks to rediscover our true identity

—Toni Blackman, NLP Master Practitioner

I want to thank you—the Core Transformation Process has been just wonderful for me. I had been identifying with my job, and this has helped me let go of that. This process has been more meaningful to my clients in the long term than any other process I've used. With other processes, people comment I've changed, but with this one people say, "This is who I truly am."

—Reverend Cherie Newland

The biggest difference as I drove away from the training was that all of me was going in the same direction. Since then some circumstances have really been challenging, and I have found that I can always come back to my heart and find out who I am. It's very powerful. My values of love and honesty are more dominant than the circumstances I am in.

—Allison Helstrup, Corporate Teambuilding, Training Development Consultant

—Acknowledgements—

I would like to thank the many people who have assisted us in bringing this book into being. My sister and co-author Tamara Andreas first proposed writing this book several years before publication. Her talent, inspiration and dedication to producing the book made it possible. Tamara wrote the first draft during a time when I was already overly busy and had given up the idea of writing a book to make this important material readily accessible. I am thankful to have had her personal sensitivity, her conceptual understanding of the Core Transformation Process, and the depth of her experience with client work and teaching the process.

Next, thanks goes to Virginia Hopkins who played a major role in everything from editing to publishing. Tamara and I were grateful to have someone who so immediately understood the heart and soul of the book, and was so skilled at assisting us in making the material accessible. Because she fell in love with the process, her devotion to making it available became at least as great as Tamara's and my own.

A big thanks to my husband, Steve Andreas, whose editing skills and ideas about organization and sequence significantly enhanced the finished product.

Thanks to the many readers who gave us detailed input, and to the office staff at NLP Comprehensive in Boulder, Colorado for many kinds of organizational support. Thanks to all the participants who have attended Aligned Self seminars, and particularly to the clients and participants who offered to share their experiences in this book. We realize how much these experiences enrich the book. Special thanks to those who have been using this process with their clients: John Parmater, Colleen McGovern, Gerry Schmidt, Mark Hochwender, Christina Boyd, Jan Prince, Jessie Milan, and Larry Iverson each contributed experiences with their clients to the personal reports we share in this book.

I thank also my many teachers over the years, including Richard Bandler, John Grinder, Leslie Lebeau, Robert Dilts, David Gordon and Judith Delozier. Their work in developing the field of NLP was the foundation upon which I developed the Core Transformation Process. I would like to especially acknowledge Leslie Lebeau, whose work has in some ways paralleled my own.

I thank my friends and colleagues Mark Hochwender, Laing Reynolds, and Richard Schaub for helping me deepen my understanding of the spiritual, as I found myself in what was for me uncharted territory.

Thanks to you the reader, for making this book worth writing.

—CONTENTS—

SECTION III
GROWING UP A PART &
BRINGING IT FULLY INTO YOUR BODY
Making Core States More Accessible

SECTION IV
COMPLETING THE PROCESS WITH ALL PARTS
Working With Every Aspect of An Issue

SECTION V
THE COMPLETE CORE TRANSFORMATION EXERCISE
Doing It From A to Z

SECTION VI
PARENTAL TIMELINE REIMPRINTING
Bringing Core States to Your Past, Present and Future

SECTION VII
ENHANCING YOUR RESULTS
Making A Good Thing Even Better

—INTRODUCTION—

Finding the Way to the Wellspring Within

The wind blows over the lake and stirs the surface of the water. The visible effects of the invisible manifest themselves.
—Inner Truth, The I Ching

In this book you will be invited to identify the behaviors, feelings and responses you like least in yourself, and use them to take yourself on a remarkably healing and uplifting personal journey within, to the depths of your beingness. This journey is called the Core Transformation Process.

Developing the Core Transformation Process came about naturally, as I was doing what I love to do best, which is exploring how people experience the world, right down to their words, gestures and facial expressions. Over the 20 years that I have been working and learning in the area of personal growth and change, I have used and developed many techniques and exercises that effectively assist people in changing unwanted behaviors, healing emotions and reaching goals. I've shared these techniques in a series of books, some co-authored or edited with my husband, Steve Andreas. The audience for these books was primarily professional—therapists, counselors, educators, and others in helping professions. This book is different. It is accessible to *anyone* who wants core transformation in their life.

The material presented in this book is a breakthrough for me both personally and professionally, and I believe it is a breakthrough in the field of personal growth, therapy, and psychology. As I explored and developed the Core Transformation Process with clients and with myself, I began to have a sense of awe and reverence for what I witnessed. Powerfully transforming states of consciousness, which I call Core States, were naturally emerging. These states seemed to be identical to the states of consciousness many people strive for in spiritual traditions, described as transcendent or spiritual experiences. Through doing the Core Transformation Process these states became more than a temporary high—they became the basis for living from a new "center."

The way these experiences emerged was surprising and unexpected. I had no intention of developing a process with spiritual overtones. I basically considered that realm of experience beyond my ability to know about, and therefore I wasn't very interested. My goal was to develop a process that went deep enough to the core of our experience to be effective with everything from the seemingly trivial to our biggest life issues. I wanted something that went deeper than what I had known before—both for myself and for my clients.

In this search I gave myself the challenge of working with people who had some major limitation they had been unsuccessfully trying to change. These were people who had struggled for years to change, without results. The issues they dealt with ranged from chronic pain and abuse to bulimia, rage, sexual dysfunction, and codependency. Some weren't so easily put into categories, like the man who felt he always held himself back from living his full potential. He already did well by most standards, but had an inner part that felt stupid and lacked the confidence to go forward in the way he wanted.

I intuitively followed a direction you'll become intimately familiar with as you read this book. The starting point was the person's limitation, and then, by going deeper and deeper into the limitation with a process that is both simple and indescribably kind, I noticed a level of experience emerging naturally, on its own, that was beyond what I had ever known before.

In seeking to find what would transform these major life issues I stumbled upon a process that went far beyond my original goals. Most of the people I took through it got the results they wanted in their lives—either complete changes or significant movement in the direction they desired. But beyond that, they wrote me cards and letters telling me things like, "It's a miracle," or, "Everything has changed." One person who didn't get what he asked for said, "I got something better; something wonderful is happening that's hard to put into words."

Discovering these incredibly powerful Core States at the center of every inner part in myself and others has certainly transformed my sense of the spiritual nature within each of us. This spiritual nature is not a belief system, it is an experience, and I want to acknowledge that you may prefer to describe your experience in other terms. You do not need to have spiritual beliefs to benefit from the Core Transformation Process. When we do this process with individual clients, or in workshops, we often do not talk about what kind of experience to expect. You will get equally strong results whether you describe your experience as spiritual, or in other terms that fit more for you.

As I was developing the Core Transformation Process I was lucky enough to have my sister, Tamara Andreas, join me in learning the process and teaching others how to do it. Her experiences both with herself, her clients, and in the Aligned Self seminars she facilitates, have added immensely to our knowledge and experience of the process, and to the content of this book.

I came to the field of personal growth work through Neuro-Linguistic Programming (NLP), a brilliant and powerful model for communication, personal growth and achievement of our potential as humans, developed in the early 70s by linguistics professor John Grinder and computer programmer Richard Bandler. Core Transformation has its roots in several NLP approaches and techniques created by Bandler, Grinder and others over the years. I am deeply grateful for my good fortune in being able to build on the work of so many good teachers, and feel that the field of NLP has greatly facilitated my ability to go deep enough to develop the Core Transformation Process.

NLP has been criticized in the past for being overly "mental," and "manipulative," which can be true if that is how people choose to use it. The Core Transformation Process takes us past the mind, past any sense of manipulation, into universally sought-after states of consciousness that evoke a sense of oneness and peace.

There are many personal stories in this book from those who have used this process, as well as interviews and actual transcripts of myself or Tamara doing the process with a seminar participant or client, which we call "demonstrations." All the accounts of personal change are presented as told to us. Although names are changed and some factual details are changed or omitted to preserve confidentiality, we were always careful to preserve the meaning. Many people were so excited about their changes that they gave us much lengthier accounts than we were able to include. The demonstrations were edited to make them easier to understand and use in written form. Complete, unedited demonstrations are available on audiotape and videotape.

You may notice as you read the demonstrations that we use unique language patterns, and have very specific ways of wording things. In these demonstrations we indicate a pause with three periods (...). This indicates that we are allowing time for the person we are working with to process information and integrate changes unconsciously. These pauses usually last a few seconds, but can last as long as a few minutes. We are guided in knowing when to go on by watching facial expressions and color, breathing patterns, gestures, and by being deeply "tuned in" to the client's state.

Knowing these verbal and nonverbal subtleties is part of the art of what we do to facilitate others in this process, but is *not* necessary to get profound benefits from the Core Transformation Process. We have had hundreds of people do the process on their own, through our tapes and videos, and report back that they got the results they wanted. However, to get the best results when you do the exercises yourself, it is important that you use the specific language we give you in the exercises, and follow the directions carefully. When you have done the Core Transformation Process many times, you will find you have intuitively created your own pace and patterns.

If you would like to find out more about these language patterns, and how and why we use them, check the resource section in the back of the book. We have a wide variety of other books, audio and video tapes, and we regularly offer seminars, workshops and trainings around the world.

As you do these exercises, be gentle and patient with yourself. Most of us have spent years developing our unwanted behaviors, feelings and responses, for very good reasons, and we want to respect that. Welcome the parts of yourself that you want to change—they are about to become your strongest and most helpful allies.

Connirae Andreas

—SECTION I—

MAPPING OUT THE TERRITORY

Keys to Core Transformation

—CHAPTER 1—

THE JOURNEY BEGINS

How Do We Get There From Here?

Don't say such changes cannot happen. A vast freedom could live inside you. A loaf of bread wrapped in a cloth for the table is just an object, but inside the human body, it becomes a gladness for being alive!
—Rumi

If you want to get somewhere, a good map can make the difference between arriving at your destination with ease and getting hopelessly lost. Let's say a friend raves about a restaurant with wonderful food, friendly people and reasonable prices, and you decide to go eat there. You ask your friend where the restaurant is.

Your friend says, "Just visualize the restaurant clearly. Post a sign on your refrigerator door that says, 'I can easily and joyfully find any restaurant I want!' That's all you need to do."

This idea may seem silly but what if my destination is "self-acceptance?" What if I want to reach a state of inner wholeness that I have never experienced before? Like the restaurant in the above example, I have heard wonderful things about it but haven't been there and don't know how to get there. Many of us have been told, "Just do it. Just accept yourself." This is a little like being told to "Just go to the restaurant," without being given any directions.

Or what if you ask how to get to the restaurant and your friend says, "Before you can find this restaurant you need to spend several months, or even years, thinking about how bad your own cooking is. You need to explore the reasons why you aren't happy with your own cooking and why you have this need to go to the restaurant. You also have to really understand how you became such a bad cook." This seems even sillier than the previous example. All you need is directions to the restaurant!

In a similar vein, many self-help approaches have asked us to spend years striving to thoroughly understand our problems. A common belief is that if we only understand the problem well enough, it will simply disappear. Yet, all too often, we understand a problem and still have it. The goal of Core Transformation is not to understand our problems, it is to go to the place within where our problems will transform. This is a "how-to" book that gives you the "how," in accessible, easy-to-use steps.

Core Transformation is not about affirmations or positive thinking. Many of us have tried to overcome our limitations by sheer will-power—simply *trying* to feel or act differently, or telling ourselves over and over that we *will* be different. That is approaching ourselves from the outside in—it's trying to change on the surface without dealing with the core of the problem. That's like taking an aspirin when we have a broken bone. We may feel better for awhile, but unless we do something to help the bone heal properly, the good feeling isn't going to last.

In contrast, the Core Transformation Process works from the inside out. It is a series of simple, step-by-step exercises that allow us to change unwanted behaviors, feelings and responses easily and rapidly, and to have an ongoing sense of well-being that occurs naturally when we experience Core Transformation.

Discovering the Wellspring

Wouldn't it be nice to have an underlying sense of wholeness and well-being whether or not things are going well in our lives in the moment? Most of us feel good when our lives are going well. Is it possible to feel resourceful even when things seem to be falling apart? Yes. We know it is possible because we have had the experience, and hundreds of our clients and workshop participants have reported back to us that they're having more and more of these experiences. This book is about developing and maintaining an inner sense of self, well-being, wholeness, and perhaps even a connection with something beyond ourselves, that sustains us in difficulty as well as in times of ease. This inner sense of fullness and integrity, and a strong, resourceful self is available to each of us, and is our own wellspring within.

We all have times when we are sad, or frustrated, or angry, or irritable—that's part of being human. But in those down times we can still have an underlying sense of well-being about ourselves. We can have an inner knowing that we have the resources to weather the storms, and an underlying sense of optimism that we will come out on the other side of our difficulties not only intact, but wiser and stronger.

All of us have personal limitations we have struggled to overcome.

With some of them it can seem that no matter what we do, they won't go away. Most of us turn away from those parts of ourselves that we don't like. We try to shove aside feelings we don't want to have. We try to "think positively" and push away negative thoughts. These approaches don't tend to create natural, lasting change. The way to our inner wellspring is *through* our limitations.

The Core Transformation Process can be used to change self-defeating behaviors, feelings or responses that have been major life problems. Many of the stories in this book tell of people changing problems they had struggled with for years. The process helps us to automatically use our limitations as the way to unveiling or releasing a deep sense of self. We resolve our limitations at the same time we experience a new sense of self that is powerfully expanding and transforming. The additional good news is that the process itself is, for nearly everyone, a profoundly pleasant experience. Although this process allows many people to quickly achieve lasting change, those who benefit most use it in an ongoing way that deepens as they continue to use the techniques.

The kinds of changes you will be making as you read this book and do the exercises will be a gentle unfolding from within. You won't be giving yourself another set of "shoulds" for how the "enlightened" person behaves. You won't be learning to think *about* yourself positively, you will be living more and more from that core nature that is truly you. You will be uncovering the wisdom and truth that is already there. As you do the process several times you will gain a trust that when you go to your core, you will discover a nature that is beyond what we usually think of as positive.

The renowned T'ai Chi teacher Al Huang talks of uncovering this nature as the goal of T'ai Chi:

> There are many basic concepts in tao that emerge in t'ai chi when you practice. One is the word "pu," which means the original material, before it's trimmed and modified, fixed and polished. Sometimes we translate this as "uncarved block." It's the raw material before it is carved into an artistic form, the essence that exists before you change it. Learn the grain of the wood before you begin to carve it. Pu is the basic substance of the real you, before it's manicured or painted over. Expose your own basic essence before you clutter it up. Don't let all the external things blind you so that you lose the uncarved block within. Every time we begin, we must find that uncarved original wood, that basic sense of what the human body is, that sense of being all together. We usually keep telling ourselves what we are, instead of just letting the pu emerge.

What Is The Core Self?

In this book we offer methods for achieving a fuller sense of what we call the Core Self, a universally-known concept that goes by many names: our inner essence, our full potential, self-actualization, our True Self, our Higher Self, the God within, and the Soul, to name a few.

I am functioning from my Core Self when:

- √ I experience wholeness, inner-peace, well-being, love, and aliveness.
- √ I am fully grounded and centered within my body.
- √ I am fully aware of my body and my emotions.
- √ I perceive the world clearly.
- √ I know what I want.
- √ I am behaving in alignment with my values.
- √ I am easily acting in my own best interest, while also respecting others.
- √ I have a positive sense of myself.
- √ I am aware of who I am, not just what I do, how I feel, or what I have.
- √ I am resourceful. I have a sense of choice about how I feel and what I do.

These descriptions of the Core Self fit for most people, and because each of us is unique, we may each have a different way of describing our experience. If you read these descriptions and say, "That all sounds good, but I'm not sure I know exactly what is meant by those words," that's OK. Using the processes in this book can lead you to an *experience* of Core Transformation that puts you touch with your Core Self.

A Map Of This Book

This book is a carefully guided journey to your own wellspring within. In Section I we lay the groundwork for you to gain the most from your inner journey. We make sure you are prepared with a few basic understandings and experiences that will allow your journey to be enjoyable and fulfilling. These basics will make it easier for you to follow the map we provide later in the book for reaching your destination within.

In Section II you will experience the Core State Exercise, the heart of the Core Transformation Process. This process will assist you in discovering

RESULTS OF THE CORE TRANSFORMATION PROCESS

Most people significantly move toward one or more of the following results each time they do the Core Transformation Process. As you read through this list, identify those results that you most want in your life. Because this process releases your Core Self, it tends to impact all areas of your life positively. When your own core inner wisdom is uncovered, you spontaneously discover you have new choices in many areas.

Emotions

√ The ability to have access to a full range of emotions.

√ An experience of greater emotional fluidity, rather than being frequently stuck in an emotion.

√ Resolution of specific emotions that are overwhelming or limiting.

√ The sense that your emotions are appropriate to present circumstances, rather than being an expression of unresolved issues from the past.

√ Having emotions that serve you and support what you do.

√ Enjoying a fundamental sense of well-being and peace.

Habits and Other Behaviors

√ Having a choice about behaviors that were addictive or habitual.

√ Having a greater ease in changing behaviors.

√ Having behaviors that are in alignment with your values.

Relationships

√ Being affirming of yourself and others without needing to compete.

√ Being able to freely express your own needs and wants and pursue them, and take into account the needs and wants of others.

√ Being comfortable around people.

√ Being able to take care of your relationships without feeling as if you depend on a relationship for your sense of well-being.

√ Being able to accept others as they are.

√ Being able to trust people appropriately, while being aware of their limitations.

√ Being able to take responsibility for making choices in the areas you have choice about, while being at peace with areas that are out of your control.

√ Being OK whether attention is on you or on others.
√ Being able to seek the truth, rather than having to be "right."
√ Being able to forgive yourself and others for mistakes and limitations, while learning from them.
√ Being OK regardless of whether others think well of you.
√ Being more honest with yourself and others.
√ Experiencing more kindness and compassion toward others.

Self-Image and Self Development

√ Experiencing more kindness and compassion toward yourself.
√ Becoming more and more the person you want to be.
√ Self-appreciation.
√ Enough security to be open to feedback.
√ Sense of equality with others.
√ High self-esteem.
√ Sense of identity.
√ Personal integrity.
√ More wholeness and balance.

Other Categories

People have resolved or made significant progress with the following difficulties using the Core Transformation Process.

√ Healing of Abuse and/or Trauma.
√ Anorexia and Bulimia.
√ Alcoholism.
√ Drug Addiction.
√ Co-dependence.
√ Depression.
√ Fears and Anxieties.
√ Post-Traumatic Stress Syndrome.
√ Hyperactivity and Learning Disabilities.
√ Multiple Personality Disorder.
√ Schizophrenia.
√ Health Concerns.
√ Resolution of specific issues and conflicts.

your own inner gifts, which will emerge out of what you thought were your worst flaws.

Sections II, III, IV and V teach you how to do the Core Transformation Process from beginning to end. We've made it easy for you by offering it in meaningful "portions" that are easy to digest. Each of the sections that have an exercise for you to do follow the same sequence, designed to make your learning comfortable and natural. The chapters in these sections are in this sequence:

- A transcript of Connirae or Tamara demonstrating the process.
- An "Understanding the Structure" chapter where you will learn the purpose of each new phase of the demonstration you just read.
- A "Doing It!" chapter or section with a "script" of easy step-by-step instructions for doing the process yourself.

Each section also includes at least one brief personal story of how someone else used this process, and the impact it had on their life. We include these to inspire you and to expand your intuitive sense of how to use the process in ways that assist you.

Section VI, Parental Timeline Reimprinting, is particularly important because it can help us forgive and love parents and others in our past, and move on to a brighter future. This part of the process deepens and enriches our experience of our Core Self, infusing the benefits of the Core Transformation Process into our family background. Once we do this, the events we experienced growing up—no matter how mundane or bizarre, tragic or serene—now support our experience of Core Transformation. People often have a sense of resolving their past after doing Parental Timeline Reimprinting.

Section VII helps us enhance the process and carry it further into our day-to-day lives. We include chapters on working with health concerns, discovering and working with basic limiting personality patterns, a variety of interviews with people who have sucessfully used the process, and how this process taps into spiritual experience.

While it may be tempting to turn right to the Core Transformation exercises, we encourage you to read the personal stories and exercises that come before it, and give yourself the benefit of creating a good inner map for your process of inner change.

—CHAPTER 2—

BEFRIENDING THE UNCONSCIOUS

Why Understanding Rarely Leads to Change

The great decisions of human life have as a rule far more to do with the instincts and other mysterious unconscious factors than with conscious will and well-meaning reasonableness.
—C.G. Jung

The unconscious speaks to us through dreams. Fairy tales stimulate us on unconscious levels. We make "Freudian slips," which come from our unconscious. What is our unconscious? For our purposes in this book, the unconscious is simply everything that is typically out of our awareness.

Making Unconscious Decisions

How often have you heard people describe their problems with great clarity and intellectual understanding, and yet you notice that they still have the problems? Have you ever made a conscious decision that you were going to change a behavior, feeling or response, only to find yourself doing it again? That's because in most cases our conscious mind alone is practically helpless to permanently change behaviors, feelings and responses that are automatic and unconscious. If we had decided to do those unwanted behaviors, feelings and responses consciously, it might be easy to change them consciously, by just re-deciding. Instead, those decisions usually happen on a more automatic level. It is as if there is an unconscious part of us that is in charge of doing those things. Because the conscious, thinking part of our mind does not run the behavior, feeling or response we don't want, the first step in changing that behavior is learning to access the part of ourselves that *does* run it. Then we learn how these parts can become inner friends.

What the Unconscious Does

Your conscious mind is good at focusing attention on a few things at once. Research indicates that we can be consciously aware of between five and nine pieces of information at one time. More than this overloads our conscious mind.

However, there is a vast amount of information that is continually streaming in through your five senses that you are not consciously aware of. For example, before you read the rest of this sentence, you were probably unaware of the weight of your body on the chair or whatever you are resting on. You were probably unaware of your breathing. You may have been unaware of objects you can see in the periphery of your vision. You may have been unaware of certain sounds around you. Your unconscious continues to notice and process this vast stream of information for you, while you are consciously attending to whatever you need to focus on.

Your unconscious keeps track of memories and plans when you aren't thinking about them consciously. For example, when you want to, you can easily think back to something that you did or someone you were with yesterday. You can think ahead to something you are planning to do tomorrow or next week. When you aren't thinking about those things, your unconscious stores them.

Your unconscious is also in charge of bodily processes that you consider automatic. If you want, you can consciously think about your breathing, and control how fast you breathe. If you forget about it for a minute, or for a year, you will continue to breathe unconsciously. Other processes, like digestion, heartbeat and even when your cells divide, are directed by unconscious processes—people do not have direct conscious control over those functions.

Your unconscious also processes information and makes decisions outside of your awareness. When we are asleep we normally spend some of the time dreaming. We don't consciously decide what we are going to dream about or exactly how the dream will unfold. Those decisions occur at an unconscious level.

Your unconscious is also in charge of a wide variety of behaviors, feelings and responses that were once learned consciously, but have become so well learned that they are now automatic and unconscious. When a child begins to learn to speak, thinking of which word to use requires full attention. The child takes great delight in saying the word that gets mom or dad to give them the thing they want. Once we have learned a language well we only need to think of what we want to say, and the right words almost always come out. We don't consciously choose exactly what words to use, or in what order to say them. That has all been learned so well that it happens automatically for us.

Another example is driving. Have you ever been lost in thought while driving and suddenly found yourself at your destination? At one time you focused a lot of conscious attention on learning to drive. Then you consciously focused attention on getting to that particular destination. Yet when I take my children to school I no longer think about where to turn, and reliably, in ten minutes, I am in the school parking lot. This is an example of how we learn things by first focusing our conscious attention on them. Once learned we can do these behaviors without thinking. They happen unconsciously.

Most behaviors that are run unconsciously are desirable and appropriate. Our unconscious takes care of many things for us that would be overwhelming to do consciously. Can you imagine how complicated it would be to walk if we had to consciously decide exactly which muscles to use, and to coordinate when each of them tightened and when they relaxed?

However, some unconscious behaviors are self-defeating or unuseful. Have you ever gotten off an elevator automatically only to discover that you were on the wrong floor? Have you ever just "found yourself" in the refrigerator when you had decided to eat less? Have you ever caught yourself biting your nails or cracking your knuckles, or doing some other behavior you consciously didn't want to do?

These and many other behaviors, feelings and responses we don't like are the ones we will be learning how to change. It is important to realize that even self-defeating behaviors that we don't like now were useful in some way when we first learned them. At an earlier time they were the best choice that some part of us had to try to achieve some useful purpose. For example, when Sam was very young he frequently heard his parents screaming at each other in anger. This scared him, and he unconsciously concluded at that time that emotions are dangerous, and decided to shut off his own emotions. That decision was now out of his awareness, or unconscious. Because it was stored unconsciously, Sam continued to experience the results of the decision: he had very limited access to his own emotions. Consciously deciding that he wanted to experience more emotions was not enough—he needed to use processes that helped him change that unconscious decision.

Becoming More Aware of Unconscious Parts

Often, people talk as if a "part" of them is running a behavior:
"A part of me makes me eat chocolate."
"A part of me gets angry at my boss."
"I knew I'd be tired the next day, but part of me wanted to stay out late."
"I really intended to stay on that diet, but a part of me just couldn't resist the dessert."

When people make these kinds of statements they are telling us they really didn't have conscious control over their behavior. It is as if some unconscious part of them has decided that the best thing to do is eat chocolate and goes ahead and eats no matter what they may consciously think they want. We find this a useful way to describe behaviors we would rather not do, emotions we would rather not feel, and negative thoughts we would rather not be thinking. When we think negative thoughts or experience emotions such as anger, envy, frustration, or guilt, we often feel as if we have no choice—it is as if some part of us *made* us have them.

When we have "mixed feelings," part of us feels one way and part of us feels another. On one hand we want to complete a project at home, but on the other hand we would rather go to a movie. We feel like shouting at the children, but we want to be loving and patient. Part of us feels intimidated when the rest of us wants to be resourceful and confident. When we say "a part of us" feels intimidated, this is a way of saying that some of our thinking and behavior is organized around feeling intimidated, while the rest of us is devoted to something else. The rest of us is probably trying hard to be calm and resourceful instead.

Although each behavior, feeling or response outside of our conscious control is generated by an unconscious part of us, it is not that we literally have separate parts running around inside. However, it's very useful to think about ourselves in terms of parts. As we go along you will learn how this idea of parts helps us come to new choices, wholeness, and resolution through the Core Transformation Process. If you prefer to use another word than "part," that's fine. Some people prefer to think about this as an "aspect" of themselves.

Recognizing and working with these parts makes it possible for us to come to wholeness. If we just try to shove aside these experiences, and "think positively" or overcome an unwanted behavior with will power, we are fighting ourselves. And when we fight ourselves, some part of us always loses.

The exercises in this book create a natural fluidity between the conscious and the unconscious. By doing them you will develop your own ability to notice when an inner part is stopping you from moving forward in your life in the way that you want to. You will be learning to work with the unconscious parts that have held you back, in a way that transforms your inner parts into inner allies in the deepest sense.

Positive Purposes

An important assumption we make in the Core Transformation Process is that every one of our behaviors, feelings or responses has a positive purpose. Even those things we like least about ourselves have some positive purpose.

Tim was having difficulty in his marriage. While he was a very successful businessman, his marriage was falling apart. His wife was about to leave him because he constantly criticized her. It turned out that Tim was constantly criticizing himself at least as harshly as his wife. We discovered that Tim had an inner voice that offered ongoing critical comments about anything or anyone within reach! It turned out that Tim's inner voice really wanted his life to improve. It wanted him to be happier and more fulfilled. Criticizing was the best way this part knew to try to make that happen for him. Tim was pleased to learn that this critical and judgmental part of himself actually wanted something positive for him. His whole attitude toward this part changed when he realized that this part wasn't something to try to get rid of, but something to work with as an ally.

Wanda was a young woman who wanted to stop smoking. She discovered that the part that made her smoke really wanted her to have a way to be a part of the group and have friends. She had started smoking as a teenager when "everyone else" was doing it and it was "cool." While she didn't want to smoke any longer, she did want to have ways to have friends and be part of a group. Fortunately, the part of Wanda that "made" her smoke didn't really care about the smoking. What this part really cared about was having a way to have friends.

Ben was uncomfortable with his flare-ups of anger. In groups, whenever someone didn't agree with his ideas, he became enraged and had to struggle not to shout them down. Ben discovered that the part of him that got angry really wanted to protect his sense of self. Getting angry was the only way this part knew to do it. Finding a fully satisfying solution meant assisting this part in preserving his sense of self in another, more fulfilling way.

Jonathan was troubled by bad feelings over having been fired from his job three years earlier. He had worked at the same job for 25 years and being fired caused considerable need for a readjustment in his life. The part of Jonathan that continued feeling bad had an important positive purpose for him. One reason he had lost his job was that he had lied about something. This part wanted Jonathan to remember how important it is to tell the truth. Feeling bad was the only way this part knew to keep reminding Jonathan. A resolution that honored his whole being meant doing more than just dismissing his bad feelings and moving on. He needed another way of knowing how important it is to tell the truth.

Sometimes There Are Many Parts

Sometimes people talk as if they have a number of parts involved in a decision. People have many different goals, or purposes. For example, I (Tamara) have goals of learning, having meaningful relationships, having a career, being comfortable, and doing interesting things. It's as if there is a part of me that cares about each of those goals. If I take care of my goal of having a career, but ignore my goal of having meaningful relationships, eventually the part of me that cares about having meaningful relationships will become dissatisfied. It's as though I am neglecting a part of myself. If I neglect that part of me long enough I might end up feeling depressed, or even doing things that sabotage my career.

If I take care of my goal of being comfortable, but ignore my goal of doing interesting things, eventually the part of me that cares about doing interesting things will become dissatisfied. If I organize my life in such a way that some, but not all, of my goals are taken care of, the parts of me that are not satisfied will interfere.

Allies instead of Enemies

Finding the positive purpose of each part is the *opposite* of what most of us usually do. We usually fight our unwanted habits and tendencies. Many approaches to self-help have encouraged us to do this even more—to use self control, or will-power to overcome our personal weaknesses. At a meeting I attended recently the speaker said he believes we all have an "enemy within," and that we need to overcome this "enemy." From my experience, I know that whenever I use that approach it doesn't work. That's because I am struggling against myself. If I am fighting myself, who loses? I do! Even if I do manage to defeat this so-called "enemy within," then I will be left with a "loser within!" *All parts of us win* when we do the Core Transformation Process. We discover the deepest positive purposes our parts have for us, and transform parts that trouble us into inner allies.

—CHAPTER 3—

FINDING POSITIVE PURPOSES

Learning to Communicate with Our Inner Allies

Your living pieces will form a harmony.
—Rumi

The benefits of doing the Core Transformation Process extend farther than just changing an unwanted behavior, feeling or response. We also have the opportunity to come to a greater wholeness within, where our thoughts, feelings and actions are in harmony and naturally support each other.

Most of us judge the unconscious parts of ourselves that are directing our unwanted behaviors, feelings and responses as "problems." When we are judgmental with ourselves we create a poor relationship with the parts that run the behaviors we don't like, creating an inner disharmony. For instance, when a part of me makes me stay awake at night, I tend to get angry at that part of myself. I may struggle against this part of myself.

The first step toward communicating with parts is learning to appreciate them for the positive outcomes they want for us. When I realize that the part of myself that keeps me awake wants something positive for me, I am more appreciative and peaceful with myself. This is the first step in befriending that part of myself. This part may want me to resolve something that remains unfinished in my day. It may have a concern for one of my children and want me to find a way to help.

The following exercise will give you the opportunity to discover the positive intention within one of your behaviors, feelings or responses.

....

Positive Purpose Exploration

1. **Choose A Part to Work With:** Think of a behavior, feeling or response that you have and don't like. You can pick an emotion you think is too extreme, or somehow "off-balance." If you have an inner voice that criticizes you, you can pick that. For this exercise, pick an issue that is mild to moderate in intensity for you. You will have the opportunity to work with issues of greater intensity after you have learned the complete Core Transformation Process.

   One way to pick an issue is to fill in the blank of one of the following sentences—whichever one is most appropriate for your difficulty. Write down your sentence.

   a. "A part of me makes me (do) _____, and I'd like to stop."

   b. "A part of me makes me (feel) _____, and I'd like to stop."

   c. "A part of me (thinks) _____, and I'd like to stop."

2. **Where, When, Who:** Write down where, when, and with whom this part of you generally comes up. For example: "A part of me makes me feel self-conscious. This happens when I am talking to a large group."

3. **Specific Incident:** Think of a specific time when this occurred. For example: "This happened last Wednesday, when I spoke to the club." Make an internal movie of yourself doing or feeling the unwanted behavior, feeling or response. Some people would rather draw a simple picture of the specific incident.

   (The following steps may be easier if you have someone read the instructions aloud. You may need to give them feedback about how fast or slow to read, and how long to pause to allow you to respond inwardly. It is generally easier to turn your attention within when the person reading the instructions talks with a soft, slow voice. If you are going to do the exercise by yourself, we recommend you read it through first and then go back and do it, moving back and forth between reading the instructions and processing. Another option is to read the instructions into a tape recorder and play them back for yourself.)

4. **Relax and Turn Within:** Take a moment to close your eyes, relax and turn within.

5. **Relive the Incident:** Mentally step into the specific incident in which this behavior, feeling or response occurred. See through your own eyes, hear through your own ears, and feel your feelings.

6. **Notice Beginning of Response:** Notice what your internal experience is as that behavior, feeling or response begins to occur. Notice the internal pictures, sounds, and feelings that go along with that unwanted behavior, feeling or response.

7. **Locate and Welcome the Part:** Since you did not consciously choose this behavior, feeling or response, it's as if a part of you did. You can begin to sense where that part of you "lives." Do you feel the feelings most strongly in a certain part of your body? If you hear an inner voice, *where* is the voice located? If you see inner pictures, *where* in your personal space do you see them? Gently invite the part into your awareness. If the part is in your body, you may want to put your hand on the area where you sense the part most strongly. This can help you welcome and acknowledge the part.

8. **Thank the Part:** Even though you do not yet know, consciously, what this part of you wants for you, you can assume that it has some positive purpose. Begin thanking this part of you for being there, doing its best to accomplish something on your behalf. Shower this part with appreciation.

9. **Ask for Purpose:** Ask the part, "What do you want for me by [Xing]?" (Fill in the unwanted behavior, feeling or response you wrote down earlier). After you ask this question inside, simply wait for a response. You may become aware of a picture, a sound, a voice, a feeling, or any combination of these. Sometimes it takes the part a little while to find its positive purpose—that's OK—this is a new experience for the part, so give it some time if it needs it.

10. **Thanks for Response:** When you get a response, thank that part of you for responding. If you think that the purpose the part already gave you is positive, thank the part for having that goal or intention for you.

11. **Continue Until You Discover the Positive Purpose:** If you do not think the purpose is positive, ask, "If you have that purpose (the answer you got in Step 9), what will that do for me that you want even more?" Thank the part each time it gives you a response. Keep asking this question until you reach a purpose that *you* think is positive.

....

Now you have discovered a positive purpose that you agree with, even though you don't like the behavior, feeling or response. For most of us, this already begins to change our relationship with our inner parts. Did you notice yourself feeling more warmth or connection with the part when you found its positive purpose? It works the same with our inner parts as it does with other people—when we find some common ground, it is easier to appreciate them as friends or allies.

For most people the exploration above is an easy way to find out the positive intention of an unwanted behavior, feeling or response. If not, you may need to do more to build a relationship with that part of yourself. One way to build this relationship is to give that part of you lots of appreciation, even before you know what its positive intention is. Often we have been shoving these parts of ourselves aside, trying to get rid of them. Inner parts, like people, get annoyed when they are shoved aside. Yet these are parts of ourselves that really want to be received and welcomed by us. Usually when we turn within, and are sincerely welcoming, these parts are eager to respond.

This exercise is the first step of the Core Transformation Process. In later chapters you will go on to explore much deeper levels of yourself through the entire process. You will find that every part of you can become a wellspring of profound states of well-being.

—CHAPTER 4—

THE FIVE CORE STATES

The Nature of the Wellspring Within

I try to help people ... experience their spiritual connectedness by helping them get in touch with both their tenderness and their power. To reach them ... we need to see that we are born to evolve. ... It is a growing thing—and there is no fear in it. Not that we haven't heard the message before. It's what Christ talked about, and the Buddha, and others. But in the past most of us ... said, "They're beyond us, they're divine...we're nothing but humans, so we can't make the same connection." But now, we're beginning to know that we can.
—Virginia Satir

As we discovered in the Positive Purpose Exploration, every part of us is attempting to get some positive outcome for us. As I (Connirae) was developing the Core Transformation Process, I intuitively began to ask parts to continue going deeper. Instead of stopping when a part gave me a positive purpose, I asked questions to find a *deeper level purpose.* I noticed that if I kept asking the part, "And what do you want through having that?" the inner part would go to a new level of depth to something more basic and more important.

As I learned more about the process I discovered that parts usually began with wanting things from the outside, like protection, security, respect, love, approval from others, or success. Soon it became clear that if I kept asking, at some point every part shifted from wanting something on the outside, to wanting a deep, inner, core feeling state. People described these states with many names, such as "Oneness," "Beingness," "Sense of Peace," "OKness" and "Love." I began calling these intense states "Core

States." A Core State is the deepest level of what our parts want for us. The irony is that our parts have been attempting to get to these Core States *through* our unwanted behaviors, feelings and responses.

The decision to pursue Core States through our limitations is not a conscious one. People don't tend to consciously decide, "Hey, I think I'll overeat so I can have a sense of inner peace!" or, "I'll just stop myself from being successful so I'll have a sense of oneness." The decision to strive for a Core State through unwanted behaviors happens unconsciously, usually in childhood.

After working with unconscious parts in hundreds of people, I found that while every part had its own unique Core State, five major "clusters" of Core States began to emerge, which are universal states of being. While these Core States are in one sense universal experiences, in another sense they are unique to each person and each part of us. When you reach your own Core States you may have your own names for them. You will find that even when two parts have Core States with the same name, they may have subtle differences in the feeling quality. We encourage you to use the experience and the name that you receive from your inner parts, rather than try to fit them into any category.

Words are only labels for experience. If we haven't had the experience, these words can sound hollow. Frequently when people get to the Core State they hesitate and struggle, because no word seems "enough" to describe what they are experiencing. In *The Aquarian Conspiracy* Marilyn Ferguson says, "The common wisdom about transcendent moments is that they can never be properly communicated, only experienced. ...Communication, after all, builds upon common ground. You might describe purple to someone who knows red and blue, but you cannot describe red to someone who has never seen it. Red is elemental and irreducible."

Recognizing this limitation, it can still be valuable to have a sense of what to expect. We will describe the five Core State clusters to you, so you will be more familiar with what usually emerges through the Core Transformation Process. This will help you *recognize* it when you get to this point in the process. What we have to say about the Core States will probably mean much more to you after you have done the exercises in Sections II and III several times.

The Five Core States

1. Being
2. Inner Peace
3. Love
4. OKness
5. Oneness

1. *BEING*

Stars burn, grass grows, men breathe: as a man finding treasure says "Ah!" but the treasure's the essence; Before the man spoke it was there, and after he has spoken he gathers it, inexhaustible treasure.
—Robinson Jeffers

When I am in a state of *being*, I am simply aware of my own presence from the inside out. It is not that I see myself or am thinking *about* myself, but rather that I just am. I experience being fully here. This state might also be described by the words "presence," "fullness," and "wholeness."

This Core State goes considerably deeper than what we might describe as our self-concept. My self-concept is what I think about myself. I might think I'm a compassionate person, an intelligent person, or a person who learns and evolves. Having a well-formed self-concept is important and useful, but this sense of being is a direct *experience* of my presence, not an idea or belief about who I am. Rather than being self-conscious, this state is one of simply being.

When I (Tamara) was sixteen years old, I spent several weeks one summer with my sister, her husband and several friends of theirs in a canyon in Utah. That summer, one of our activities was hiking through beautiful red rock canyons that showed no sign of civilization.

One evening as we were planning a hike down Line Canyon for the next day, I decided to hike alone. The next morning a driver dropped off everyone else at the top of the canyon, and an hour later, the driver dropped me off. I had experienced a lot of hiking, but this was unique. Before, I had been very aware of the other people on the hike. I would pace myself according to their pace. If I got too far behind, I was aware that I was probably holding back the group. If I got ahead, I was aware of how I might look to the people behind me. I checked with others to know when it was time to eat a snack or get a drink of water.

This time as I hiked the four-mile trail I had a new experience. I became more and more aware of my own presence. As I responded to the beautiful scenery I was in, and decided how to make my way through, I had a growing sense of self that was independent of other people, their expectations, what they might think of me, and how well I thought I was doing. I just was. The experience was so strong—I felt both euphoric and grounded. You may have also had some experience in which you felt a sense of being that was so strong it stood out as different from your usual experience. Some people experience this state doing sports when they become totally involved and totally present with what they are doing.

2. *INNER PEACE*

If we are not able to smile, then the world will not have peace. It is not by going out for a demonstration against nuclear missiles that we can bring about peace. It is with our capacity of smiling, breathing, and being peace that we can make peace.
—Thich Nhat Hanh

When I (Tamara) was a student, I remember riding a bus one day when a father, mother and a boy and girl boarded the bus. Both the father and the mother carried white canes and wore sunglasses—they were clearly blind. The parents sat on the left side in the front of the bus, and the children sat quietly across from them. I noticed that the children were very calm, and they were watching their parents.

I thought to myself, "If I were blind, having kids would be very difficult. How would I ever know that they were doing OK? What if the kids got into things that were dangerous?" As I continued watching them, I heard the father say quite nervously, "Nancy! Danny! What are you doing? Are you sitting down while the bus is moving?" He was flustered and agitated.

The mother felt out to touch his knee with one hand and responded, in a calm, clear voice, "The children are doing fine." As she spoke, she exuded a sense of peacefulness that brought a smile to my face as I sat there on the bus. I was touched by this woman, who had the inner peacefulness that allowed her to trust her small children, even in a world she could not see. Being in her presence, a part of me resonated with her. I began to feel peaceful myself.

Have you met a person who exudes a peaceful quality? Perhaps you have had this experience when holding a contented baby, feeling a peaceful sensation that comes from within yet transcends personal boundaries. Having a Core State of *inner peace* is having a calmness or tranquillity within, in all kinds of surroundings. We often refer to this state as calm centeredness. Indira Gandhi said, "You must learn to be still in the midst of activity, and to be vibrantly alive in repose."

In his book *Teach Only Love,* Gerald Jampolsky describes the importance of having inner peace: "Instead of judging everything and trying to twist people and circumstances into appearances we like, the way of peace proceeds quietly and simply. Whenever life surprises us, our first reaction is now to consult that calm place within our heart. We stop and rest for a moment in God's love. Then, if action is needed to restore our inner peace, we take the course that comes to us from out of our calmness."

3. *LOVE*

Let the disciple cultivate love without measure toward all beings. Let him cultivate toward the whole world, above, below, around, a heart of love unstinted....For in all the world this state of heart is best.
—Buddha

What a great experience it is, to love and be loved! For thousands of years, storytellers, poets and song writers have spoken and written about the value of love and the desire for love. Most of them talk about loving others, or others loving them. The kind of love we experience as a Core State is much more complete and encompassing than the feeling we normally mean by the word "love." It is deeper than romantic love, deeper than loving and being loved. It is also deeper than self-love. With self-love, I am loving myself—one part of me is loving another part of me. The Core State of *love* includes everyone and everything. It is the love spoken of by many prophets and mystics; one that transcends boundaries within myself, and boundaries between people. It is unconditional and neutral. It just is. As self-help author John-Roger says, "When you get high enough in consciousness, everyone has the same name. That name is Love."

4. *OKNESS*

"I'm OK, You're OK"
—book title

The developers of Transactional Analysis discovered that we can enjoy life more fully by having a basic sense that we are "OK." The kind of *OKness* we are describing as a Core State is unusual. Often, when we talk about feeling OK, we mean that something we do makes us OK, or that someone judges us to be OK. For example, I may get a good grade on a test, or be complimented on a haircut, and feel worthy and OK in that situation.

OKness usually means *satisfying* an inner or outer judge. However, the kind of OKness that emerges as a Core State transcends judgment. It is a sense of being OK, on a very deep level, just as I am. It is a deep sense of worthiness that arises out of our very beingness, not from doing anything or having anything. It is a deep level of intrinsic worthiness.

5. *ONENESS*

Why, when a housefly flaps his wings, a breeze goes round the world; when a speck of dust falls to the ground, the entire planet weighs a little more; and when you stamp your foot, the earth moves slightly off its course. Whenever you laugh, gladness spreads like the ripples in a pond; and whenever you're sad, no one anywhere can be really happy.
—*Norton Juster,* The Phantom Toll Booth

Many people in our seminars have discovered Core States within them that they call by different names, including "oneness," "spiritual connectedness," "being filled with the light," "grace," "oneness with God," "Nirvana," and others. For the sake of discussion, we will call this Core State *oneness.*

Experiencing this state of oneness is different from a *belief* that we are all one. In the experience it is as if personal boundaries dissolve. I am everything and yet nothing in particular at the same time. When we look, listen, and feel in ordinary reality, we experience ourselves as separate beings. It is easy to observe differences and feel separate; I'm me, and you're you. Yet all of the major spiritual disciplines describe another deeper reality in which we realize we are all one. When people describe profound spiritual experiences, they usually describe an incredible sense of oneness with everything: "I am everything, everything is me, there is no separation." Sometimes this is described as "recognizing the God within me, that is also within everything."

Peace Pilgrim described oneness well when she said, "It does not matter what name you attach to it, but your consciousness must ascend to the point through which you view the universe with your God-centered nature. The feeling accompanying this experience is that of complete oneness with the Universal Whole. One merges into a euphoria of absolute unity with all life: with humanity, with all the creatures of the earth, the trees and plants, the air, the water, and even earth itself. This God-centered nature is constantly awaiting to govern your life gloriously. You have the free will to either allow it to govern your life, or not to allow it to affect you. The choice is always yours!"

In *The Way of the Peaceful Warrior,* Dan Millman describes his experience of oneness, "Open your eyes and see that you are far more than you imagine. You are the world, you are the universe; you are yourself and everyone else too! It's all the marvelous Play of God. Wake up, regain your humor.... You are already free!"

Although this experience of oneness usually has spiritual overtones, we have found that it does not conflict with spiritual beliefs people already have, nor does it require any spiritual beliefs to benefit from the experience. When I (Connirae) presented the Aligned Self seminar in London recently, I worked with a wonderful woman named Margo. When she reached her Core State, she said—with a strong blush—"I've got it, but this is really terrible! I don't want to say what it is." I let her know that she didn't need to tell me what the Core State was if she didn't want to. We could continue with the process without me knowing. However, Margo decided she really did want to say what it was, and told us, "Well, my part says it wants *oneness with God.* But I'm an atheist!" I assured Margo that it was fine for her to be an atheist. She didn't need to change her beliefs to do the process. The only important thing is to acknowledge whatever Core State we receive from the part. There is no need to be concerned about what we believe or what is "really going on."

Going Directly to the Core

Probably more has been written about the five Core States above, than about anything else in history, yet for most of us, having direct and immediate access to states such as these is only a dream. Many people experience some of these, some of the time. Perhaps you have had a Core State experience in the beauty of nature, the miracle of a baby being born, or the first blush of being in love. Wouldn't it be nice if we didn't have to wait for the right life circumstances to produce these states?

One of the predominant features in our culture is the use of drugs. This includes relatively accepted drugs, like nicotine, caffeine, alcohol, sleeping pills and prescription narcotics, anti-depressants and tranquilizers, as well as the illegal street drugs society frowns on. Many people use drugs to try to induce inner states similar to the Core States we have described—a sense of being, peace, love, OKness, and oneness. Unfortunately, using drugs for this purpose creates a variety of problems, including physical side-effects, addiction, loss of mental capacities, financial cost and—for some drugs—legal problems. The fact that so many people in our culture rely on drugs, despite the problems they create, shows how strong the desire is to experience inner well-being.

The Core Transformation Process has given many people a direct and immediate *experience* of oneness and other Core States that they have never had before. At a recent seminar a man came up to me during a break. His eyes were alight and he seemed to be almost bursting with excitement. "Do you realize what this process is doing for the people in this room?" he asked. "They are reaching states in minutes that people go sit on mountains for years to try to attain!"

Embracing Our "Ugliness Within"

Many personal growth and spiritual approaches tell us we need to control or eliminate our "ugliness within." They tell us we should quit thinking negative thoughts and stop ourselves from doing negative behaviors. Taking that approach leads to more inner separation which makes it impossible to feel oneness and wholeness.

Those behaviors and responses we most dislike and criticize in ourselves are the very qualities that open into Core States. The doorway to our Core States leads us *through* our "ugliness within," *through* our most unwanted qualities; those behaviors, feelings and responses we have called our limitations or problems. Equally important, through the Core Transformation Process these states become more than just brief emotional highs. We actually discover how having an awareness of our Core States can transform our daily experience.

—SECTION II—

THE CORE STATE EXERCISE

The Heart of the Core Transformation Process

—CHAPTER 5—

A DEMONSTRATION WITH CATHY

Having It Your Way

I'm free to be me. I'm free to surrender. I'm free to allow other people their blessed differences.
—Cathy

In this chapter Tamara guides a woman named Cathy through the Core State Exercise. This exercise will take you through the first five steps of the ten-step Core Transformation Process. Cathy wanted to change an emotional response in her work situation. She was so concerned about getting results and took on so much responsibility that she made herself "nervous and uptight." She noticed this most strongly when she came back to work after being away from it.

When most people go through the Core State Exercise they find it easiest to sense their inner experience if they talk very little. However, to give you a more complete understanding of how the Core State Exercise can be experienced, in this case we asked Cathy in advance to describe each state she went through in detail.

....

Tamara: What is a feeling, behavior or response that you would like to change?

Cathy: This is a recurring issue. I have a new business as a consultant, and have been attending a four-day weekend training, once a month. During these four-day weekends everything is completely taken care of. I know where I'm supposed to be, I eat out so the meals are taken care of, and everything is planned. There is a real sense of safety and security, having all of that taken care of. When I get home, for the first three or four days after the training, my tendency is to start to get nervous again: "Am I going to make it, is my business going to prosper, am I going to be able to help all my clients?" Then, after three or four days of working, I feel like I can relax again. I don't want to feel uptight while I'm working, and be looking forward to the days when I can relax so I can get geared up to work again.

Tamara: OK. Now, I'd like you to mentally put yourself into the time when you get nervous and uptight. Imagine that you just came back from the training weekend and you are starting to think about the appointments you have coming up. *(Cathy closes her eyes and furrows her brow.)* What do you notice happening internally as you begin to feel nervous? What inner pictures, sounds, or feelings go with the nervousness?

Cathy: There are two things I'm doing physically. One is I'm breathing in shallowly, and then forgetting to breathe out. I'm holding my breath. The other thing is my left shoulder muscle tenses up, gets sore. When I touch it, I can actually feel a knot.

Tamara: OK. Now, you aren't consciously trying to get nervous in that situation, right?

Cathy: No, not at all.

Tamara: So we can think about it as if there is an unconscious part of you that is creating that response for you. As you know, whenever we feel, think or do something we don't like, the part of us that creates that experience has a positive purpose. That part of us wants something really wonderful for us. So, I'd like you to go back inside, back to the time when you notice the nervousness, the shallow breathing, and the tension. *(Cathy closes her eyes and begins breathing more shallowly. Tamara speaks more slowly and softly.)* Notice where in your body you have those feelings, and thank this part of you for being there and having some positive purpose for you. It's doing its best to accomplish something really positive for you through this response of nervousness. So you can give it lots of appreciation for having some positive purpose, even though we don't know what that purpose is yet. ...

And as you feel the appreciation, ask this part, "What do you want, through getting tense and nervous?" After you ask that question, allow your inner part to give you an answer. Notice what pictures, sounds, or feelings you get as a response.

Cathy: It said that it wants to do a good job.

Tamara: Good. So thank this part of you for being there and for wanting that for you. *(Cathy nods.)* Now, ask the part, "If you have the experience of doing a good job, fully and completely, what do you want through doing a good job that's even more important?"

Cathy: Now the part says that I get to relax. *(Cathy takes a deep breath.)*

Tamara: Great. Thank this part of you for wanting that and for doing its best to get that for you. *(Cathy smiles and nods.)* Now ask this part of you, "If you have the experience of relaxing, fully and completely, then what do you want, through relaxing, that's even more important?"

Cathy: The part says that I get to be more creative. The more I relax, the more new ideas start to form.

Tamara: OK, more creative. Ask that part of you again, "If you get to be more creative, fully and completely, what do you want, through being more creative, that's even more important?"

Cathy: *(More slowly and softly.)* I get to do really good work. I'm picturing these new ideas really making a difference in my work.

Tamara: Great. And thank that part of you again. Now ask that part, "If you get to really have this whole set of things—you get to relax, you get to be more creative, and you get to do really good work, what do you want, through doing really good work, that's even more important?"

Cathy: ... I didn't get words this time, but I became aware of a sense of freedom. There's a wider space of possibility. I feel like I've just come out of a tunnel, and now I can see the whole countryside! My body can move in any direction. It's really nice.

Tamara: OK. Thank this part of you for that response. We don't really need words from this part—the important thing is that this part of you *experiences* the answer to the question. *(Cathy nods.)* Now, ask this part of you, "When you have the sense of freedom, fully and completely, just in the way that you, this part, want to experience this sense of freedom, then what do you want to experience, through having this sense of freedom, that's even more important?"

Cathy: *(Softly.)* Umm. I get to connect with lots of different people on lots of different levels. I feel as if I've moved closer to people. I can see and hear them much more clearly.

Tamara: You get to connect with lots of different people on lots of different levels. Thank this part of you again, and ask it, "If you have that connection with different people on different levels, fully and completely, what do you want to experience through connecting that's even more important?"

Cathy: *(As Cathy breathes more deeply, her body relaxes even more.)* The experience of a loving oneness. ... All of the worry and anxiousness is flowing out of my head and shoulders, dropping down to a place in my center, just below my belly button, that's much more grounded. ... It's not worry and anxiousness anymore. As those sensations flowed into my center, they turned into loving oneness!

Tamara: Loving oneness. What a wonderful thing! And ask this part now, "If you get to have loving oneness, fully and completely, and you're just filled with loving oneness, is there anything you want to experience through loving oneness, that's even more important and even deeper?"

Cathy: *(She turns within and pauses.)* No. There are lots of nice consequences of having loving oneness, but there isn't anything that's deeper and more important.

Tamara: Great. Thank that part of you again. Now invite this part of you to consider this idea. It's as though this part of you got the idea that it had to go through this whole series of steps in order to get to its Core State of loving oneness. Unfortunately, this doesn't work very well. Usually, parts don't get to experience their Core State very often when they go about it in this way. What's more effective in actually getting the experience of loving oneness is to simply have it as a starting point—as a way of being in the world in an ongoing way. So ask this part, "Would you like to have that loving oneness, as a starting point, in an ongoing way?"

Cathy: *(Laughing.)* The part says, "Yes, yes, a thousand times yes!"

Tamara: *(Laughing with Cathy.)* So thank this part of you. What a wonderful part it is! And ask that part, "How does your already having loving oneness as a way of being make things different?"

Cathy: *(Turns within to notice the answer to this question. A soft smile spreads across her face.)* ... Those ways are just flooding into my awareness. That feeling of loving oneness changes how I feel and what I do in so many situations! Images of different situations are coming in, some of them challenging situations, and the loving oneness transforms those images.

Tamara: And now, ask this part, "When you already have loving oneness as a way of being, how does it affect your experience of connecting with lots of different people on lots of different levels?"

Cathy: ... It makes those connections relaxed and meaningful.

Tamara: Great. So thank that part of you, and now ask this part of you, "How does just having that loving oneness with you in an ongoing way transform your experience even when you're with someone that you don't feel as connected with?

Cathy: *(Turns within to check.)* ... That's the whole point of loving oneness. It makes it easy to remember that we all have our different paths, and the connection is on a deeper level than our personalities. I'm picturing being with someone who's acting kind of belligerent, and I am aware of a deeper connection between us. That deeper connection makes it easy to let his belligerence bounce off of me.

Tamara: Great. So thank that part of you again, and ask, "How does your already having that loving oneness enhance or enrich your sense of freedom?"

Cathy: Incredibly. I'm free to be me. I'm free to surrender. I'm free to allow other people their blessed differences. ... That loving oneness helps me drop down, out of my head and into my center, and I slow down.

Freedom comes from having time to absorb what the other person says, and having time to let my response bubble up from me. My reaction is deeper, which comes from being slower.

Tamara: Great. And thank that part of you again, and now ask, "As you start with loving oneness, how does that make it even easier to be more creative?"

Cathy: ... Oh, the channels for creativity are much more open, because I get to take my time.

Tamara: OK, and thank this part of you again. Now ask this part, "How does already having loving oneness enhance your sense of relaxing?"

Cathy: Oh! *(Laughs.)* They're lovingly one and the same! ... Loving myself and loving every other part of this universe is the same. There is no separation, there's a flow between us. ... I'm caring enough about *myself* to relax and take my time, and at the same time I'm caring enough about *them* to do that.

Tamara: OK. Thank this part again, and ask, "How does starting with loving oneness transform the Intended Outcome of doing a good job?"

Cathy: ... Well, I'm doing good work anyway, and I'm really relaxing in the process. I can feel the work coming from deep inside of me. It's coming up from my center and out of me. I can feel the burden of responsibility moving away from my shoulders because I know I'm doing the best I can. It's easy to see what I might do differently the next time, and what I might change, too. There's a real difference in my experience now that I'm right here in the present with my client, as opposed to being off in the future, thinking, "Is it working?" I'm right here, doing the best I can, knowing that my best can keep changing and evolving. I know everything is just right, just the way it is.

Tamara: Great. Ask this part of you now, "When you have loving oneness already there as a way of being, how does that change your experience even when you do something you don't consider to be such good work, or you make a little mistake?"

Cathy: ... What this allows me to do is relax, step back, take the time I need to reformulate or apologize or change what I'm doing. It allows all of that to happen at a pace that's very comfortable for me. ... I'm letting some past mistakes I've made come to mind, noticing how I respond to them differently with the loving oneness. ...

Tamara: Good. Ask this part of you, "How does just starting with loving oneness transform the original situation? How does it change your experience when you are just coming home from a four-day training?"

Cathy: Oh, it really connects me to remembering *myself,* as well as the tasks at hand. It's blended—I'm important *and* what I'm doing is important. It's a connection of me and the world. We're together, co-creating something.

Tamara: Great! Thank this part of you, again, for bringing you this state of loving oneness. Now, what is it like to think about the times in the future when this loving oneness will make a difference?

Cathy: I can see myself going out into the future—into tomorrow's two appointments, into tomorrow's social engagements, out into Sunday, which isn't even planned yet, and more importantly into Monday, when "work" resumes.

Tamara: Notice what happens through the next training weekend and beyond.

Cathy: I see myself during the weekend, relaxing with everything taken care of. And then I'm arriving home, choosing to take Tuesday off, because that takes care of me. Then, Wednesday begins from this place of loving oneness. I see myself being with clients, knowing what I'm responsible to do, which is bringing my best work forward, trusting that they will take care of their responsibility, and knowing the difference. I'm staying with the process, seeing how well I allow this work to sustain me, and not drain me.

••

You have just read a demonstration of the Core State Exercise, which is the heart of the Core Transformation Process. After doing the complete Core Transformation Process, Cathy commented that her goal is to do consulting full-time into her nineties. She had been concerned that getting too "nervous and uptight" about doing well enough and focusing so intently on her clients without taking care of herself could have interfered with her plans. Now she feels that she has the freedom to take care of herself as well as her clients in a balanced way.

A few weeks later, we asked Cathy how she was experiencing her work. She told us the following:

> I definitely feel better about my work. I feel differently, and it's manifesting itself in good work. I am simultaneously respecting myself and the other person.
>
> The measure of change for me is in how I feel after I have met with a client. In the past, I would feel very accomplished, but it would put me through the wringer. I wasn't aware of how tense my muscles were, how hyper-vigilant I was. I often held my own breath as my clients were responding to me. Then, after the meeting, I collapsed to regroup. Now the work isn't taking as much out of me. In fact sometimes I actually feel rejuvenated after consulting with a client.
>
> In addition I now have the ability to shift gears. Having recently started my business, I have to wear a lot of hats in addition to consulting. There's the advertising hat, the copy-writing

hat, the networking hat, the free consultation hat, the learning and creative hat, the administrative hat, the hat of creating a pleasant environment for clients, and then on top of that I have a private life. In the past, I took all of those hats with me when I met with a client. I couldn't switch gears fast enough to stay totally present. And now that's not happening. The minute a meeting begins, everything else drops away and I'm focused on my client. "That was then, this is now." I'm so aware of what I'm there for.

I used to have certain days when I "couldn't" schedule any client meetings, so I could focus on administrative things. Today, I have set aside the day to take care of a lot of administrative things, but if someone calls and needs to see me, I could set an appointment. I'm much more flexible. I know I could completely switch gears and focus on a client if I needed to. If someone cancels unexpectedly, I can switch gears easily and do administrative work.

Something else that's changed is how I react to mistakes. Before, making one mistake could cause a domino effect. One mistake affected the next thing I did, making it shaky, and that effected the next thing, and things continued going downward. Now when I make a mistake, I am matter-of-fact about it. I have a voice inside that says, "Oh OK, where do we go from here?" with a real sense of acceptance, no judgment. The mistake is completely behind me, and I can move on from there. It's easy to think of other things I could do next time.

This demonstration with Cathy helps lay the groundwork for you to do this exercise for yourself. Each person's Core Transformation Process is unique. It is an opportunity to work creatively with yourself. What is important is to use this process to find *your* intended outcomes, and *your* Core State. Then you will discover how your Core State transforms each of your intended outcomes.

—CHAPTER 6—

THE CORE STATE EXERCISE

Understanding the Structure

It is only with the heart that one can see rightly.
What is essential is invisible to the eye.
—Antoine de Saint-Exupery, The Little Prince

We will use Cathy's demonstration to explain the basic structure of the Core State Exercise. The first four steps take Cathy to her Core State:

Step 1. CHOOSING A PART TO WORK WITH

Cathy began by noticing a response she didn't like, which was feeling nervous about her work.

a) **Experiencing the Part:** She imagined herself in a situation or context where she felt nervous about her work, then noticed what feelings, images or sounds emerged. When we do this process it is important to begin with the experience we have—some feeling, inner voice or inner image that gets in our way. This is the automatic and unconscious part of us that we will work with and transform.

b) **Receiving and Welcoming the Part:** She thanked and appreciated the part for being there and having a positive purpose for her. Most of us have had no idea that when we have a behavior, feeling or response that we don't like, it is actually our best attempt to get something positive. When we welcome and receive an inner part we have been fighting with, we already begin to change our relationship with this part. You may notice a small shift in your feelings already when you have done this step.

Step 2. DISCOVERING THE PURPOSE/FIRST INTENDED OUTCOME

She asked the part, "What do you want through getting nervous?" Cathy's part responded by telling her it wanted her to do a good job. We call this answer the first *Intended Outcome* of the part. Sometimes we get the answer in words, as Cathy did. Other times we receive a feeling, an image, or a sound that is the answer we are seeking. You can find examples of each of these kinds of responses in the demonstration with Cathy.

Step 3. DISCOVERING THE OUTCOME CHAIN

Next, she asked her part, "If you have the experience of doing a good job, fully and completely, what do you want through doing a good job that's even more important?" The answer to this question is the part's second Intended Outcome. By continuing to ask, "What do you want through [Intended Outcome] that's even more important," for each Intended Outcome, Cathy discovered what we call her part's Outcome Chain.

CATHY'S OUTCOME CHAIN

Part to Work With: Nervousness
Intended Outcome 1 (Purpose): To do a good job
Intended Outcome 2: To relax
Intended Outcome 3: To be creative
Intended Outcome 4: Sense of freedom
Intended Outcome 5: Connect with people

Notice that all of Cathy's Intended Outcomes were positive and useful. Sometimes our parts begin by wanting something that *we* don't like, such as to have power over others, to fail, to make someone else look bad, to intimidate someone, or even to destroy someone. It is important to include these outcomes. And, when we continue to ask, "What do you want through that," at some point the answers *always* flip to something positive.

Step 4. THE CORE STATE: REACHING THE WELLSPRING WITHIN

The final and deepest outcome Cathy's part intends for her is called her Core State, which is loving oneness.

When we continue asking our inner parts, "What do you want through having that?" we uncover increasingly important and wonderful purposes within the very behaviors we dislike most in ourselves. We discover that our limitations are actually our part's best attempt to get to a profound way of being in the world that we call a Core State. Cathy's part was seeking "loving oneness."

Step 5. REVERSING THE OUTCOME CHAIN WITH THE CORE STATE

In working with hundreds of people and thousands of inner parts, I have found the same pattern repeated. Our inner parts somehow get the idea that their best chance of getting a wonderful Core State is to begin with a behavior, feeling or response we don't like, and then proceed through a long series of Intended Outcomes. This method usually doesn't work at all. Cathy's nervousness did not bring her to a full experience of loving oneness.

Once we have discovered the Core State our inner part wants, we are in a position to transform the basis of our inner life. Now the process guides us in literally turning our old pattern around. We can *begin* by having what we were hoping we could somehow get to if we worked hard enough at it. We can *begin* with the Core State— the wellspring within. We invite the part of ourselves we are working with to step into its Core State and have it. Then we invite our inner part to notice *how already having the Core State as a way of being in the world* transforms each of our Intended Outcomes. Finally, we notice how already having the Core State naturally transforms the original behavior we didn't like. Each purpose that our parts have becomes transformed by the Core State.

For Cathy, the process of turning her old pattern around looked like this:

a) **For Each Intended Outcome** she asked, "How does already having loving oneness as a way of being transform or enrich [the Intended Outcome]?" When we already have our Core States, we are already whole and fulfilled; we have what we most deeply want. Our motivations become very different. Rather than acting out of need or lack we act out of fullness. When we let the Core State transform each Intended Outcome we allow this fullness or completeness to radiate through each sphere of our lives that our part is concerned with. Positive Intended Outcomes become enriched with the Core State present. Intended outcomes that seem to be negative are transformed. We never force or try to change these areas to something we like better; we simply invite our part to notice what *naturally happens* when the Core State is already there.

b) **Transforming the Original Context:** Cathy is asked, "How does just starting with loving oneness transform the original situation? How does it change your experience when you are just coming home from a four-day training?" This is the step that brings about the change Cathy was seeking.

When we do this process we don't force anything. We never decide ahead of time what our part's Core State "should be" or how this Core State will transform our earlier outcomes. The change comes from within. The original feeling does not always change completely, as it did for Cathy. Sometimes when I have started with anger, in the end I am still angry, but the quality of my anger is different. I am cleaner and clearer about my anger and the need to blame the other person drops away. *I* am angry, but I recognize on a deep feeling level that the other person is not wrong. It's just that *I* don't like something.

CRITERIA FOR THE CORE STATES

Reaching and recognizing the Core State is what makes it possible for the Core Transformation Process to get dramatic results so quickly. Once we reach the true Core State, the rest of the process usually goes very smoothly. Here are some guidelines to help you know when you have arrived at the Core State.

1. The key criterion is that the Core State is always an internal state that has a being quality. States like OKness, lovingness, beingness, peace and oneness, just *are*. They are not dependent upon anything external such as doing, getting, giving, or knowing. In contrast, success, recognition and appreciation are all things we can *get* from others. Contributing and achieving are things we *do*. While they can be important, they are not Core States. Understanding or knowing are not Core States because they are in relationship *to* some*thing*. Freedom is not usually a Core State because it is *from* or *to* something. A Core State just is; it is not in relationship to anything else.

2. The Core State is always something that can be experienced through time. Happiness, for example, is usually not a Core State because it wouldn't fit through every moment of time. If I am happy it is usually *about* something and has a "because..." attached to it: I am happy because I received a gift, or because a friend called and invited me to dinner, or because I shared a special moment with my children. A Core State happens at a deeper level. Inner peace, beingness, or OKness, for example, can be present through *every* moment of time, independent of outer circumstances. A Core State can be present through any moment of time, no matter what is happening in my life—even when I am sad or angry! When I have a Core State present my anger is likely to be cleaner. I will be owning it rather than losing control or blaming someone else.

3. Most people feel they have tapped into something very deep and important when they experience a Core State. Some are visibly touched and moved to tears when they tap into the Core State, clearly going to a deeper level than an Intended Outcome. There is often a sense of it emerging from deep within ourselves and radiating through our entire being and beyond. You may or may not immediately experience a Core State fully when you first discover it. If you don't experience it fully at first, the steps in the process that come after discovering the Core State make it easy to gain the full experience. When observing a Core State in others you may feel a sense of awe and privilege at being part of the experience. After an Aligned Self seminar one woman told me, "When someone else goes into a Core State I feel chills going up my spine and I get goose bumps."

4. Once you have reached the Core State, when you ask the part the question, "What do you want through having that?" the part either:

> **a.** Cannot go any further. Your inner part may tell you, "There is no more," or just stay with the last Intended Outcome it got. Or,
>
> **b.** starts describing the *consequences* of having the Core State, such as, "Then I can do what I want to do in my life."

In the next chapter a questionnaire will assist you in discovering a part to work with and give you a better sense of the variety of issues you can bring to the Core Transformation Process.

—CHAPTER 7—

A QUESTIONNAIRE

Finding An Unwanted Behavior, Feeling or Response to Work With

It is better to know some of the questions
than all of the answers.
—James Thurber

No matter what we experience as our limitations or problems, the Core Transformation Process can make a tremendous difference to us. You may already know areas in your life that are less than fully satisfying and that you want to work with. If you already know what limitation you would like to work with first, feel free to skip the questionnaire for now, or skim through it. You can always come back to it later.

The following questionnaire gives you an easy way to focus in on and observe some areas in your life where the Core Transformation Process can be powerfully effective. The function of these questions is to stimulate you to think of areas and issues that would be a good starting point for the Core Transformation Process.

Who Decides What You Should Change?

You do. If you see something on this list that is true of you but do not consider it to be a limitation, you certainly do not have to change it. You are the one who decides which things are important to have more choices about.

How Do You Eat An Elephant?

One bite at a time. As you read through the questionnaire you may notice many areas you want to resolve. If you want to prioritize these areas so you know what to work with first, you can check off the ones that apply to you, then go back and rate the level of intensity or "stuckness" each one has for you, on a scale of one to ten. The first time you do this process we recommend you identify a limitation that is a five or less on your intensity scale.

When you have done the Core Transformation Process a number of times, and four's and five's on the rating scale go smoothly and easily, you can use your own judgment to decide when to work with more intense difficulties.

THE QUESTIONNAIRE

Emotional Areas

- Do you get stuck in an unpleasant emotion or mood such as depression, anger, rage, grief, jealousy, hurt, fear, anxiety, loneliness, emptiness, intimidation?
- Do you have difficulty feeling your emotions?

Addictions/Habits

- Do you have difficulties with eating, such as overeating, bulimia, or anorexia? Do you "fight with yourself" about what to eat or how much to eat?
- Are you over-attached to smoking, drinking, sex, relationships, money, things, or something else?
- Do you have "nervous" habits or mannerisms, such as biting your fingers or fingernails, drumming the table, a "nervous laugh," etc.?

Relationship Areas

- Does it make you feel bad to know someone else is better at something than you are? Do you feel driven to look the best, have the best/most, be the most popular, etc.?
- Is it difficult for you to ask for what you want? Do you usually go along with what others are doing, even if you don't like it? Do you sometimes say you agree with others, even if you don't really agree?
- Is your attention usually on pleasing others? Do you do things for others at your own expense? Are you willing to do almost anything to gain the love and approval of others?
- Do you often avoid being with people? Do you ever feel unsafe around people who are no threat to you?
- When you are with people, are you reluctant or afraid to fully "be yourself"? In intimate relationships, do you find yourself pulling back from the other person to avoid intimacy? Do you have difficulty being "present" with another person?

- Are you afraid that you will be abandoned?
- Does it seem as if you could not live without another person? Does it seem like your life would fall apart if a certain person wasn't there? Do you find yourself relying on someone else to make decisions for you?
- Is it difficult for you to trust anyone? Do you often assume that others have evil motives? Do you regard only a few people as "good people"? Do you tend to say things like "Men are jerks," or "Women are devious"?
- Do you tend to trust people inappropriately? Do you ignore other people's limitations in ways that injure you? Do you try to convince yourself that someone is more mature or evolved than they really are?
- Do you usually want to be the one in charge? Does it anger you when people do things you can't control?
- Does it upset you when someone else seems to be on a power trip?
- Is it difficult for you to keep commitments? Is it common for you to say "yes" and regret it? Do you ever say "yes" and then back out?
- Do you strive to be in the limelight? Do you feel uncomfortable when someone else is getting all the attention? Do you ever feel compelled to take credit for things you did not do?
- Do you get into arguments about "who's right?" Do you cling to your position, even when it is clear to you that the other person is right? Is it difficult to admit that you made a mistake?
- Do you often think about problems in terms of whose fault they are? Do you argue about who is at fault? Do you think other people should take the blame and admit they caused problems for you? Do you tend to judge others for mistakes or limitations? Is it difficult to forgive someone else?
- Do you tend to blame yourself for other people's mistakes or feelings? Do you sometimes judge yourself for making mistakes? Is it difficult to forgive yourself?
- If someone does something you don't like, do you try to get even? Do you feel compelled to push people's buttons? Are you often sarcastic? Do other people often take offense at things you do or say, even though you don't know what they're so upset about?

- Is it incredibly important that others think well of you? Are you tempted to stretch the truth or even lie, in order to maintain a positive image?
- Are you tempted to be dishonest in order to get what you want from others?

Self-Image

- Is it difficult to accept yourself unless you are "perfect?"
- Are you overly critical of your behavior when you make small mistakes?
- Do you think of yourself as better than other people and look down on others?
- Do you think of yourself as inferior to others, and look up to others?
- Are you ashamed of yourself or of your behavior?
- Would you like to improve your self-esteem?
- Do you lack a sense of who you are?

Other Categories

- Do you have a physical illness that you suspect could be related to unexpressed emotion or stress?
- Have you defined yourself as co-dependent?
- Are you abusive toward others?
- Are you or have you been a victim of physical, sexual, mental or emotional abuse?
- Do you find yourself behaving in ways that are self-defeating?
- Are you over- or under-achieving?
- Are you preoccupied with money issues?
- Do you experience a lot of inner conflict?
- Do you have obsessive thoughts about something?

—CHAPTER 8—

DOING IT!

THE CORE STATE EXERCISE

Reaching the Wellspring Within

Action will remove the doubt that theory cannot solve.
—Tehyi Hsieh

This exercise works most easily with two people when you are first experiencing the process. One person is the "explorer" and the other is the "guide." The explorer picks something to work with, and the guide reads the script of the exercise. If no one is available to assist you and you want to do it on your own, you can play both roles, shifting back and forth between being the guide reading the instructions and being the explorer of your inner experience. Whether you have a guide or are doing the exercise by yourself, we suggest you read this exercise through at least once and then come back and do it. In the following chapter, "Going Solo," you will find more information on doing the exercise by yourself.

You (explorer) can prepare by making yourself physically comfortable, relaxing, and turning within. This process is usually easier with your eyes closed. As you ask the questions internally, pause and be aware of any response. You may get a picture, a sound, a voice, and/or a feeling. As you get closer to the Core State, your responses are likely to have a strong feeling component. If you think you have a response but you are not sure, you can ask the part, "Is your response this? Or is it something else?"

The guide can facilitate the process by talking a little more slowly than normal, with a soft tone of voice. After each instruction, pause to give the explorer time to respond internally. Write down the key words or phrases to track the Intended Outcomes of the explorer. When you are the explorer, you can let the guide know if you want to go faster or slower.

If you are doing the exercise on your own you'll want to have paper and something to write with, so you can keep track of your Intended Outcomes.

If you are the guide, notice that when we have put a phrase or sentence in italics in the following instructions, you do not need to read it out loud.

....

Step 1. CHOOSING A PART TO WORK WITH

a) Identify the part you want to work with. Pick something you feel, think or do that you don't like. The first time you do the exercise, pick something that is mild to moderate in intensity. *Write this down in a word or two. We will refer to this as [behavior, feeling or response X] in this script, and you can fill in what this part does.*

b) When, where, and with whom do you have this [behavior, feeling or response X]? *Write down the answer in a few words.*

Experiencing the Part

c) Take a moment to close your eyes, relax and turn within. Mentally step into a specific incident in which [behavior, feeling or response X] occurred. As you enter this experience, relive the incident, and begin to notice your inner experience. You may notice inner pictures, sounds, and feelings that go along with this experience.

d) Since you did not consciously choose [behavior, feeling or response X], it is as if a part of you did. You can begin to sense where that part of you "lives." Do you feel the feelings most strongly in a certain part of your body? If you hear an inner voice, <u>where</u> is the voice located? If you see inner pictures, <u>where</u> in your personal space do you see them? Gently invite the part into your awareness. If the part is in your body, you may want to put your hand on the area where you sense the part most strongly. This can help you welcome and acknowledge the part.

Receiving and Welcoming the Part

e) Receive and welcome this part of you. Even though you don't know what the purpose of this part is, you can begin thanking it for being there, because you know it has some deeply positive purpose.

Step 2. DISCOVERING THE PURPOSE/FIRST INTENDED OUTCOME

a) Ask the part of you that [X's], "What do you want?" After asking, notice any image, voice or sound, or feeling that occurs in response. You may get the answer instantly. Or, sometimes it takes the part a little while to find its purpose—that's OK—this is a new experience for the part, so give it some time if it needs it.

b) *Write down the answer you get from the part.* This is your first Intended Outcome. Thank the part for letting you know. If you like the part's Intended Outcome, thank it for having this Intended Outcome for you. Sometimes the first Intended Outcomes that emerge don't seem to be positive. However, by continuing to ask the part what it wants, positive purposes always emerge. It is important to include and acknowledge any negative outcomes that emerge. The outcomes that we don't like will be transformed before we finish with the process.

Step 3. DISCOVERING THE OUTCOME CHAIN

a) Ask this part of you, "If you have [Intended Outcome from previous step], fully and completely, what do you want, through having that, that's even more important?" *Wait for a response.* Thank this part for having this Intended Outcome for you. *Write down this Intended Outcome.*

b) *Repeat Step 3a until you get to the Core State. Each time, you'll get a new Intended Outcome and write it down. Each time you ask the question you'll use the new Intended Outcome.*

Step 4. THE CORE STATE: REACHING THE WELLSPRING WITHIN

a) When you reach the Core State take the time to experience it and enjoy it fully; then go on to step 5.

Step 5. REVERSING THE OUTCOME CHAIN WITH THE CORE STATE

a) Somehow our inner parts get the idea that in order to experience core states of being, they first have to go through a whole series of Intended Outcomes. Unfortunately, this doesn't work very well. We don't experience our Core States very often when we go about it that way, because a Core State of beingness is not something that it is possible to earn or to get through actions. The way to experience a Core State is just to step into it and have it.

CRITERIA FOR CORE STATES

Having clear criteria for recognizing a Core State is important, because without this, people tend to stop eliciting the Outcome Chain either too soon or too late. If one does either, the process does not work as well. You can tell you have arrived at the Core State by the following characteristics:

1. It is always a state of beingness, in contrast to doing or having or knowing or relating. People use many different words to describe these states. Most Core States are something similar to beingness, peace, love, OKness, and oneness.
2. It is not dependent on others, like, "appreciation from others" or "love from others."
3. It is not reflexive like, "loving myself."
4. It is not a specific emotion, such as confident, hopeful, satisfied, courageous, proud.
5. When you do step 3a with the Core State, one of two things will happen: 1) the part can go no further, 2) The part begins to describe the consequences of having the Core State, such as, "My whole life will be different."
6. Physical changes take place, such as relaxation, skin color changes, changes in breathing, changes in tempo. If you are doing this yourself you will probably notice a strong change in the way you feel. (Some people find that although they like their Core State, they don't feel it as fully as they want to. This usually means there are other steps in the process that still need to be taken. We will show you how to take those steps in Sections III and IV.)

b) General: Invite this part to step into [Core State] now, and ask your part, "When you just have [Core State] as a beginning, as a way of being in the world, how does already having [Core State] make things different?" *Pause to give the explorer time to enjoy the experience.*

c) Specific: *Let the Core State transform each of the Intended Outcomes, one at a time, beginning with the one next to the Core State.* Ask the part, "How does already having [Core State] as a way of being transform or enrich [Intended Outcome]?" *Pause each time to allow the explorer time to enjoy and integrate the experience.*

TRANSFORMING YOUR INTENDED OUTCOMES

The question in step 5c is the "generic" way of transforming Intended Outcomes. In some cases you will need to vary this question:

1. **Dependent Intended Outcome:** When an Intended Outcome is dependent on other people, such as "appreciation from others," or "being loved," you'll ask the part two questions:

   a) "How does already having [Core State] transform your experience when you are getting [dependent Intended Outcome]?"

   b) "How does already having [Core State] transform your experience when you are *not* getting [dependent Intended Outcome]?"

   Example: Intended Outcome of "Appreciation from Others"

   "How does already having Oneness as a way of being transform and enrich your experience of receiving appreciation from others?"

   "How does already having Oneness as a way of being transform a situation where another person is not able to appreciate you?"

   Example: Intended Outcome of "Being Loved"

   "How does already having Peace as a way of being radiate through your experience of receiving love?"

   "How does already having Peace as a way of being transform situations when another person is not able to give the love that they have inside?"

2. **Negative Intended Outcome:** When an Intended Outcome does not serve you well, such as "revenge" "control" or "being perfect," ask the part, "How does already having [Core State] transform this whole area that <u>used to be</u> [negative Intended Outcome]?"

   Example: Intended Outcomes of "Revenge" and "Control"

   "How does already having Beingness radiate through and transform this whole area that used to be revenge?"

   "How does already having Oneness transform this whole area that used to be control?"

Transforming the Original Context

d) *When you have asked about each of the Intended Outcomes in sequence, you are ready to discover how the Core State transforms the limitation you began with.* Ask the part, "How does already having [Core State] as a way of being in the world transform your experience [in the context where you used to X]?" *Give the explorer time to enjoy the difference. If the original unwanted behavior, feeling or response is not satisfactorily changed, this is most likely a signal that you need the additional steps taught in Section III and IV.*

....

Working With the Process

Now you have completed the Core State Exercise once. You have done the first five steps of the ten-step Core Transformation Process. Whether you noticed a lot of change or a little change, or even no change this first time through, we want you to know how to get more from this book. The new steps added in later chapters will enrich your experience significantly.

Many people have reported that their response becomes fuller or more complete as they do the process several times. Our unconscious begins to understand what the process is all about, and the inner pathway to the Core States becomes more obvious and automatic. This is much like the way water flowing over the same ground creates a deepening channel over time.

—Chapter 9—

GOING SOLO

Doing the Core State Exercise With Yourself

There is no reality except the one contained within us. That is why so many people live such an unreal life. They take the images outside them for reality and never allow the world within to assert itself.
—Herman Hesse, Demian

Now that you have experienced the Core State Exercise we will give you a brief example of how a woman named Julianne did the exercise with herself. As you read this you can invite your own unconscious to apply this experience in ways that fit for you. In the following paragraphs Julianne talks about what part she chose to work with, how she discovered her Outcome Chain and her experience of the Core State:

> I started with feeling resentful and irritated at my husband. He has a tendency to publicly take credit for *my* ideas. This time we were having a party to celebrate completing a new addition on our house. We were giving our guests a tour. When a friend said how much he liked the placement of a window with a view of the hills my husband thanked him, as if he had done it, when in reality I had spent days figuring it out! I watched how the light came in through the day, figured out where the sun would hit at different times of the year, and even where it would catch the rising moon in the spring! He knew all of that, and he knew I was standing right there! I was angry!
>
> When our guests left I told my husband how I felt and he apologized, but I still felt really "unfinished." I decided to take

the part of me that was angry through the Core Transformation Process. First, I just sensed the part and welcomed it. As I really received the part, I could feel the part being furious. I let the part really feel the anger fully, and asked, "If you really get to be as angry as you want to be, what do you want through being this angry, that is more important?"

The answer didn't come immediately, but when I let the part just feel the surge of anger, pretty soon in the middle of that, emerged the answer, "To fully express myself." This part wanted me to have full expression of all qualities of emotion. This was different from what I expected. I thought the part would want respect and recognition.

I asked the part, "Do you want respect or recognition?" This part clearly did not resonate with that. This part wanted "To fully express myself."

I invited the part to step into experiencing this and asked, "If you get this experience of fully expressing yourself, just the way you want it, what do you want through having that, that is even more important?" The part stayed with this experience of fully expressing itself for a while, then the answer emerged: "I will experience full, strong vitality."

I invited this experience to fill the part, and asked, "If you have this experience of full strong vitality the way you want it, what do you want through having that, that's even more important?"

In answer, I got a warm golden glow that permeated this part of me. As I invited this part to experience the golden glow fully, I asked, "And if you have this experience, is there anything even more important that you want through this?" Nothing came at first. Then as I stayed with the golden glow experience, through the middle emerged an experience that is even harder to describe. The closest I can come is that it is an experience of *liquid light.* This liquid light seemed to be moving, with a quality that has the fullness of honey, yet infinitely purer and smoother. As I invited the part to step into this experience, I was surprised by a vibration movement. It was as if the atoms of my physical being were no longer organized in the same way--they were no longer organized around me being a separate individual—they were in some kind of wave motion. This is an attempt to put into words something that is of a different level of reality, and these words do not fully describe it. This was my Core State.

JULIANNE'S OUTCOME CHAIN

Part to Work With: Anger
Intended Outcome 1: Fully Express Myself
Intended Outcome 2: Full, Strong Vitality
Intended Outcome 3: Golden Glow
Core State: Liquid Light

At this point in the Core State Exercise, Julianne has discovered what her part really wants: more than anything, this part wants her to experience the state she calls liquid light. This part thought that being angry would lead her along a path, through the other Intended Outcomes, that would eventually get her this valued experience.

Next Julianne reverses her Outcome Chain. This enables her inner part to *begin* by already having the Core State it wants. She is given the opportunity to experience how already having the Core State transforms or enriches each Intended Outcome, including the original feeling of anger. This ensures that Julianne naturally and automatically uses her liquid light experience in her ongoing living.

Let's go back to Julianne's experience:

> As I continued with the process, I invited this part to experience how already having this liquid light experience as a way of being makes things different.
>
> Next I let its impact wash back up through the Outcome Chain. I let the liquid light experience radiate through the experience of golden glow that was at an earlier level. Then I asked "How does your already having this liquid light experience as a way of being transform, enrich and radiate through the experience of strong vitality?"
>
> Then, "How does already having this liquid light as a way of being transform and enrich having a full range of expression?"
>
> I just let this integrate unconsciously. I don't know what changed from that, but I noticed the experience was much fuller, and somehow both stronger and more peaceful.
>
> Then I got to the last step and invited this part to notice how already having the liquid light transformed the original situation that I was angry about. I thought I might be more cleanly angry. I was surprised that as the liquid light radiated through this context, I felt a laugh emerge from deep within me. It was one of those laughs that is both very full, and yet silent at the

same time. It was as if the laugh permeated everything without making a sound.

I don't know what this will mean, exactly. I don't know what I will do. Yet I clearly don't feel "attached" to my ideas in the way I was before. I noticed right away that I felt an openness toward my husband that was new.

DOING THE CORE STATE EXERCISE SOLO

Some of you will have a partner to read the Core State Exercise and guide you through the process, and some of you will be doing the process on your own, with yourself. When you do the process with another person acting as your "guide" it is easy to stay on track and complete the exercise.

We have found that it takes more focus to do the Core Transformation Process solo—it's easier to become "spaced out" in our wonderful, nonverbal Core States! You will get the most benefit from the process if you do it all the way through. It will be helpful if you have a pencil and paper handy to write down your part and Outcome Chain. Here is an example of brief notes made by Tina, who did the process on her own. You can enjoy following along with her experience.

Step 1. CHOOSING A PART TO WORK WITH

a) I will work with the part of me that feels intimidated when my co-worker is strong in her opinions.

Experiencing the Part & Receiving and Welcoming the Part

b) I notice I feel intimidated in my stomach area—it feels tight and churning. I welcome and receive this "part" of me. As I do this I feel slightly warmer in my stomach, as if this part is cocooned, protected.

Step 2. DISCOVERING THE PURPOSE/FIRST INTENDED OUTCOME

a) I ask, "What do you want for me?" The part answers, "To be safe." I have a feeling of the part being enclosed in a safe area.

Step 3. DISCOVERING THE OUTCOME CHAIN

a) I ask the part, "If you are safe, fully safe, just the way you want to be, what do you want, through being safe, that is more important?" The part answers, "Then I can be present." I sense the part just being present, fully here in the moment—there is a warm sensation and a sense of clarity that goes with this.

b) I ask the part, "If you can be present the way you want to be, fully and completely, what do you want through this experi-encc that is even more important?" The part answers, "Live fully." I sense the part moving freely, without constriction, and I feel excited.

c) I ask the part, "If you have this experience of living fully, then what do you want through having that, that is even more important?" The part answers, "Be whole," and I feel as if I'm surrounded and permeated by a sphere of warmth.

Step 4. THE CORE STATE: REACHING THE WELLSPRING WITHIN

a) I ask the part, "If you experience 'be whole' fully, completely, what do you want through being whole that is even more important?" The part goes to an expansive infinity state that keeps going, without boundaries. I feel weightless and as if I exist in every atom of the universe. I sense that this is my Core State.

Step 5. REVERSING THE OUTCOME CHAIN WITH THE CORE STATE

a) I start to reverse the Outcome Chain and I ask my part, "How does already having expansive infinity as a way of being, make things different?" When expansive infinity goes into the part, it is as if something drops away, the part is freed in some way.

b) I ask my part, "How does already having expansive infinity radiate through the experience of being whole?" I experience wholeness as much bigger.

c) I ask my part, "How does already having expansive infinity transform and enrich living fully?" It is calmer, yet more enriched.

d) I ask my part, "How does already having expansive infinity transform being present?" I have a sense of even more warmth and greater clarity.

e) I ask my part, "How does already having expansive infinity transform and enrich your whole experience of safety?" Now the walls drop away more completely, there is more light, there is a sense of safety being a given in a different way. The barriers are irrelevant. Safety just is.

Transforming the Original Context

f) I ask my part, "How does already having expansive infinity transform the original situation of being with a co-worker?" There is a feeling of this part almost jumping up and down eagerly, really ready to be with the other person. It's completely different. I can't say completely what's different, but it is. I don't see the other person the same way anymore. They are just another person like me.

—CHAPTER 10—

PUTTING CORE TRANSFORMATION INTO PRACTICE

How the Core States Can Change Unwanted Behavior, Feelings and Responses

Considering the intensity of the problem we were dealing with,
I was surprised that the process was really easy.
It was very gentle, even though it was extraordinarily powerful.
—Russell

When we are living from our Core States many other limitations, in addition to the one we started with, tend to fall away. We simply don't need them anymore. People have often been surprised to discover other habits or feelings that changed seemingly on their own. Throughout the book we have included interviews with people who have gone through the Core Transformation process, to give you some idea of what usually happens.

Russell's Story

Russell, a businessman, did the Core Transformation Process with anger that he considered to be inappropriate. This is how he described the changes in his life a year after doing the process.

> It's a very powerful process. I had an issue of temper. I experienced unbelievable anger in circumstances that were totally inappropriate. Anger would just come up at the wrong times, and I would do dumb things—things that I would regret, things that didn't get me anywhere—they made it worse. Like getting angry at people in automobiles, or someone who was ahead in line and taking too long.

Because people attract the same type of personalities that they are, I attracted some angry people. I have found angry people to be a group of people I do not want to be around. They tend to cause the same kind of problems that I caused myself, so attracting those kinds of people to me compounded my problems. They sometimes got angry right along *with* me about a situation and fueled the fire: "Yeah, yeah! Go get 'em!" Sometimes they drew in circumstances which got me angry and upset. All of which didn't take me towards any objectives or useful outcomes. This was really destructive.

The worst example of this happened on a project with a subcontractor. The subcontractor had done something that was a little bit questionable and might have cost the project some extra money and a delay. Because I and the people I was involved with were so angry, everybody goaded everybody else on and we said, "Well, let's go get this guy!" It became a cause of its own, and the objectives of the project sat idle while this vindictive program was carried out. It involved lawyers and lawsuits and on and on and on. The final result was that the project suffered. We didn't have a sustainable claim. We could never have gotten a lot damages anyway. It was just something born out of anger and carried out from anger, and it was costly to everybody involved.

The total project we were involved in was quite significant. It was a project whose potential return was in the hundreds of millions. They were very big numbers. So when things slowed down and the focus went away from the objectives of the project, this was very damaging. In this particular instance, the legal fees, the waste of time, the waste of energy, the wasted opportunities, the costs of not moving forward were very, very high. Without a question, that one incident cost us millions of dollars.

For me this issue of anger was a subject that was very hard and angular and brutish and nasty and involved some not pretty memories. But the Core Transformation Process itself is easy and gentle and flowing. We were asking, "What is the higher good being sought here?" Considering the intensity of the problem we were dealing with, I was surprised that the process was really easy. It was very gentle, even though it was extraordinarily powerful. I didn't have to go through hell—I never had to get into the anger state at all.

Since the Core Transformation process, I've had—as we all have—a number of opportunities to let somebody know my displeasure. It is very different now. I will start to feel anger, and then, instead of blowing it, in a fraction of a second there's sort of a check list that appears in my mind, and a voice says something in my ear like, "What are you doing? What is this going to accomplish? Is it appropriate to lose your temper? Will a show of anger actually help this situation? What do you really want out of this? What is going to be an effective behavior mode to get what you need or what you want?" It happens in a nanosecond, but it's there. It catches me. And 99 percent of the time, I have a new kind of response. My inner voice says, "Let them re-cook the steak; let the guy dart in front of you; let the guy have the parking place."

I did this process a year ago, and the results are spectacular. I've been attracting people that are focused, not upset, not angry. I no longer waste energy. I don't get involved in things that are inappropriate, that take time. I don't have to go back and mend fences. I don't have to constantly be on guard about lashing out at things. Things have become much more easy, effortless. It doesn't mean I don't work. I put in the time, but the results have been incredible. More positive things have happened in the last year than have happened in a long time.

A couple of projects that we're working on have flowed really easily and effortlessly. We've written four books since April. I'm turning in another manuscript in May. There is a large market potential for these particular books. We are expanding our mail-order business. We were able to hire a top-flight chief operating officer, with fourteen years' experience in marketing with major U.S. corporations. He joined us and he doesn't have any of those anger issues. He's not upset with the world. Because we are focused and not upset, we are attracting in more people who are not upset. They are focused and look at things in a much more functional and appropriate way. I just can't say enough. It's been fantastic.

Working with this process has changed a number of areas in my life—the anger issue is only one. The ease with which the process works and the length of time that it takes is appropriate for the 1990s.

Kimberly's Story

Kimberly did the Core State Exercise with a part of her that wanted to be more accepting of somebody she felt deliberately hurt her. The story demonstrates how her beliefs about the other person were changed as a result of having her Core State. It is clear that this process is not about having another intellectual understanding of what we "ought to" experience. It is about reaching our wellspring within—something that has always been there—and allowing this inner wellspring to naturally ripple through our being.

> Intellectually I knew I should accept people I perceive as being hurtful and mean. I knew they just hadn't reached a place of knowing how to be nice, and that they had a positive intention behind their behavior. But I didn't have an *experience* of what I knew intellectually. I couldn't really think about this person in that way. It was more like, "So what! Even if that positive intent is in there, they're still being a jerk!"
>
> During the process, one of the Intended Outcomes was that my part wanted "to love and be loved." The Core State was *total love,* and there was a golden-silver light that came before it. It was *very* different from the Intended Outcome of "to love and be loved."
>
> When I did the Outcome Chain Reversal and took the Core State into the part that wanted "to love and be loved," I *also* saw the Core State inside of the person who had been hurtful to me. It went into their stomach area and surrounded the part of them they hadn't found yet. I could see it light up, and that it was a very small child in them. I experienced very deeply a level of compassion for this person that I had never felt before.

Natural Changes in Beliefs and Experience

As Kimberly and Russell have described, as we go through the Core Transformation Process, we usually experience spontaneous natural changes in our beliefs about ourselves and the world. Our limiting beliefs are found embedded within our Intended Outcomes. Without even knowing what our limiting beliefs are ahead of time, or changing them directly, it is as if the Core State washes them clean.

For example, safety and protection are Intended Outcomes that many parts strive for. Like small children, our inner parts tried to become safe and protected by walling themselves off or by walling us off from others in some way. We may try to protect ourselves by "hiding" and not speaking our mind, or by forming a "tough" exterior where we do not show ourselves. After living from the Core States, we usually experience safety and protection entirely differently. If, for example, my Core State is oneness, then when I am "one with everything," in one sense there is nothing left that I need protection from.

Needing something from others, such as love, recognition, or approval, is also very different. Let's assume again that our Core State is oneness. When I am living from the experience of being one with everything, it makes no sense to need something from someone else that I perceive as already a part of me. Most of our limiting beliefs can be thought of as arising out of the assumption that we are separate. When we experience ourselves as one with everything, much is transformed. Most of the Core States have a quality of oneness within them, even if that is not the word we use to describe the state. The kind of peace, OKness, beingness or love that is present when we reach our Core States has a universal quality.

—SECTION III—

GROWING UP A PART
&
BRINGING IT FULLY INTO YOUR BODY

Making Core States More Accessible

—CHAPTER 11—

INTRODUCTION

GROWING UP A PART

Gaining Resources and Wisdom

The child is the father of the man.
—Alfred, Lord Tennyson

The Japanese Soldier

During World War II, at the height of Japanese expansion in the Pacific, there were Japanese garrisons on literally thousands of tiny islands scattered across an enormous expanse of ocean. When the tide of battle turned, many of these were overrun and defeated, but some were entirely missed. On other islands, small groups of soldiers or isolated survivors hid in caves in inaccessible areas. A few years later, the war was over. But since these survivors didn't know this, they continued to struggle, maintaining their rusting weapons and tattered uniforms as best they could, totally isolated, yearning to be reunited with their command.

In the years immediately following the war, many of these soldiers were discovered when they shot at fishermen or tourist boats, or were found by natives. As the years passed, these discoveries became less frequent. The last one was some thirty years after the war had ended.

Consider the position of such a soldier. His government had called him, trained him, and sent him off to a jungle island to defend and protect his people against great external threat. As a loyal and obedient citizen, he had survived many privations and battles through the years of war. When the ebb and flow of battle passed him by, he was left alone or with a few other survivors. During all those years, he had carried on the battle in the best way he could, surviving against incredible odds. Despite the heat, the insects, and the jungle rains, he carried on, still loyal to the instructions given to him by his government so long ago.

How should such a soldier be treated when he is found? It would be easy to laugh at him, and call him stupid for continuing to fight a war that has been over for 30 years.

Instead, whenever one of these soldiers was located, the first contact was always made very carefully. Someone who had been a high-ranking Japanese officer during the war would take his old uniform and samurai sword out of the closet, and take an old military boat to the area where the lost soldier had been sighted. The officer would walk through the jungle, calling out for the soldier until he was found. When they met, the officer would thank the soldier, with tears in his eyes, for his loyalty and courage in continuing to defend his country for so many years. Then he would ask him about his experiences, and welcome him back. Only after some time would the soldier gently be told that the war was over, and that his country was at peace again, so he would not have to fight any more. When he reached home he would be given a hero's welcome, with parades and medals, and crowds thanking him and celebrating his arduous struggle and his return and reunion with his people. (This story was reprinted from *Heart of the Mind,* by Connirae and Steve Andreas. We offer it with thanks to Greg Brodsky.)

Growing Up A Part

When I (Connirae) first developed the Core Transformation Process, I noticed that some people followed the steps in the Core State Exercise, but didn't feel connected with the results. It was as if some part of them got to experience the Core State, but this part was still separate from them. The part experienced the Core State, but *they* didn't experience the Core State. The steps in this section fully connect and integrate the part you have been working with. I have noticed that these steps help everyone complete and amplify their results—even people who already experienced dramatic results from the Core State Exercise.

Being younger is one way that a part can still be separate from us. Most of us can easily identify behaviors, feelings and responses in ourselves that come from an earlier age. It's as though parts of us are "out of touch" with the experience and wisdom we have as a grown person. These isolated parts are the ones in charge of the behaviors, feelings and responses we want to change! At the time we learned these coping strategies, they were the best choice that we could come up with to deal with a difficult situation. Just as the Japanese soldiers had been left behind, it is as if that part is still stuck at that early age, isolated from the skills, information, and wisdom that we now have.

If we ask our inner parts, "How old are you?" many of them will give an answer from early childhood or infancy. If we leave a part at a younger age, even though it has its Core State, we are not likely to experience this Core State as fully as possible. (You will learn how parts are formed in more detail in Chapter 27, "How Parts Are Formed.")

Nearly all of the behaviors, feelings and responses we have that we don't like are remnants of an earlier age. As adults, most of us are ready to move beyond these kinds of reactive states. In the next few chapters you will learn how to take the Core Transformation Process a step further, bringing greater healing to these younger parts through their Core States. When we grow up a part in the Core Transformation Process we are lovingly and gently communicating that it is now safe and natural for a new, more resourceful behavior, feeling or response to emerge.

Bringing the Part Fully Into Your Body

The other major way our inner parts can remain separate from us is if we experience them as literally in a separate location. For us to experience the Core State fully, the part needs to reunite with us completely—to flow into our entire physical body and fill us. In this section we will learn to notice where our parts are located, and then make sure our parts are completely reunited with us.

As long as our parts are somehow separated from us by age or by location, we are not yet the complete, integrated being we are intended to be. When we are fully reunited with our parts, we can fully receive the gifts they have to give.

—CHAPTER 12—

A DEMONSTRATION WITH LISA

The Value of Growing Up Parts

When you're one with God, then you also tend to see the God in other people, whether they are treating you like a Daddy, a Mommy, a son, or like a mosquito!
—*Connirae Andreas*

In this demonstration two new steps are added to the Core Transformation Process: "Growing Up A Part," and "Bringing the Part Fully Into the Body."

Before Connirae demonstrates these new steps she guides Lisa through the Core State Exercise. We offer this second example of the Core State Exercise to assist you in understanding the process more fully.

Imagine that you just arrived here from another planet and have only seen one plant. Having only seen that one plant you have no way to appreciate the variety of growing things here. You wouldn't realize that some plants are flowers, some grasses, some trees, some shrubs. However, once you've seen a few plants you will easily recognize a new one, even if you've never seen that particular variety before. Botanists could list all the specifications that make it a plant, but without knowing the list you already know from your experience that it is a plant. In the same way, reading through this demonstration with Lisa will help your unconscious understanding and recognition of how the Core Transformation Process can work for you.

This demonstration takes place in an Aligned Self seminar. Commentary that has been added to the transcript appears in *(italic and parentheses)*.

....

Choosing A Part to Work With

Connirae: So, Lisa, what is a behavior, feeling or response that seems young to you, that you'd like to have more choice about? Younger, but not delightful.

Lisa: I don't like it when someone treats me like they're a Daddy. I don't like it when someone tries to tell me what to do. *(Lisa looks annoyed.)*

Experiencing the Part

Connirae: OK. When this happens, what is your response?

Lisa: It's a feeling in my throat. *(Lisa touches her throat as her breathing becomes faster and sharper.)*

Connirae: In your throat. OK.

(To the group.) Notice that we already have access to this part of Lisa. She's got it, right away. If she hadn't already accessed this part of her, we would ask her to think of a specific incident in which she had this response.

Receiving and Welcoming the Part

(To Lisa.) What I want you to do, Lisa, is let your attention turn within, so you can begin to welcome this part. Before, you may have been in conflict with this part, and wanted to shove it aside. ... *(Lisa nods.)*

Discovering the Purpose

Connirae: With this sense of welcoming now, you can ask this part, "What do you want?"

Lisa: ... Stand up for myself.

Connirae: OK. This part creates a feeling in your throat, and it wants, "Stand up for myself." That sounds like an important thing for all of us to have. Lisa, you can thank this part for wanting this outcome for you. ... *(Lisa nods and turns within.)*

Discovering the Outcome Chain

Connirae: Now ask this part, "If you *get* this purpose for me, just the way you want it, what do you want for me, through *having* this ability to stand up for myself?"

Lisa: ... Value. I think standing up for myself has to do with having a sense of value—it's that these things I think or have to say have value. That's what standing up for myself is.

Connirae: It wants you to have a sense of value? Standing up for yourself has to do with having a sense of value?

Lisa: ... Yes.

Connirae: Now, Lisa, you can thank this part, and ask it, "If you, this part of me, get *all of this,* value and standing up for myself, then what do you want through having this, that's still more important?

Lisa: There's a feeling of love that comes up then.

Connirae: There's a feeling of love that comes up then. That's a nice feeling. So, as you turn within now, Lisa, and thank the part for having this outcome for you, ask, "If I get this experience, of *having this feeling of love,* then what do you want to experience, through having this, that is even more important?"

Lisa: I'm getting a new awareness of what I got before, a feeling of love.

Connirae: That's fine. *(To the group.)* Some of the rest of you may find this to be true, also—that you get the same answer twice. Almost always, however, there will be something unique about the second answer that's significant. So it needs individual attention. Usually the feeling quality is deeper or fuller the second time. So you can tell me what it is.

The Core State: Reaching the Wellspring Within

Lisa: *(She has her eyes closed, and is sensing on the inside.)* ... And then it goes to sense of enlightenment. And then, *being one with God.*

(Rather than answer my question, Lisa's part has gone on to the next two answers. As Lisa reports these answers, she looks like she has already tapped into a wonderfully blissful state of being. "Being One With God" is clearly the Core State of Being for this part.)

LISA'S OUTCOME CHAIN

Part to Work With: Feeling in throat when someone tells me what to do
Intended Outcome 1: Stand up for myself
Intended Outcome 2: Sense of value
Intended Outcome 3: Feeling of love
Intended Outcome 4: Feeling of love (more deeply)
Intended Outcome 5: Sense of enlightenment
Core State: Being One With God

Reversing The Outcome Chain With the Core State

Connirae: *(In a warm, resonant voice.)* OK. Great! You can thank the part for wanting all of these wonderful things. Now you can ask the part, "What is it like to just *have* this experience of being one with God as a way of being in the world?" ...

Yeah, kind of nice, huh? Having it is much nicer than not having it. Notice how that makes a difference ... and also notice how already *having* the experience of being one with God enriches and supports the sense of enlightenment. ...

(Lisa nods.) And how having the oneness with God already, supports and enriches a new awareness of love. ...

(Lisa nods.) Yes Lisa, that's right.

(To the group.) And as I guide Lisa in having the Core State present in each of her Intended Outcomes, I let myself go through each step along with her. That helps my words be more appropriate. I let my words and tone of voice work for me, and also watch to see if they work well for Lisa. Doing it along with her means I also get all kinds of good states out of this!

(To Lisa.) You can invite this part to also experience how already having oneness with God radiates through the state of love, because it is different, already having oneness with God there. And how already having Oneness with God radiates through having a sense of value. ... And how already having oneness with God adds to or transforms the whole situation about standing up for yourself, and what you see as worth standing up for, and so on. Noticing how already having oneness with God transforms that whole thing. *(Lisa's breathing deepens and becomes fuller, her body relaxes. She is becoming more visibly radiant with each step.)*

(To the group.) Notice that there are some Intended Outcomes where what makes sense is that the oneness with God is going to support and enrich, and make automatic. And there are other Intended Outcomes which the oneness with God is going to completely transform. It's going to become a whole different thing. When you already have oneness with God, what is this thing about standing up for yourself? I mean what more do you need! It's just not that big a deal.

(Although Connirae speaks to the group, her purpose is to support Lisa's integration. Connirae is watching Lisa's nonverbal response, to know what most facilitates Lisa's change process. When Lisa's nonverbal changes settle, Connirae asks her for a report.)

So what happens with "standing up for yourself?" *(Lisa nods slowly and smiles.)* Here you are, what more do you need? It's not that big a deal. Standing up for yourself has already happened in a deeper way. In a different sort of way, you already *are* stood up for.

Transforming the Original Context

Connirae: Also notice how already having this oneness with God transforms those original situations, making those different. Now the oneness with God permeates through the context so that we let it be how it is now, with this oneness with God there, and you can just notice how it is.

When you're one with God, then you also tend to see the God in other people, whether they are treating you like a Daddy, a Mommy, a son, or a like a mosquito! It doesn't matter too much what their thing is. We all have our things. And there's a recognition of that, too. ... *(Lisa opens her eyes and looks at Connirae expectantly.)*

Connirae: *(Laughs.)* I was just pausing, because I thought it would be rude to keep talking given the kind of wonderful state you look like you're in. I will go ahead and ask you the next question now if that's all right.

Lisa: *(Smiles and nods.) (Lisa has been signaling Connirae primarily nonverbally. Most people prefer not to talk much in the kind of intense state she is in.)*

Growing Up the Part

Connirae: Lisa, now, as you turn within, I'd like you to ask this part this question: "How old are you?" And find out what answer emerges.

Lisa: *(Long pause.)* Two years old.

Connirae: Now you got that answer a long time ago, right?

Lisa: Yeah, first four came up, and then I got some other ages, and two was the earliest one.

Connirae: All right, good. *(To the group.)* If you get a series of ages, take the earlier age as Lisa just did.

The interesting thing about this is that we all have these parts. They are generally much younger than our current age—often really young, like two years old, and they're in charge of a really important Core State—like, in this case, oneness with God. So, here we've got this two-year-old, and we say, "OK, your job is this! Do it, all right?" *(Laughter.)* And they don't have the resources that come from all the rest of our experiences—our evolution through time.

(To Lisa.) Is this part a he, a she, or an it?

Lisa: *(Turns within to check.)* It's not a he or a she—I guess it.

Connirae: OK, then I'd like you to ask the part—to support having oneness with God fully for you in an ongoing way if it would like to evolve forward through time so that it has complete access to your full range of experience and wisdom. *(Lisa turns inward to check, then nods.)* Great, great. Let your unconscious allow that to happen now, having this Core State fully available, while this part evolves forward through time, all the way to your current age, letting you know whenever this part has arrived at the age you are now. ... And as it evolves through time, it has that Core State already there. Through each moment of its life more resources are collected, more experience is accessible, to bring to manifesting that Core State even more fully as a way of being, with no need to realize just how that's happening or what else is also transformed and colored by it as it evolves forward through time. ... *(Lisa nods to indicate the part is finished.)* Great. And it is much easier to allow our unconscious to do that, than to do it consciously, because the transformation can be easier and more complete when it happens at that level.

Bringing the Part Fully Into Your Body

Now, where do you sense this part is located in space? Is it outside of you, or within you? At this moment where is it?

Lisa: It's in me. It's here *(Gesturing to her throat.)* and all over. It's strongest in my throat and it's throughout my body.

Connirae: So it's there, throughout. Good. Now you can allow this Core State to flow through your body even more, radiating through your whole being, through every cell, through your entire nervous system, through all of your neurons, muscles, blood vessels, bones, all of your organs, bathing every cell, permeating every cell from the inside out, from top to bottom so that being one with God is there, deeply throughout your being. You may also have a sense of it radiating beyond your skin.

Reversing the Outcome Chain With the Grown-Up Part

(To the group.) Now that her part is current age and fully throughout her body, I'm going to invite Lisa to invite her part to repeat taking the Core State through the Outcome Chain. Often we can experience this more fully once the part is our current age.

(To Lisa.) Lisa, now that this part is fully throughout your being, at conscious and unconscious levels, having oneness with God already there as a way of being, you can sense how that amplifies and enriches the sense of enlightenment, and you can experience how that can happen even more thoroughly. You can experience how already having oneness with God adds richness to the new awareness of love, now, even more than it did before. ... That's right, you can just let that spread, and let yourself really appreciate that and be touched by it. *(Connirae pauses—Lisa is clearly very moved by what is happening. Her eyes are moist, and her breathing is increasingly full and deep.)*

Are you ready for the next one? *(Lisa nods.)*

Now you can experience how already having oneness with God amplifies the sense of love, ... how already having oneness with God radiates through the sense of value ... how already having oneness with God really does transform even more deeply and completely, the whole thing about standing up for yourself, and how already having it changes those situations around people. ... You can stay there even longer. *(Connirae pauses to give Lisa more time, since she is experiencing the state very powerfully.)* That's right, really breathing in those changes, and letting that experience radiate.

And whenever you're ready, you can make sure that this part, and the sense of oneness with God, is already flowing fully through your whole body, through every cell. Sometimes people have a sense of it radiating beyond. *(Lisa nods.)* Yes, ... it's through the bone marrow, through the blood, through the cells, and beyond. It's nice to notice that it's already flowing through us from the top of our being to the bottom, from the front to the back, side to side, so that we can fully enjoy the benefits in every aspect of our being. *(With each step of this process, Lisa has become more radiant. She now looks like she is completely in this state of oneness with God.)*

And that, Lisa, is as intense as we're going to get for this moment! Of course, you're free to do more if you like! *(Laughter.)*

....

Lisa's Results

Lisa spoke with us about a year after doing the above Core Transformation Process with Connirae:

> My life has changed in so many ways. My behavior changed in very nice ways, and sometimes I just want to pinch myself and say, "Is this real?" because life is happier every day. Now, instead of waking up dreading something, I wake up wondering, "What great things can I be and do today?" A lot of ideas I'd had before were just dreams and wishes. This year, they have all become reality. Before, it was, "Gosh, I really wish," and, "Wouldn't it be neat," but it didn't seem possible. There were obstacles and problems and "yuck" that I thought I had to go through before I could have what I wanted.
>
> One of the main issues I'd had was if anyone wanted me to do something I had a lot of resistance. I didn't like what I'd call commands or have to's. This came up with bosses, as well as in personal relationships. I am in sales, where people get crazy and demanding. A lot of my days were spent with a lot of anxiety and physical pain. I would choke up and get to the point that I couldn't breathe. I used to have what I called "mini-heart attacks." I had terrible, incredible pain in my chest, without having an actual heart attack—because I didn't know what to do. I was asked to do things that were impossible to do.
>
> I also used to have this voice in my head that would start panicking, saying, "What am I going to do? How am I going to do this?" and, "I hate my job! I need to find something else to do."
>
> Here's one example: We had a job to print a million catalogues for a large company. It takes two weeks to print them. Before we could begin printing they had to give me the materials I needed to get it done. They didn't get the materials to me when they said they would; they were a week late. Then they still wanted the job done by the originally agreed upon date. That gives us *one* week, instead of two weeks, to print the catalogues. But they still wanted them, and there were a million of them,

and there were six colors, and they wanted everything to match perfectly. This happens twice a year with this client.

The biggest problem was that I couldn't personally fulfill the demand they were making, because I'm just a sales rep. But in order to keep my customer happy and keep the account, I then had to go back to the company I work for and put the demand on them. Because of my intense emotional and physical reaction to the demand, I had a very difficult time selling my company on what had to be done to keep my customer happy. In order to sell my company on the idea, I would have to know a way, in my mind, that it *could* work. And I wasn't in a state of creativity; I was stuck.

Being in the business as long as I have, I know what can and cannot be done in a certain time-frame for a certain amount of money. What was demanded could not be done in the amount of time they wanted, based on the way I had been taught this business.

This situation at work is just one example of this issue. I had the same reaction to a lot of other work situations, and the same thing happened in personal relationships if I was being asked to do something that I didn't think could be done, or should be done.

This is the issue I worked on with Connirae. Afterwards a lot of people came up to me and said I was glowing, that I'd made changes that were obvious and everybody could see—it must have been something!

After the seminar I didn't think about the change, I just went home and went about my life, but I have found that whenever I am in a situation in which demands are placed on me, my response is entirely different. I can clearly understand what is being asked, why it's important, and what needs to be done. I can get really creative immediately, instead of having those awful physical symptoms, having a lot of resistance and resentment, and feeling I'm being controlled.

The last time this happened with that client was just before I went to the seminar, and it was awful. Now, the same thing happened again, and this time I have responded totally differently. I have been very creative. This time, when they didn't get the materials to my company on time, and the days were slipping by, and my company still had to get the finished product out, the feeling that I used to get in my heart didn't happen. The choking feeling that I used to get in my throat didn't happen. I didn't have the problems with breathing. This time, without even thinking about it, I started breathing really deeply—where before I didn't breathe. This time, I had a "knowing" that I could still get this done, instead of the old voice in my head that said "It's impossible." Now I have a knowing that says, "Yes, we can do something. I will work on it."

Before doing the Core Transformation Process, I had tried everything. I'm 35 years old and I have been studying self-help methods since I was sixteen. I'm the type of person who will read every book, listen to every tape, and try anything that I can think of to be a happier person and enjoy my life. I was raised a good Catholic girl, so I tried praying, too. I'd tried crying, getting upset. I tried "being positive." I told myself that everything would work out fine, I told my client that everything would be OK, and then went back to my company and tried to motivate the people around me. I told them, "Yeah, you can do this, I know it's impossible but we can get it done." That was my positive way of trying to "rock the boat," and trying to get people to see it my way.

That didn't work at all. It drained me. No one believed me because I didn't believe it. So people at the office began taking sides. People were saying that I didn't care for the company because I was putting these pressures and demands on them. They felt I should have fielded off the demands, I should have told the customer "no."

Now I feel much more neutral. I'm able to see everyone's side and I don't get into the emotions of it. And I love my job again! That's important. Last year, before I did the Aligned Self seminar, I was at a point in my life where I thought the change needed to be something outside myself. I was looking for anything to change but myself. So I was thinking I needed a new career, and that was really scary because I've been doing this for twelve years, and I'm good at this and I like it. It was very disturbing to me to think about changing careers. So now I have my life back.

What I love is that when I did the technique, I changed and it has lasted. I don't have to think about taking deep breaths. I don't have to consciously do anything; it's all automatic. It's like I have a new *me.* I don't have to think anything—my new response is just me now.

Stopping Smoking

An unexpected bonus from this workshop was that I stopped smoking as a result of the Core Transformation Process that I did as an exercise with two of my group members. I had smoked a half pack to a pack a day. It went in spurts. If I was around girlfriends who were smoking, I might smoke two packs. If I was busy and working, I smoked more like a half to one pack. I had smoked since I was sixteen years old. I didn't go into the process with the idea of stopping smoking. Of course, I knew smoking wasn't good for me. The message "stop smoking, stop smoking," is everywhere. However, I didn't feel any need to stop smoking.

I went into the exercise with the idea of my body as a vehicle, and I was in it. I'm always into feelings and learning and growing, and I've always thought of all of that as "me," and my body was just the way I got around. I was curious about what benefit I could have from being one with my body, instead of seeing me and my body as two separate parts.

I was very surprised by what I found out. After I did the process I experienced my body in a new way—it's like a filter. Information and energy comes in through it and goes out through it. Then a realization came up about smoking. The smoke was filtering the information and the energy. The smoke was in the way! It was like a fog. I got a clear picture of the inside of my body, with all these blood vessels and muscles, and there was this fog on the inside. The idea was that I would see more clearly, hear more clearly, and feel more clearly if this fog was gone.

What happened—and this is what I just love about the procedure—is that afterwards I didn't want a cigarette! The desire was gone! I didn't decide to quit, I just didn't want one. I had no withdrawal symptoms at all.

Better Relationship

I have been dating the same person for ten years. The situation is that I have been married twice, and he has been married twice, and we won't live together, that's too close for comfort, and there was a lot of yuck happening in the relationship. Now, we're living together! I sold my house and we have a beautiful farm now.

This has changed in that before I went through the Core Transformation Process, even though I could wish for the way I wanted things to be, it wasn't that way all the time. After the process I was able to communicate with my partner about how I wanted to relate and how I wanted life to be. And I could paint a picture for him that was very clear to me and to him. It was a really nice picture. Then it was a matter of "Do you want to paint this picture with me, and does this picture match your picture? And if it doesn't, that's okay." That was a first for me. Before, it was never okay with me for him not to want what I wanted.

Before, my attitude was "If you don't want it, I'll be heartbroken, and I'll just hang around and be miserable forever. Someday, maybe, you will see the light."

My new attitude is "It's okay, because I'm now me and I'm whole. And I can have a life whether you want to be in it or not." That's what has changed. And what's even greater is that once I became whole and let him go, he came to me!

—CHAPTER 13—

GROWING UP A PART

Understanding the Structure

...no sooner was it done than the fox turned into a man, and was none other than the brother of the beautiful princess, freed at last from the spell under which he had lain. And now there was nothing lacking to their happiness, so long as they all lived.
—The Juniper Tree and Other Tales From Grimm

Genuine transformation comes from having full access to our Core States throughout our body. When we do the Core Transformation Process with parts that have been split off from us we are welcoming them back within us. Having the Core States present gives these parts the acknowledgment, warmth, acceptance and love that they needed when we were young. The next step is to grow them up. This gives them the benefits of our experience and wisdom so they can be fully integrated into the wholeness of who we are. Our parts are then "freed from the spell" they have been under.

In this chapter we will enrich your understanding of the two new steps you were just introduced to in the demonstration with Lisa: "Growing Up A Part" and "Bringing the Part Fully Into the Body." These are steps six and seven of the ten-step Core Transformation Process.

Step 6: Growing Up A Part

When Lisa's two-year-old inner part gained access to its Core State, "being one with God," this part was deeply transformed and Lisa felt the results quite strongly. However, since this part was only two years old it was still somewhat separate from Lisa. When Lisa allowed her inner part to evolve forward through time to her current age, her part gained an enriched experience of being one with God. For some people and some parts this step is particularly powerful. At a younger age the part can't fully bring the Core State into current everyday experience. When you do the exercise you will have the opportunity to notice what kind of a difference growing up your part makes for you.

Having the Core State available *while* growing up the part is very important. Before I knew anything about tapping into the Core State of a part, I frequently invited younger parts of my clients to grow up. Without a Core State, younger parts often had objections to growing up. As a part grew up it would frequently encounter a life situation that it didn't want to go through. The inner part would object, "That was terrible, and I don't want to go through that now." These "terrible" life circumstances are why the part split off in the first place. While I always found ways to help these young parts grow up, it was sometimes difficult, and the results were not as dramatic.

I was fascinated to discover that when an inner part gains access to its Core State, this and other objections to growing up rarely occur! The process almost always goes very smoothly and quickly. Our Core States are our ultimate solution—they tap into a quality of experience that goes beyond the ordinary conflicts of daily living. When our parts have a Core State as a felt experience, ordinary difficulties tend to melt away.

When you grow up a part it is not necessary to consciously move through your life history. The growing up often happens at such a deep unconscious level that most people don't even have a sense of going through specific parts of their personal history. We suggest that you simply invite your part to evolve forward through time as outlined in the exercise in the following chapter, without needing to know how your part does this.

Step 7: Bringing the Part Fully Into Your Body

If we check where our inner parts are located we usually discover that they are separate from us. It is easy to observe this by asking inwardly where in the space around us we see, hear, feel, or "sense" the part we are working with. Many parts are either outside our body or restricted to a small area within our body. When our parts are completely outside of our body—in front, behind, to one side, above, or below—allowing them to flow back into our body gives us much greater access to our Core States.

When Lisa had finished growing up her part it was already located in her body, yet she noticed that it was most strongly present in her throat. It did not fill the rest of her body as fully as in her throat area. By inviting her part to flow and radiate through her whole body Lisa gained a fuller experience of oneness with God.

Step 8: Reversing the Outcome Chain with the Grown-Up Part

This step enriches our experience of how the Core State naturally and automatically impacts our daily living. When we have the Core State and take it through our Intended Outcomes we traverse through all the life situations this part is concerned with. Lisa experienced how being one with God transformed enlightenment, love, value, and standing up for herself—this time with her part reunited with her whole body. As I explained to Lisa and the group, we can usually experience this more fully once the part is current age. A two-year-old part won't have access to the same ways to "stand up for herself" for example, that are available to the adult Lisa.

Parts That Object to Growing Up

When your part has rediscovered its Core State, it almost never objects to growing up. The Core State seems to provide an inner solution, or healing ointment, to the life difficulties that caused the part to split off at a younger age. If a part has difficulty or objects to growing up, this may be a sign that you haven't really gotten to your part's Core State. There is probably another state this part wants that is deeper.

Another possibility is that an objecting part is afraid of losing its positive childlike qualities. Alicia, a workshop participant, initially balked at the idea of inviting parts of herself to grow up. She said, "Won't they lose something important if they grow up? They know how to have fun!" It is true that children spend more time having fun and being spontaneously themselves than grown-ups. Many people assume that loss of these childhood gifts as we grow up is inevitable. They, like Alicia, want to keep younger parts as a way to have access to those childlike qualities.

Ironically, we have found that the loss of the choice to be childlike and spontaneous happens only to the degree that we are cut off from parts of ourselves, and cut off from our Core States. When we split these parts off from ourselves, and keep them at a younger age, we *don't* get full access to these wonderful childlike qualities. We leave them in a separate part, rather than taking them into who we are now. Once a part of ourselves has stepped fully into its Core State it can grow up while keeping the choices it already has, and gaining new ones. I explained to Alicia that her part could keep its two-year-old ability to have fun, and add to it the three-year-old ability to have fun, the four-year-old ability to have fun, and so on. After growing up one part of her, Alicia commented, "It's like that part of me came fully back to life!"

—CHAPTER 14—

DOING IT!

THE "GROWING UP A PART" EXERCISE

Embracing Inner Children Who Were Left Behind

Action should culminate in wisdom.
—Bhagavad-Gita

Personal integration happens when three elements come together:
1. We have access to our Core States.
2. All our parts are at our current age.
3. All our parts are fully associated throughout our bodies.

You have already learned the first element, how to access a Core State. Now you will add the other two elements. While you are doing this part of the Core Transformation Process you can use the same guidelines as for the Core State Exercise: making yourself physically comfortable, relaxing, and turning within. You can use the same part that you used in the Core State Exercise. You will be adding steps 6, 7 and 8 of the full process.

If you are reading this as a guide for someone else, you do not need to say the italicized words out loud. Remember to speak in a soft, slow voice when you are talking to someone's inner part. You can experiment with stepping into and experiencing each Intended Outcome and the Core State. This usually makes it easier for your partner.

....

Step 6. GROWING UP THE PART

a) Begin with a part you have already taken through the Core State Exercise in Section II. *This is very important. The exercise is very simple* *and powerful when the part's Core State is already present. (The exercise will not work with a part that hasn't been through the Core State Exercise.)*

b) Turn within and welcome and receive this part as it is now. Relive your experience of getting to [Core State]. You may experience it as a fast action movie, as you quickly sense your part going from one Intended Outcome to the next, all the way to [Core State]. When you are finished with this step you will be in the state you were in when you finished the Core State Exercise with this part.

c) Turn within and ask this part, "How old are you?" Notice what answer emerges. If you are not sure whether you have the correct age, that's OK. You can invite your part to just notice unconsciously what age you were when it was first formed. *Write down the age of the part. If the part is already current age, skip to step 6.*

d) This part is usually much younger than you are. This means it doesn't yet have the full benefit of the wisdom that comes from all the experiences you have had in the years since this part stopped growing up with you. It also means that this part doesn't yet have full access to you. This part wants to give you the gift of [Core State], and yet it's separate from you. Being separated at a younger age, it can't give you this gift as fully as it would like to. So, ask this part if it would like to have the benefits that come from evolving forward in time to your current age, with this [Core State] fully present. *If you get a "yes," you are ready to go on. In the event that the part doesn't want to have these benefits, ask what its objection is. Make sure any objection is satisfied before going on. An objection is usually a simple misunderstanding. For example, the part may think it has to give up having fun.*

e) Invite this part of you to begin by having [Core State] fully present now. When it is fully present, you can invite your unconscious to allow this part, with [Core State] present, to evolve forward through time, from whatever age it is, all the way forward to your current age, having [Core State] there through every moment of time. You can allow that to happen now. Have the part let you know when it has arrived at your current age.

Step 7. BRINGING THE PART FULLY INTO YOUR BODY

a) Notice where the part is located now. Where, specifically, is it located? Is it inside your body or outside your body?

b) *If the part is inside your body, skip to step 8.* If the part is outside your body, allow this part of you to now flow into your body, so that [Core State] flows into your physical being. Notice where the part naturally flows into you.

c) Noticing where this part already fills your body, allow it to spread and flow fully through every cell, so that every cell of your being is filled, nourished, and bathed by [Core State]. You may notice how, as this [Core State] radiates from the place it began, throughout your whole body, the more it radiates through your body the stronger it becomes in the place where it began. And as [Core State] fills every cell, you may already sense how it is as if this is now a part of your emotional coding—the ground of your being.

Step 8. REVERSING THE OUTCOME CHAIN WITH THE GROWN-UP PART

a) *Briefly repeat the Outcome Chain Reversal with the grown-up part.* Now that the part is current age, and fully in your body, [Core State] can even more completely transform your experiences in the present. Invite this part to notice how already having [Core State] as a way of being, as a way of moving through the world, transforms and enriches [Intended Outcome].

Continue the Outcome Chain Reversal, bringing the Core State into all Intended Outcomes and into original context. (See "Reversing the Outcome Chain With the Core State," in the Core State Exercise, Chapter 8, if you need to refresh your memory on how to do this.)

b) Now you can experience how having this part grown up, and having [Core State] throughout your body as a way of being in the world, transforms [Original Context].

—SECTION IV—

COMPLETING THE PROCESS WITH ALL PARTS

Working With Every Aspect of An Issue

—CHAPTER 15—

INTRODUCTION

COMPLETING THE PROCESS WITH ALL PARTS

Integrating Core States More Deeply

All which we behold is full of blessings.
—William Wordsworth

Most people find that allowing a part to discover its Core State, growing it up, and bringing it fully into the body, is deeply moving. When people experience these processes in seminars, they often respond by saying, "How could there be anything beyond this?" That reminds me of the old children's riddle: "What makes more noise than a happy hog in a mud puddle?" Answer: "Ten happy hogs in a mud puddle!"

If you have had difficulty getting the process to work easily and smoothly for you, this section may give you the information you need. The important issues in our lives often have more than one part. To have the most complete, lasting change it is important to work with all of the parts of ourselves involved with an issue. In this section we will give you several ways to identify all the parts involved.

After we have worked with all parts involved with an issue we add one last step to solidify the results of this process even more. This last step is called Timeline Generalization. In this part of the process we spread the Core States throughout our past, present and future.

—Chapter 16—

A DEMONSTRATION WITH GREG

Inner Peace As A Way of Being

The most exciting part was the discovery that I didn't have to go outside myself to get inner peace. The things I used to get outraged about still happen, but they are not a hot button for me anymore.
—Greg

This transcript gives you an example of an entire client session of the Core Transformation Process. When the client, Greg, set up the appointment, he said he wanted to work with a major issue—something he had worked with for several years and nothing had made a difference. After doing the Core Transformation Process with one part, Connirae helps Greg identify a second part which also needs to be worked with to fully resolve this issue. Greg's wife Ann is also present during the session. As you read Greg's experience, if you choose you can invite your unconscious to lay the groundwork for the inner changes that will matter most to you. Commentary that has been added to the transcript appears in *(italic and parentheses)*.

....

Choosing A Part to Work With

Connirae: Briefly, what is it that you want?

Greg: We have a lot of stress in our relationship. Not just the relationship—we have a lot of stress in our life. Ann and I have a good relationship, but my stepson Eric effectively manages to push all my hot buttons to a point that it damages the relationship between the two of us. I've been working on changing this pattern for two years. The situation with Eric, coupled with everything else going on is just more than I can handle. Specifically I would like to find a way to deal with my anger towards Eric. I would be much happier if I could see the things that are going on and let them just roll off my back.

Connirae: OK.

Greg: The second thing that I would like is to feel more solid overall. I have got all kinds of stress going on in my life. Business-wise, we have tremendous success on the one hand, and we've got a lawsuit on the other hand. It is getting nasty. We will have a jury trial that will probably take a half-day or a day. I would like to feel more centered so that I don't give that other party my energy to feed on.

Connirae: All right. Which of these issues is the most important to you? Which will make the most difference to you if it is handled?

Greg: The one with my stepson.

Connirae: We will take that one then. It sounds like you want things to roll off your back and not irritate you. *(As Connirae asks Greg questions, she is also watching and listening to him attentively. His choice of which issue to work with fits with his deeply felt responses to his stepson.)*

Greg: He does a lot of small things that shouldn't be that big a deal.

Connirae: But some part of you gets hooked in.

Greg: What he does conflicts with my belief system.

Ann: The last time it happened, my son stayed after school to work. He is yearbook photo editor and graphics editor of the school newspaper. He called to see if he could get a ride home and Greg spoke with him first because I was out getting groceries and was not feeling well. Greg blew up at him, and said, *(In a loud, angry tone.)* "Your mother is out getting groceries, and you can take your chances and try again later." *(Sounding upset.)* I can't understand why Greg flipped out about it.

Connirae: Let's stop right here, because Greg doesn't understand why he got upset either. So we can explore and find that out. Is that what you would like to know, too?

Ann: Yeah.

Connirae: Now let me ask you something else. Once Greg has shifted so that this behavior is not a hot button, he may still decide that he is not available to pick up Eric some night without flipping out about it. Or there may be several relapses, so to speak. Would you like to have it so that even if he has a relapse, you don't have to be pulled apart by it?

Ann: Yes.

Connirae: OK. So that can be your goal for yourself.

Greg: I would like to acquire some more power and be congruent with my belief system.

Connirae: How have you been incongruent with your belief system?

Greg: Well, what triggers me is when he does things that I believe are irresponsible. Rather than giving up my beliefs about common courtesy and consideration and responsible behavior, I think I would rather acquire a level of tolerance, and remember that maybe he just hasn't learned yet to be responsible. I want a sense of patience and tolerance.

Connirae: OK. So there are things that he does that are inconsistent with what you feel is common courtesy, and you would like to have a different response to him.

Greg: Yes. I don't want to change Eric. I want to change the way I respond. I want to be tolerant and patient.

Connirae: OK. There is only one problem with those two words. Very few people can actually carry them out. Very few people who are described on the outside as being patient *feel* like they are being patient on the inside. They don't feel patient at all, because usually patience and tolerance are things that you have to try to *make* yourself have against your inclinations. It is usually very hard to have success at that. So we will have success at something else.

Greg: OK. That is why we are here.

Connirae: OK, so when your stepson does one of these things, on one hand you would like to be patient and tolerant but on the other hand you get angry. How do you manage to do that? What do you have to think about to get angry?

Greg: Well, I probably run through a little history of everything that has occurred before.

Connirae: Yeah, if I do that it works for me! I can start getting angry that way.

Greg: So it is a good warm-up?

Connirae: Yes, that is a good warm-up! *(Greg, Connirae and Ann laugh together.)* So you run through all the past examples.

Greg: Yeah, and all the times I have asked him to do things in a different fashion, and then I feel the emotion welling up, I guess.

Connirae: OK. Now when you run through the examples, what conclusion do you come to?

Greg: Well, I look at what my son Randy has done, and I look at my old belief system about what I consider to be considerate and responsible.

Connirae: And it makes sense that it would lead to being frustrated. You are comparing your stepson's behavior that you consider irresponsible with a sense of what, for you, is ideal behavior. OK. When you are comparing differently, what things do you notice that are better with Eric than with Randy?

Greg: That's difficult for me. I do identify the positive intent behind his behavior, but then I am reluctant to share that with him.

Connirae: OK. ... What are some things Eric has *done* that you feel are positive?

Greg: Well, he has done some things I think are very considerate. For instance, we went out to dinner and we let him drive and he dropped us off at the door. I thought that was really considerate, but I don't think I told him that. *(Greg looks tight and reluctant.)*

Connirae: So you haven't been in the habit of keeping track of the considerate things like you've been keeping track of the inconsiderate things. So we just have to put your noticing skills to better use here.

Greg: Yes.

Connirae: Greg, I'm noticing two parts that have emerged that we could work with to get the change you want in your relationship with your stepson. One is the part that feels angry and outraged sometimes. The other is the part that holds you back from telling him when you think he's been considerate. You know which part I mean? *(Connirae pauses to give Greg time to check inwardly and notice the experience that goes with this. Greg nods.)*

So I'd like you to turn within *now* and ask your unconscious to let you know which part will be most key for us to begin with today. ... You can close your eyes and simply be receptive to whatever response you get from your inner wisdom. It may be the part that feels outraged at your stepson. ... Or the part that stops you from acknowledging your stepson when he does positive things. ... Or some other part that we're not aware of yet.

Greg: The part that stops me from sharing with him when I'm pleased with what he does.

Experiencing the Part

Connirae: OK. Now take a moment to close your eyes and step into that time when Eric dropped you off at the door. What stops you from sharing with him when you are pleased with something he does that you think is considerate? Think about that right now. Take a moment to feel that out. What are your inner pictures, sounds, and feelings? Where is that part of you located? *(Greg closes his eyes and turns within. He furrows his brow, defocuses his eyes, breathes deeply, and his face flushes slightly. He puts a hand on his stomach area.)*

Receiving and Welcoming the Part

Connirae: OK. Now you can thank this part for having a purpose for you, even though you don't know what that is yet. *(Greg nods.)*

Discovering the Purpose

Connirae: Ask this part of you, "What do you want for me by stopping me from sharing with Eric something he does that I think is considerate?"

Greg: ... When I forget about the logic and just go with the gut level feeling, I think that if I acknowledge things that he has done well, I am giving up control.

Connirae: OK. So the part's purpose is to have control.

Greg: But I know that's not true, it doesn't make sense. That is just what popped up.

Connirae: That's good. That makes it *more* valid. The fact that it popped up and doesn't quite make sense to you makes me think that it is right on. It has a definite logic but it is not conscious mind logic. I would like you to thank your inner part for letting you know that it wants to have control, and would feel like it was giving up control if you mentioned positive things to your stepson.

Discovering the Outcome Chain

Connirae: On the inside, ask this part of you, "If you have control, fully and completely, the way you want it, what do you want through having control, that's even more important?"

Greg: ... The word that pops up is respect. My fear is that I might be considered an old softy, and I don't want that.

Connirae: OK. So this part wants respect?

Greg: Yes. Absolutely.

Connirae: Good. So thank this part again for letting you know so clearly, and then ask this part another question. "By getting respect, what do you want through having respect, that is even more than that?"

Greg: ... I am getting a one word answer. "Comforting."

Connirae: So this part wants comforting?

Greg: I guess. That's what popped up.

Connirae: OK. So thank this part of you for that information and let's find out if there is something even more core that this part wants. Ask this part of you, "If you get respect and you get comforting, what do you want through having that, that is positive and that you *really* want?" This part wants something that is really core.

The Core State: Reaching the Wellspring Within

Greg: ... *Inner peace* comes up.

Connirae: OK. Inner peace.

Greg: That is something that is important to me.

Connirae: So this is a very important part, a very core part. So you can turn back within and thank this part of you for wanting such an important state in you. Let this part know that you feel very grateful and you are glad that you have such a wonderful part of you, and ask it, "If you have inner peace, fully and completely, is there anything else that you want through inner peace, that is even more?"

Greg: Nothing else comes up.

GREG'S OUTCOME CHAIN

Part to Work With: When Eric does something positive, I don't share that with him.
Intended Outcome 1: Control
Intended Outcome 2: Respect
Intended Outcome 3: Feel Comfortable
Core State: Inner Peace

Reversing the Outcome Chain With the Core State

Connirae: Good. It seems clear that inner peace is your Core State. Now, it sounds like this part has made the assumption that you have to *do and get* certain things—to have control and get respect—in order to have inner peace. So this part has probably been working very hard to get something that is very important to you. (*Greg nods emphatically.*)

Ask this part of you, "What is it like to just begin by *having* inner peace rather than working to have it? ... This way you aren't leaving something that important up to other people. It's a lot nicer than going to all that effort and work to get others to respect you first. Inner peace is something worth just *having* at the beginning.

So what happens when you invite this part to step into experiencing inner peace as a way of being in the world—because it is something that is important to you? How are things different, when you begin with this feeling of inner peace?

Greg: It is easier to be comfortable. It makes the control and the respect less of an issue. I get a picture and sound now and a sense of being able to enjoy my stepson.

(Greg has visibly changed. His response indicates that he has taken his Core State through his other Intended Outcomes, and that it has transformed his original behavior. Nevertheless, Connirae still guides him explicitly through these steps to be sure he has all the benefit from them.)

Connirae: Great. And now you can invite this part to notice how already having inner peace, as a way of being in the world, transforms feeling comfortable.

... And you can invite this part to notice how already having inner peace, as a way of being, radiates through the experience of respect, transforming it even more fully.

... And invite the part to notice how already having inner peace, as a way of being, transforms the experience of control even more. *(Greg nods, indicating he is finished.)*

Transforming the Original Context

... And invite this part to experience how already having inner peace fully there radiates through the experience of being with Eric when he does something you like.

Greg: I feel more warmth toward him, and like I want to reach out to him.

Growing Up the Part

Connirae: OK. Now, turn within and ask this part, "How old are you?"

Greg: The part has been there my entire life. It is my age.

Connirae: OK. Greg, usually these parts of ourselves form at a very young age, and even if they have grown up with us, they have grown up *separate* from us, and *without* their Core State. Does that make sense? *(Greg nods.)* So ask your part if it would like to have the experience of having inner peace present all the way through time. *(Greg nods.)* You can invite your unconscious to allow that to happen *now.* This part can go back to before the time when it was formed, and have inner peace fully present. ... With inner peace there, it can evolve forward through time all the way to your current age. ... Experiencing and enjoying how it is with inner peace present. ... Your unconscious can let you know when that is finished, and you can nod so I'll know. ... *(Greg nods.)*

Bringing the Part Fully Into Your Body

Connirae: Now that your part has inner peace as a way of being, it no longer needs to stay separate from you. So, now you can let inner peace flow into you and spread throughout every cell of your body. And as it spreads, this inner peace becomes available to every part of you. Sometimes it's as if 99% of our parts have access to it, but then there is one part that really wants the inner peace but it doesn't have access to it. It still thinks that it has to struggle to get it. So as all of your parts really have inner peace to begin with, now, things become easier.

Greg: This is kind of strange. Another part of me is asking, "What prevents me from having it to start with?"

Connirae: Good question.

Greg: And the answer is really "nothing," my parts just step in and have it.

Connirae: Yes. And that's what we're doing now. Often parts think that they have to do certain things and get certain responses from others and then you get to experience inner peace. The problem is, usually inner peace doesn't come that way. Once a part realizes how just beginning with inner peace makes it easier to then go and do the things that may end up gaining respect from others, the part is delighted to do it that way. And fortunately, it becomes less important to get the respect and control and so on, because the part already has the inner peace. It already has what *really* matters. ... Now that all parts of you have this inner peace, where in your life will it make a difference?

Greg: Probably everywhere. I'll be more relaxed about the things that I do. It will affect my dealings with that court issue. I will be able to do what I need to do without getting upset about it.

Connirae: Things like that can still be a nuisance and a lot of work, but when you begin with the inner sense of inner peace, it is easier to have inner clarity. The whole situation becomes easier.

Greg: This is fascinating. This is the first time the question has been posed, "What happens when you have inner peace to start with?" That inner peace has always been something that I sought.

Connirae: Yes.

Greg: This new process works! Everything else was a struggle.

Connirae: What can make it a struggle is that somehow, on the unconscious level, we get confused about which things involve work and which things are just core states of being. Inner peace is a Core State. You don't have to work at Core States, you just have them. People often spend their lifetime working to get a Core State and they never get it! Even if they succeed at the things they thought would get them the state, it just doesn't get them the state. That's because work doesn't bring about Core States. Just stepping into those states and having them, on the unconscious level, brings about Core States.

(Connirae's goal in saying more about having Core States rather than working for them is to deepen the unconscious change Greg is already demonstrating.)

Greg: It is so simple.

Connirae: It is simple, and what makes it effective is getting access to the parts of yourself that have been struggling to get their Core States.

Reversing the Outcome Chain With the Grown-Up Part

Connirae: Greg, now that this part is grown-up and fully throughout your being and your body, at conscious and unconscious levels, you can sense how having inner peace already there as a beginning, as a way of being in the world, makes things different. ... *(Greg nods.)* And now you can sense how that inner peace amplifies and enriches feeling comfortable, ... and you can experience how that now radiates through your new awareness of respect, and how already having inner peace transforms your experience even when you are not getting respect. ... *(Greg nods and smiles.)* That's right, you can just let that spread, and let yourself really appreciate that and be touched by it. Now you can experience how already having inner peace transforms having control, and even when you are not feeling in control, how already having inner peace as a way of being in the world transforms that experience. ... *(Greg nods and smiles.)* That's right, and now, how does already having inner peace transform, enrich and radiate through, even more deeply and completely, sharing with Eric when he does something positive, and how already having it changes those situations with him. … *(Greg breathes deeply and nods. He has become very relaxed and still. Connirae gives him a few moments to enjoy this state.)*

Checking For Objecting Parts

Connirae: Now ask inwardly, is there any part of me that objects to my just having inner peace *now* as a way of being in the world?

Greg: … A little tiny part says it doesn't want to lose control.

Experiencing the Objecting Part

(When we find an objecting part, we work with it in exactly the same way that we worked with the first part. When we find what its Core State is, and go through the process so that it can have its Core State, it will no longer have an objection to the first part's Core State.)

Connirae: Good. We want to find out all the objections, so if there are any more we want those, too. Where do you sense this part? Did you hear this, feel it, see it?

Greg: Yes. I heard it *(gesturing in front of him)* and then I physically felt it.

Receiving and Welcoming the Objecting Part

Connirae: OK. First you can thank that part of you for letting you know it has an objection. This part will end up being a very important ally for you. … *(Greg nods.)*

Discovering the Outcome Chain of the Objecting Part

Connirae: We already know this part wants control. Now ask this part, "If I get control, what do you want, through having control, that is more important?"

Greg: … It is taking a long time to respond. It says something which doesn't make sense consciously: "respect of others." The reason I have trouble with this response is because I think I have that already.

Connirae: That's OK. For this process it doesn't matter whether you have it or not. What's important is that the respect of others is the next step in what this part *wants.* Ask the part, "If you get the respect of others, what do you want through having this respect, that's even more important?"

Greg: Sense of security.

Connirae: OK. Thank the part for wanting that for you, and then ask this part, "If you have respect from others, and the sense of security, what do you want through having both, that is really positive and even more core?"

Greg: I hear, "to feel good," and then, "inner peace."

Connirae: *(Nodding.)* That's the same Core State that your first part had. It's not unusual to have several parts with the same Core State, but since they are different parts, they need individual attention. This second part also needs the experience of having the Core State as a beginning.

(It may seem strange that a part that just objected to having inner peace as a way of being now wants the same thing. Parts that object frequently end up wanting the same Core State they objected to. It is as if the part's attention is so focused on the first several outcomes that it has lost track that it really wants the same thing. Once all parts reconnect with their Core State, the objections vanish. Even when Core States are not identical they are always mutually supportive of each other.)

THE OBJECTING PART'S OUTCOME CHAIN:

Part to Work With: Objecting to having "inner peace" as a way of being in the world.
Intended Outcome 1: Control
Intended Outcome 2: Respect from Others
Intended Outcome 3: Sense of Security
Intended Outcome 4: To Feel Good
Core State: Inner Peace

Reversing the Outcome Chain With the Core State

Connirae: Thank this part of you for letting us know so clearly. Now, this part has been listening in on what we have been doing with the first part, but it hasn't yet discovered how having inner peace already present makes things different for this part. So, turn within and ask this part, "How are things different when you begin by having inner peace as a way of being in the world?" *(Connirae's voice becomes full and soft. She shifts into letting a state of inner peace fill her, so that her voice tone will reflect this state and invite Greg to experience this state even more richly.)*

Greg: Yes, it likes the idea. That is what it wants.

Connirae: So invite this part to notice, "How does already having inner peace as a way of being in the world enrich the experience of feeling good?" ... *(Greg nods.)* And now ask this part, "How does already having inner peace as a way of being enhance your sense of security?"

Greg: ... Now it's just there.

Connirae: Good. ... Now invite this part to notice, "How does already having inner peace as a way of being in the world transform the whole area of respect from others?" *(Greg turns inward and then nods.)*

"When you already *have* inner peace, how is it different to receive respect from others? ... *(Greg nods.)*

"And when you already *have* inner peace as a way of being, how does it transform a situation where another person isn't able to be respectful?" ... *(Greg nods.)*

And perhaps getting respect becomes less important?

Greg: Yes. Now it's less important.

Connirae: OK. Now ask, "How does beginning with inner peace transform the whole area of control?"

Greg: ... Now that's less important, too.

Connirae: OK. Now ask, "When you begin with inner peace does that make it OK for other parts to begin with inner peace?"

Greg: Yes, the part says that's OK now.

Growing Up the Part

Connirae: OK. Now ask this second part, "How old are you?"

Greg: The part said, "I was born when you were seven." I got a picture of what I was doing when this part first appeared. This control issue started when I was seven. My dad started working night shifts and I was the man of the house.

Connirae: And looking back on that, you can probably appreciate what this part did for you that was positive at that time. You can also notice the ways in which things are different now. This part was born when you were seven. Does it still have the sense of being that age?

Greg: No, it is grown up now.

Connirae: OK, that's fine. So again, you can invite this part of you to begin at the age of seven this time, with inner peace present ... fully ... and this part can evolve forward through time, now in another way, having inner peace available all the way to your current age. ... *(Greg nods when he is finished.)*

Bringing the Part Fully Into Your Body

Connirae: All right. Now ask this part if it is ready to be your ally by giving you the full experience of inner peace, now that it knows that is really what it wants for you.

Greg: Absolutely.

Connirae: Good. Now, this part of you already has the full experience of inner peace. *(Greg nods yes.)* Where is this part located now? Is this part still outside of you, in front?

Greg: *(Greg nods.)* I see the part up here, *(Gesturing in front of him.)* but it is not physically outside—it is still inside me.

Connirae: So you feel it in you, as well as seeing it outside?

Greg: Yes. There is still a sense of it internalized.

Connirae: Great. Usually if we see a part of ourselves that is still outside our body, when we bring it in, we get a more complete experience of our Core State. So let's discover if that happens for you. Now you can invite this part to flow into you, so you can experience inner peace even more fully, ... so that every cell is really intimately familiar with inner peace. ... And as inner peace spreads through every cell of your body, you can allow *this* inner peace to integrate with the inner peace of the first part. ... What is your sense of that?

Greg: It is like a flow.

Checking for Objections

Connirae: OK, good. Now let's check by asking if there is any other part that has any objections whatsoever to your just having this inner peace in an ongoing way.

Greg: *(Turning within to check.)* ... There are no more objections.

Timeline Generalization

(Up to now this transcript has demonstrated portions of the Core Transformation Process you are already familiar with. Timeline Generalization is a new phase of the process. Its purpose is to give Greg the experience of having his Core State of inner peace available throughout time.)

Connirae: Now we'll do something to make your experience of inner peace even richer, fuller and more automatic. It's called Timeline Generalization. I'd like you to let your whole past flow behind you in a line or pathway, and your entire future out in front, and you are right here in the present. We'll call this your timeline or your time pathway. *(Greg nods.)*

Having inner peace fully throughout your being, let yourself float up over your timeline. When you've done that, you can float back over your timeline, floating past younger and younger times in your life, back to just before you were conceived. ...

Now you can let yourself drop back down into time, into the moment of your conception, having inner peace already there as a way of being. ...

As soon as you are there, you can allow yourself to move forward through time, letting inner peace color and transform and radiate through every moment of your experience. ...

At the unconscious level you can notice and feel the way inner peace becomes fuller and richer, building and amplifying, as your whole past is changed by inner peace radiating through every moment of experience, as your unconscious moves all the way to the present. And when you reach the present you can envision yourself moving forward on the same trajectory into the future, sensing how it is also colored and transformed by having inner peace already there. ... And if you want to, sometimes it is useful to cycle back through that again. *(Greg nods.)*

This time through, you will be starting with this new level of inner peace, and letting that become even more complete, as you float up over your timeline again, back to before the moment of your conception, dropping into time, and then letting yourself go *(Connirae makes a "sshooop" sound.)* all the way to the present. ...

And on into the future. *(sschooop)* ...

If you want to, you can do it at least once more, very quickly this time. *(Greg nods, pauses.)*

Do you have anything to report on that you were aware of consciously?

Greg: There is nothing focused that I'm consciously aware of.

Connirae: Good. If your unconscious wants you to have even more inner peace it can give you dreams, exploring what difference inner peace will make in various situations.

Checking Results

(The next questions Connirae asks are designed both to find out if the changes Greg has made are complete, and to support further integration of the change. Both Greg's nonverbal response and his verbal report are clearly much different than at the beginning of the session.)

Connirae: What happens now when you think about Eric doing something that you like?

Greg: *(Pausing to check inwardly.)* I enjoy it and find pleasure.

Connirae: Good. And now what is it like when you think about Eric doing one of *those things*—the ones that used to push your hot buttons? *(Greg shrugs as if it is now trivial.)* No big deal? OK. Now, from this state of beginning with inner peace in an ongoing way, what does it feel like to look back on the way that you did things before? Is that something that seems really strange to you, or do you have a sense of compassion for your past self?

Greg: I have compassion and understanding.

Connirae: So looking back on that old you, you have a sense of understanding.

Greg: *(Nodding.)* There was nothing wrong with the goal I was going for.

Connirae: Great. Now, as a parent you have in mind a direction for yourself, and you also have a direction for the children that you are parenting, is that right? *(Greg nods.)* How has your positive direction for him shifted?

Greg: ... I don't have a new direction for him. I still want him to be happy and successful, but I don't feel any pressure or tension. In the past I felt responsible.

Connirae: It was as if you were the one to make that happen.

Greg: Yes. I didn't want him to make the same mistakes I had in the past.

Connirae: So as you think about your stepson, think about the attitude you have toward him now.

Greg: ... Somehow I don't have the pressure. Now the issue isn't being responsible for him, it's how I relate to other people.

Connirae: That is what really is important.

(Sometimes when we pick one key part to work with out of several that come forward at the beginning of a session, the other parts are automatically transformed. At the beginning of the session Greg looked and sounded irate when he thought or spoke about certain things his stepson did. At the end of the session he looked and sounded peaceful when he thought about these same things. This change happened without working directly with the part that got irate, and follow-up let me know that change lasted. If it had not, it would have been desirable to work directly with the part that got irate.

Since this was a couple's session, and Greg had clearly made some major positive shifts, Connirae now turned to Greg's wife, Ann, to offer her the opportunity for similar changes in the areas most important to her. That session is not included here.)

....

Follow-Up

One week after his session, Greg gave us the following feedback about the results of the Core Transformation Process: "It was so impressive to me, I'm excited about it still. Everything's different. There has been such a positive change this week. All these things happened that would normally tear me apart, and it just didn't happen. I guess we really changed some old beliefs!"

One year after his session, Greg had this to say: "The most exciting part was the discovery that I didn't have to go outside myself to get inner peace. It made a tremendous difference at the time, and it still does. The things I used to get outraged about still happen, but they are not a 'hot button' for me anymore."

OVERVIEW OF GREG'S SESSION

GREG'S GOAL: To change my relationship with my stepson.

1. **CHOOSING A PART TO WORK WITH:** When he does something positive, I don't acknowledge him.

   Experiencing, Receiving and Welcoming the Part

2. **DISCOVERING THE PURPOSE/FIRST INTENDED OUTCOME**

3. **DISCOVERING THE OUTCOME CHAIN**

4. **CORE STATE:** Inner Peace

5. **REVERSING THE OUTCOME CHAIN WITH THE CORE STATE**

6. **GROWING UP THE PART**

7. **BRINGING THE PART FULLY INTO YOUR BODY**

8. **REVERSING THE OUTCOME CHAIN WITH THE GROWN-UP PART**

9. **CHECKING FOR OBJECTING PARTS**

   SECOND PART TO WORK WITH: Objecting to having inner peace as a way of being in the world.

   Discovering the Outcome Chain and Core State

   Reversing the Outcome Chain

   Growing Up the Part

   Bringing the Part Fully Into Your Body

   Checking For Objecting Parts

10. **TIMELINE GENERALIZATION**

—CHAPTER 17—

COMPLETING THE PROCESS WITH ALL PARTS

Understanding the Structure

Weapons cannot cleave him,
Fire cannot burn him,
Water cannot wet him,
Wind cannot dry him away.
He is eternal and all-pervading,
Subtle, immovable, and ever the same.
—The Bhagavad-Gita

In the demonstration with Greg you experienced the complete ten-step Core Transformation Process. Often when we do just The Core State Exercise, Growing Up A Part, and Bringing A Part Fully Into the Body, we get powerful and lasting results. However, sometimes other parts are involved with an issue. You are more assured of in-depth change that will last when you do the Core Transformation Process with all of the parts involved.

Step 9: Discovering Objecting Parts

When Greg had finished working with his first part—the one that stopped him from sharing positive comments with his stepson—he looked as if he was finished with the process. But it was important to check if another part was involved. When we have another part involved in an issue and it doesn't have its Core State, this part is likely to interfere with getting the results we want.

Discovering Objecting Parts is very simple. When you have finished working with the inner part you began with, you inwardly ask the question,

"Is there any part of me that objects to my having *[Core State]* as a way of being in the world?" If the answer is "yes," you then take that part through the Core Transformation Process.

The Gift of Objecting Parts

When people discover an objecting part in themselves they sometimes feel disappointed or annoyed. This is because we have the illusion that objections are something that get in our way. When objecting parts come forward they are actually giving us what we need for Core States that are full, rich and strong enough to transform our lives. When Greg had inner peace not only from his first part, but also from the second part that objected at first, the quality of his Core State was greatly enriched.

Each of our inner parts represents a certain amount of our energy or vitality. When we include all of our inner parts we literally gain strength and vitality. Our energy begins to move in concert, rather than in discord.

Each time we do the Core Transformation Process with ourselves our parts unfold in a slightly different way. In the next chapter, "How To Recognize Parts That Need To Be Included," you will find many more valuable examples of how people's parts have unfolded. This will help prepare you to honor and respond to the unique and individual ways your own parts unfold.

Step 10: Timeline Generalization

After all parts involved in an issue have their Core States, have become your current age, and are fully in your body and being, it is useful to do Timeline Generalization. This process helps amplify the Core State by giving you this way of being throughout time—past, present and future. This helps us heal past events that were troubling or unpleasant, and helps make sure the Core States are easily and automatically available throughout many different kinds of future situations.

—CHAPTER 18—

HOW TO RECOGNIZE PARTS THAT NEED TO BE INCLUDED

Guidelines and Examples

Human beings do have a higher nature. By really knowing and appreciating ourselves in all our parts, we can reach that higher nature.
—Virginia Satir, The New Peoplemaking

Over the two decades that I (Connirae) have been involved in personal growth work I have used and taught many processes. In my experience the Core Transformation Process is the most nearly foolproof. By this I mean that if you follow these techniques there is almost always a simple way to get significant results with any issue you bring to the process. By going to the Core State of each part, we get beyond the realm in which limitations exist. If things are not going smoothly it usually means you aren't yet working with the part that needs your attention first. It is time to look for another part.

In this chapter we will offer you many examples and guidelines that will assist you in discovering when more than one part is involved in an issue. You can also use these examples to find parts to work with.

Before the Process: Parts That Are There From the Beginning

Sometimes you will know you have more than one part to work with before you begin. Off-balance parts often come in pairs. These pairs usually appear to be opposite sides in an inner conflict. One woman complained that part of her wanted to be the center of attention all the time, while another part of her felt like hiding in the wallpaper and becoming invisible.

Darla had been stuck in a career decision. Part of her wanted to leave the large company where she worked. There were many things about her work environment that she was unhappy with. Yet, despite her unhappiness, Darla remained at the job. The fact that she hadn't left her job was a clue that another part of her was involved—a part that was keeping her at the job. This other part of her wanted the security her position gave her. She felt stuck because these two parts were at odds with each other. She was unable to be completely happy and whole with either decision. It was as if she had to choose one part of herself over the other. If she left the company, it was as if a part of her would be left behind.

Darla did the Core Transformation Process with this issue. She discovered that the Core State of both parts was "being at peace." Through the process those two parts integrated into her. This gave her the congruence to make her decision from a position of wholeness. A month after doing the Core Transformation Process with these two parts Darla became very clear that she wanted to leave the company. Because she was now more integrated, she could make a decision that was good for her as a whole person. Instead of suddenly quitting or acting in ways that would get her fired, she spoke honestly with her boss. He chose to lay her off and give her three months' severance pay and health insurance, which made it easier for Darla to make the transition into a new job.

One way to find out if a part is one of a pair is to check for the opposite of the part you started with. If you are working with a habit you will probably begin with the part that "made you do it." You can then check for another part that tries to *stop* you from doing the habit. Brenda had one part that wanted to overeat and binge on junk food, and another part that was overly strict about eating and liked to fast. The strict part felt badly if she ate anything but bran and fruit juices. For Brenda to come into balance, she needed to work with both parts.

Michele had several parts that were very dependent on other people liking her. She found herself doing things she didn't really want to do in order to "manipulate" people into liking her. We discovered that there was another part of her that wanted to totally avoid people.

Craig had a part that wanted to be completely in service to other people. This part wanted to have no selfish desires at all. Then we discovered another part of him that wanted to do things only for himself, and never think of others. Again, both parts were important to include in order for him to experience wholeness.

Usually, when we have a part of us that is extreme in one direction, there is another part of us that is just as extreme in the opposite direction. Often we are more aware of one side or the other side. We may even consciously think one side is "good" and the other side is "bad." However, we have found that we become the most aligned and balanced by working with both sides of the issues, integrating both extremes together into a balanced whole.

Objections That Are Obvious

In the demonstration with Greg, after working with one part, you probably noticed that Connirae guided him to inwardly ask the question, "Is there any part of me that objects to my just having inner peace now as a way of being in the world?" An objecting part can emerge in response to this question, as it did with Greg. He discovered another part that wanted to be in control, and its Core State was also inner peace.

A second part may come forward with an objection at any time during the process, even if you are not asking for it. Objecting parts make themselves known in many ways, including pictures, words, sounds or feelings. Mary Jo heard a loud inner voice saying, "Stop!" when she was in the middle of working with a part. Ben stopped in the middle of the process and said, "It's as if a brick wall came between me and this part, and I can't get answers anymore." When you have a strong objection it is usually easiest to shift to working with the part that objects, and then return to finish with the original part.

When we think of objecting parts that get in the way most of us think, "Oh no, I don't want those!" People often begin by trying to shove aside objections or by trying to talk those parts into going along with what they want. Usually neither of these approaches is successful. Inner objections that aren't dealt with are likely to get in the way of the changes we want and sabotage them. Many approaches to personal change consider objections to be a problem. People often label objections as "resistance," and then try to overcome or break through it. It is much more useful to welcome these objecting parts as our allies. In Core Transformation we assume that every part is important, valuable and necessary for the person to become whole. By doing the Core Transformation Process with objecting parts we give them whatever inner state they deeply need, and honor them for being resources.

Bonnie wanted to work with rage. As she was beginning to work with the part that created this rage, she felt it as heat in her head and neck. The part told her that the purpose of the rage was to control everything and everyone. Then Bonnie heard a loud, panic-stricken voice in her left ear that said, "No way! I don't want to be controlled! This part has to be stopped!" She worked with that objecting part, which wanted safety, freedom, and then a sense of "being." Once Bonnie had finished with this part, and it had access to what it *really* wanted—this sense of being—it was happy. Bonnie could now return to her part that wanted to control everything, with this new part present as an inner ally. Bonnie discovered that her part wanted to control everything so that it could feel safe. It wanted to feel safe so that it could "just be," so that it could "connect with all," and experience a sense of "oneness." Because Bonnie guided both parts through the Core Transformation Process, she ended with two Core States to transform her experience.

Zack had a part of him that stopped him from dating women. Whenever he thought about dating women he felt nervous and self-conscious. As he began working with the part that made him nervous he found out it wanted him to be safe, so he could feel loved. Then another part of him objected, saying, "This is ridiculous! You'll never feel loved! There's no point in fooling yourself." He worked with that part, which had a Core State of "unconditional loving." Next he completed the process with the first part, and discovered that it had the same Core State.

Nadine, a surgeon, worked with a part that stopped her from having emotions. She experienced this part of her as a suit of armor in front of her. As she got closer to the Core State the suit of armor became softer and softer until it looked like a velvet dress. Then suddenly she saw a black screen between her and the velvet dress. She asked the black screen what it wanted for her, and it said, "I want to keep you from becoming vulnerable." She worked with the black screen first, and then went back to work with the velvet dress.

During the Process: Subtle Kinds of Interference from Parts

If doing the process is somehow difficult for you, guess what? This difficulty can very easily become the source of a new inner part and a new inner blessing. All you need to do is notice what kind of difficulty you are having, and think of it as another part that can benefit you.

Kevin worked with procrastination. While he was discovering his Outcome Chain he found it hard to concentrate on the process and complained of feeling "spacey." Kevin thought perhaps the process just wouldn't work with him. I explained to him that feeling spacey was just another part that needed to be included, and asked him to notice where and how he felt spacey. He noticed a sensation in his head, as if a part of him were beginning to float away. He asked that part, "What do you want by floating away?" This part of him said, "Protection." Kevin commented that this made sense to him. He recalled some images of himself getting spacey at school and at work when he didn't know what was going to happen. He completed the process with that part, which had a Core Outcome of "oneness with God," and then went on to finish working with procrastination.

If you experience "interference" the easiest way to honor yourself is to shift immediately to working with the interfering part. You can pause, let the part you started with know you'll return to it and finish, then do the full process with the part that is getting in the way. This will eliminate the struggle.

Subtle interference may also show up as a headache or other body pain, a sudden strong emotion, restlessness, a recurring thought, or anything else that interferes with the process. Other common types of subtle interference from parts that we will cover in more detail include "Mind Chatter," "Wanting to Figure Things Out" and "Judging Ourselves."

Mind Chatter

A common kind of interference is "mind chatter." Sometimes when we turn within, our mind may start to focus on everything but the part we want to work with. We find ourselves wondering if we turned the stove off at home, or worrying about an upcoming meeting, or rehashing an upsetting argument with a friend.

Rather than work against this mind chatter, you can discover how to make it your ally. Treat the mind chatter itself as an inner part. Begin by asking, "What do you want?" and you will be on your way to discovering the Core State for this inner part. When you work with these kinds of parts you will be benefiting much more than if you just worked with the problem you began with. This mind chatter part has probably gotten in your way in other situations as well. When this part is able to come from its Core State, it will be your ally.

Wanting to Figure Things Out

Some people discover that when they turn within to ask a part "what do you want?" they immediately try to consciously "figure out" the answer instead of waiting for the response from their inner part. Analyzing and figuring things out is a common part of American culture and it is a useful skill in many other contexts. It is not that we *intend* to interrupt the process, but if we have a habit of automatically analyzing, this can get in the way. It is very easy to turn this interference into a blessing by treating this automatic urge as another part of us and discovering the Core State of that part also.

A woman named Beth was struggling every step of the way. I noticed that rather than just turning within and receiving the response that came inside, she immediately tried to "figure out" the response in a more mental way. Rather than reporting back her inner experience, she would tell me what she was "figuring out." She would say things like, "Well, *I think* the part wants protection for me, because protection has really been what this is all about." Beth was attempting to figure out what made sense, rather than just turning within and noticing what the part actually expressed. She felt the pull to figure things out very strongly. When I talked to Beth about it, she agreed it would be better to just turn within and notice, but she really couldn't do it. She automatically started to calculate and compute what the answer must be. What made a difference was working with the part that "automatically has to figure things out." After working with this part, Beth noticed that she still felt the urge to figure things out. When she checked, she noticed that this was a second part, with the same behavior. The first part had been a voice speaking to her from the front of her forehead. The second one was a voice located in the back of her skull. When both of the parts that wanted to figure things out had their Core States, Beth's other parts could then express themselves without being second-guessed and the rest of the process flowed smoothly.

When I (Connirae) first did this process with myself I had great difficulty getting messages back from my parts. I noticed that I was doubting and questioning every response I got. I wanted to be so *sure* the answer was right that it was difficult to go on. I decided to treat this tendency as a "part" and work with "the part of me that doubts each response." I have found a number of parts like this within myself that I have worked with over time. Taking these parts to their Core States has made it much easier for me to get responses with other parts. Now the process usually flows smoothly and easily for me.

Working with these "interfering" parts offers us much greater value than just making the process go smoothly. These parts are usually important aspects of our way of being in the world. For example, as I worked with those parts that doubted the answer, I began to realize that this had been a "life theme." I had doubted *myself* in many ways in my life. Working with these inner parts has given me an ability to move through the world with greater comfort and assurance.

At one point in my (Tamara's) relationship with my boyfriend, he told me he felt a part of me wanted to control his behavior in certain ways. At the same time, he felt that another part of me wanted to protect his freedom and independence. This happened during a period when I wasn't sure I liked some of the changes that were occurring in our relationship. I had never thought of myself as being controlling of others, but since he sometimes experienced me that way, I wanted to explore the possibility. As I began asking on the inside whether there was a part of me that wanted to control his behavior, I quickly became aware that some part of me was trying to figure out the answers to my question without waiting for unconscious responses. I switched gears and worked with that part of me. I asked this part, "What do you want for me by figuring out the answers for the other part?" I found out that this part wanted to decide the answers in order to control my life. As the Outcome Chain unfolded, it looked like this:

Part to Work With: Decide the answers for the other parts
Intended Outcome 1: Control my life
Intended Outcome 2: Protection
Intended Outcome 3: Safety
Core State: Being

As I was doing this, I got an image of a four-year-old Tamara who was hiding behind a wall for protection. I then invited this part to just have the experience of "being" as a beginning. That felt wonderful! It made protection and safety less of an issue. The image of the wall dissolved. As this part of me grew up, filled with the state of being, I got the sense that this part's orientation was shifting from "controlling" my life to "taking care of" my life. When I again focused on the part of me that wanted to control my boyfriend, I found it had already shifted! Now, instead of wanting to "control" my relationship, it wanted to "take care of" my relationship. It was more like taking care of a garden, in contrast to controlling a robot. As a result, the part of me that wanted to protect his freedom could relax, too.

Before doing this process, whenever my boyfriend was angry with me, I got angry with him for being angry. Anger had always been an emotion that I had difficulty accepting in other people. After this process I noticed a definite shift in my automatic response to his feelings. When he got angry, I could just let him be angry, and respond in other ways than by being angry back at him. I had always intellectually understood that it's better to be accepting of other people's emotions, including anger; now I actually *felt* more accepting.

Judging Ourselves

Jerry was very motivated to communicate with his inner parts, yet the answers were not forthcoming. I noticed that each time Jerry turned within to ask a question he had a scowl on his face. Then when he told me what happened, he sounded irritated; "The part won't talk to me!" he said. It became clear that he was feeling very impatient with his inner parts. If they didn't give him a clear message immediately he became annoyed. This made it difficult to sense the responses that were coming. After we recognized the "part of him that felt impatient and annoyed" and did the process with this part, Jerry easily went through the process with his other parts.

Any part that judges our experience as wrong can be noticed and included. We may have one inner part that is angry, or feels abandoned, or feels rebellious. Then another part may feel "That is wrong! I shouldn't feel that!" This extra layer of judgment can be worked with as a part that then becomes our inner ally. We always assume that every interrupting part has some very positive, valuable function for us that needs to be preserved. In fact most of the time, the part of us that started out by "interrupting" ends up playing a crucial role in helping the process work more fully.

At the End of the Process: Taking A Cue From Your Body

When you have finished the Core State Exercise, and grown up the part, you invite it to fill your body. Occasionally people tell me, "It's filled my right side, but not my left." Or they say, "It's filled everything but my heart area," or "It's going into my body, but not my head." Whenever an area of the body won't receive the Core State it is a sign that another part is involved. Some other part wants to be included before it is really appropriate for the Core State to go into that area. You can discover this part by asking inwardly, "What part of me objects to the Core State going into this area?" and noticing what part emerges.

When you have gone through the Core Transformation Process and are finished with a part, your body feels and looks as if the Core State is flowing through you as one unit. If you aren't finished integrating the Core State your body may feel and look like one part is feeling one thing and one part another. For example, when people talk they often gesture with one arm and hand but not the other, or it may look like only the head is expressing an idea, but not the rest of the body. When the Core State is fully accessed, the entire body is moving in harmony. Movements may be very small and subtle, but the movements that do happen tend to come from the whole body. Gestures are likely to include both sides of the body simultaneously, rather than only one side.

After the Process: Are You Still Doing the Original Behavior?

Many limitations change after the first time you work with them. Some limitations change after you work with them twice. If the limitation you began with is still present in your life, it is useful to assume that another part or parts need to be worked with.

Phil wanted to feel less judgmental toward his children. He noticed that he always felt himself cringe when they did something he considered "wrong." He could feel his index finger getting ready to point at them in blame, and the impulse to shout. He wanted to feel accepting of them so he could set limits for them clearly, out of an inner attitude of acceptance. The first time Phil worked with this issue he noticed two parts. The first part wanted to jump in and find fault with his children. This part was ready to blame anyone for anything. He could hear this part speaking to him from just outside his left ear. The second part, Phil noticed, felt vulnerable to being blamed. This was a very young part that had been blamed a lot by his own parents. After working with both parts Phil noticed he felt a tenderness and closeness to his children he hadn't felt before. He also noticed a feeling of ease in other areas of his life that he appreciated. However, Phil still felt the impulse to blame his children when they did certain things. When he turned within, he found yet another part that wanted to blame. This part spoke to him from his right ear. After working with that part also, Phil got the results he wanted with his children.

Tracking Our Parts

When we do the Core Transformation Process our objective is to find the easiest way to discover all of the parts involved with an issue and lead each one to its Core State. The following two examples are of people who had at least three parts. Notice how these parts emerged, and how simple the process can be even when more than two parts are involved.

Beverly had quite a few objections as she was doing the process. A theme we noticed was that her parts didn't want to have their Core States as a starting point. This is a little unusual—most of the time, parts are delighted to be able to have the Core State they've always wanted to experience. On a hunch I had Beverly ask inwardly, "Is there a part of me that believes that everything has to be a struggle?" She got a "yes." When we discovered this part's Outcome Chain, we found that by struggling to get things this part wanted to have the sense that Beverly really earned what she had. Through that sense of earning it wanted to have a sense that what she had was really hers and couldn't be taken away. When we found out all of this it was really understandable that this part had objected to her just having these Core States without doing anything to earn them.

We then found out that this objecting part's Core State was "sense of being." This objecting part's Outcome Chain was like this:

Part to Work With: Objecting to starting with Core State.
Intended Outcome 1: Struggle to get things.
Intended Outcome 2: Feeling that I earned what I have.
Intended Outcome 3: What I have is mine and can't be taken away.
Core State: Sense of Being.

When Beverly asked her part, "How does having that 'sense of being' as a starting point enhance your experience?" this part found that starting with that "sense of being" made life much easier. When this part started with "sense of being," it no longer needed to struggle for everything. After working with this part the rest of the Core Transformation Process went very easily for her. It was as if this part was the key to making the process work.

Charlotte chose to work with a part that created a nervous tic. Everything went smoothly until she got to the Intended Outcome of "running and playing." Charlotte suddenly got very tense and said another part had come up. "It's out here," she said, gesturing toward the right side of her face, "and it says, 'I wish that part would just grow up and do what it needs to do.'" This was an objecting part. I told Charlotte, "Welcome this new part of you and let it know that we are glad it is here, and that we know it also has important purposes for you. Let it know that we want to include it also, to help it get whatever it truly wants for you. Ask it, 'Are you willing to wait while we finish with the first part, or do we need to switch now and work with you instead?'"

The objecting part told Charlotte that it was willing to wait, so we proceeded with the first part. When we got to the Intended Outcome of "feeling a part of everything," Charlotte reported that she felt as if there was something very intense in front of her, blowing her over. For Charlotte this blowing sensation was a communication from a third part of her. Because the sensation of being blown over was intense, we decided to switch gears and work with this third part next. It got to a Core State of "being OK." After we reversed its Outcome Chain, it no longer had an objection to the process we were doing. We grew it up and let it spread fully through the body, then we went back and completed the process with the first part. Then we went back to the second part which had originally objected and wanted the first part to "grow up and do what it needed to do." It was now fine, and no longer had any objection.

If many parts emerge when you are working with an issue you may not want to work with all of them in one sitting. You can always take notes and return to working with the part later in the day, or on the following day.

When There Are Many Parts

Sometimes an issue seems to be the focal point for *many* parts. It is almost as if a lot of inner parts gather themselves around a certain limitation and use it. The main issue Donna worked with was losing weight, and a whole cluster of parts emerged around it. The work was intense and powerful, and Donna was pleased with the results in her life. She felt a greater sense of self and well-being in many situations. However, Donna didn't lose the weight she wanted to. A year and a half later Donna again did the Core Transformation Process with her issue of losing weight. She shared with me how pleased she was at the additional progress she was making and said a whole different set of parts was coming forward for her to work with. Later we heard from Donna, who said she was excited that she was doing the things that she expected would result in gradual weight loss: she was exercising regularly, eating in a healthy, balanced way, and working with her emotions rather than eating when she was unhappy. These lifestyle changes were all new for Donna.

Sometimes interference and interruptions are coming from many different parts that want to do the Core Transformation Process. One way to handle this is to explain to all the parts that you will need to work with one at a time to be sure they all get what they want. Then find a sequence they all agree to. Another possibility is to work with all of your parts at once. You will learn how to do this later in the book. (See Chapter 30, "Generalizing the Core Transformation Process.")

Summary of Working With All Parts

The following is a summary overview of the different ways you can discover and work with more than one part involved in an issue.

1. **Before the Process—Parts That Are There From the Beginning:** At the beginning it may be clear that two or more parts are involved in an issue. These are often opposite sides of an issue.

2. **During the Process:**

   a) Parts That Object Overtly make themselves clearly known as you do the process. They may communicate in words, feelings or images that seem to block the process.

   b) Subtle Kinds of Interference From Parts: If the process isn't going smoothly, notice what you are doing that might be getting in your way and treat this as an inner part.]

   Examples are:

   Mind Chatter

   Wanting to Figure Things Out

   Judging Ourselves

3. **At the End of the Process—Taking A Cue From Your Body:** If the Core State doesn't fill the body at the end of the process, work with the part that blocks the flow of the Core State.

4. **After the Process:** If after doing the process the unwanted behavior, feeling or response hasn't changed, treat the recurrence as a new part.

—SECTION V—

THE COMPLETE CORE TRANSFORMATION EXERCISE

Doing It From A to Z

—CHAPTER 19—

DOING IT!

THE COMPLETE CORE TRANSFORMATION EXERCISE

Putting All the Steps Together

i thank you God for this amazing
day: for the leaping greenly spirits of trees
and a blue true dream of sky; and for everything
which is natural which is infinite which is yes
—e.e. cummings

This chapter is an outline of the entire Core Transformation Process. If you need more detailed directions and explanations, you can refer back to the specific section or chapter on that piece of the exercise. When you do this exercise we encourage you to begin by sitting in a quiet, comfortable place where you won't be disturbed. If you are doing the exercise by yourself, have a piece of paper handy for writing down your Outcome Chain. Keeping track of where you are on paper is especially helpful if you have more than one part. If you are reading these instructions as a guide for someone else, parts that are italicized do not need to be read aloud. When you are the guide you can help create an ambience that will assist your partner by entering one of your own favorite Core States.

By now you are aware that the Core Transformation Process can unfold in many different ways. You may spend ten minutes working with one part on a minor issue, or you may spend three hours working with many parts connected to a major issue. Give yourself the freedom to explore!

....

Step 1. CHOOSING A PART TO WORK WITH

a) Identify the part you want to work with. *We will refer to this as [behavior, feeling or response X] in this script, and you can fill in your experience of this part.*

b) When, where, and with whom do you have [behavior, feeling or response X]? *Write down the answer in a few words.*

Experiencing the Part

c) Take a moment to close your eyes, relax and turn within. Mentally step into a specific incident in which [behavior, feeling or response X] occurred. As you are there, relive the incident, and begin to notice your inner experience. You may notice inner pictures, sounds and feelings that go along with [behavior, feeling or response X].

d) Since you did not consciously choose [behavior, feeling or response X], it's as if a part of you did. You can begin to sense where that part of you "lives." Do you feel the feelings most strongly in a certain part of your body? If you hear an inner voice, where is the voice located? If you see inner pictures, where in your personal space do you see them? Gently invite the part into your awareness. If the part is in your body, you may want to put your hand on the area where you sense the part most strongly. This can help you welcome and acknowledge the part

Receiving and Welcoming the Part

e) Receive and welcome this part of you. Even though you don't know what the purpose of this part is, you can begin thanking this part for being there, because you know it has some deeply positive purpose.

Step 2. DISCOVERING THE PURPOSE/FIRST INTENDED OUTCOME

a) Ask the part of you that [X's], "What do you want?" After asking, notice any image, voice or sound, or feeling that occurs in response.

b) *Write down the answer you get from the part.* This is your first Intended Outcome. Thank the part for letting you know. If you like the part's Intended Outcome, thank it for having this Intended Outcome for you.

Step 3. DISCOVERING THE OUTCOME CHAIN

a) Ask this part of you, "If you have [Intended Outcome from previous step], fully and completely, what do you want, through having that, that's even more important?" *Write this down.* Thank this part for having this Intended Outcome for you.

b) *Repeat Step 3 until you get to the Core State. Each time you will get a new Intended Outcome and write it down. Each time you ask the question you'll use the new Intended Outcome.*

Step 4. THE CORE STATE: REACHING THE WELLSPRING WITHIN

a) *When you have reached the Core State, take time to enjoy it; then go on to step 5.*

Step 5. REVERSING THE OUTCOME CHAIN WITH THE CORE STATE

a) *The guide reads this aloud.* Somehow our inner parts get the idea that in order to experience core states of being, they first have to go through a whole series of Intended Outcomes. Unfortunately, this doesn't work very well. We don't experience our Core States very often when we go about it that way, because a core state of beingness

ALTERNATE QUESTIONS FOR TRANSFORMING INTENDED OUTCOMES WITH CORE STATES

1. Intended Outcome That Is Valuable In and Of Itself:

"How does already having [Core State] transform, enrich, or radiate through [Intended Outcome]?"

2. Intended Outcome That Is Dependent On Other People:

a. "How does already having [Core State] transform your experience when you are getting [dependent Intended Outcome]?"

b. "How does already having [Core State] transform your experience when you are not getting [dependent Intended Outcome]?"

3. Intended Outcome That Does Not Serve You:

"How does already having [Core State] transform this whole area that used to be [negative Intended Outcome]?"

is not something that it is possible to earn or to get through actions. The way to experience a Core State is just to step into it and have it.

b) ***General Reversal:*** Invite your part to step into [Core State] now, and ask your part, "When you just have [Core State] as a beginning, as a way of being in the world, how does already having [Core State] make things different?"

c) ***Specific Reversal:*** *Let the Core State transform each of the Intended Outcomes, one at a time, beginning with the one that came just before the Core State.* Ask your part, "How does already having [Core State] as a way of being transform or enrich [Intended Outcome]?"

Transforming the Original Context

d) *When you have asked about each of the Intended Outcomes in sequence, you are ready to discover how the Core State transforms the limitation you began with. Ask the question,* "How does already having the [Core State] as a way of being in the world transform your experience of [the context where you used to X]?"

Step 6. GROWING UP THE PART

a) Turn within and ask your part, "How old are you?" *Write down the age of the part.*

b) Ask this part if it would like to have the benefits that come from evolving forward in time to your current age, with [Core State] fully present. *If you get a "yes," you are ready to go on. In the event that the part doesn't want to have these benefits, ask what its objection is. Make sure any objection is satisfied before going on.*

c) Invite this part of you to begin by having [Core State] fully present, now. Then you can invite your unconscious to allow this part, with [Core State] present, to evolve forward through time, from whatever age it is, all the way forward to your current age, having [Core State] there through every moment of time. You can allow that to happen now. Have the part let you know when it has arrived at your current age.

Step 7. BRINGING THE PART FULLY INTO YOUR BODY

a) Notice where your part is located now. Is it in your body or outside your body? Where specifically?

b) *If the part is outside your body, do this step.* Invite this part of you to now flow into your body. Welcome this part, noticing where it wants to flow into your being, allowing you to experience [Core State] more completely.

c) Noticing where this part already fills your body, allow it to flow completely through every cell, so that every cell of your being is filled, nourished, and bathed by [Core State]. You may notice how, as this [Core State] radiates from the place it began through your whole body, that the more it radiates through your body the stronger it becomes in the place where it began. And as the sense of [Core State] fills every cell, you may already sense how it is as if this is now a part of your emotional coding—the ground of your being.

Step 8. REVERSING OUTCOME CHAIN WITH THE GROWN-UP PART

Briefly repeat the Outcome Chain Reversal with the grown-up part fully in your body.

a) ***General Reversal:*** Invite your part to step into [Core State] now, and ask your part, "When you just have [Core State] as a beginning, as a way of being in the world, how does already having [Core State] make things different?"

b) ***Specific Reversal:*** *Continue the Outcome Chain Reversal, bringing the Core State into all Intended Outcomes and into the original context, asking the question,* "How does already having [Core State] as a way of being transform or enrich [Intended Outcome]?"

c) ***Transforming the Original Context:*** "How does already having [Core State] as a way of being transform your experience of [the context where you used to X]?"

Step 9. CHECKING FOR OBJECTING PARTS

a) Ask, "Is there any part of me that objects to my just having [Core State] now as a way of being in the world?" *If the answer is "no" you are ready to go on to step 9b.*

If the answer is "yes." This means you have another part with something valuable to contribute to this process. Notice how you are aware of this part. Do you see, hear or feel something? Where is it located? *Go back to step 2 and do the Core State Exercise with this new part.*

b) If you already know of other parts involved in this issue, now is the time to go back to step 1 and do the Core State Exercise with that part. *When all parts have finished step 8, go on to step 10.*

Step 10. TIMELINE GENERALIZATION

If you have worked with more than one part, and two or more Core States have emerged, list each Core State when you see [Core State(s)] in the following step of the exercise.

a) You can have a sense of your entire past flowing behind you in a pathway or line. All of your past is in that pathway, including what you remember and don't remember consciously. Your entire future can flow straight out in front, with you right here in the present. This is your timeline.

b) Having [Core State(s)] fully throughout your being, let yourself float up over your timeline. Float back over your timeline, floating past younger and younger times in your life, back to just before you were conceived. ...

c) Now you can let yourself drop back down into time, into the moment of your conception, having [Core State(s)] already there, as a way of being. ...

d) As soon as you are there, you can allow yourself to move forward through time, letting [Core State(s)] color, and transform, and radiate through every moment of experience. ... At the unconscious level notice and feel the way [Core State(s)] become(s) fuller and richer, building and amplifying, as your whole past is colored by [Core State(s)] radiating through every moment of experience, as you move all the way to the present. ...

e) Now you can allow these Core States to flow into the future, noticing how that is also colored by having [Core State(s)].

f) It is useful to cycle back through the Timeline Generalization several times. Each time it will go faster. Each time you can allow the changes to happen on a more and more unconscious level. When you are finished, re-orient in the present.

g) Congratulations! You have completed the Core Transformation Process with this part or parts. Your Core States are now radiating through your past, available in your present, and waiting for you in every moment of the future. Give yourself some time to relax and enjoy your Core States! Some people like to go for a walk or find another way to allow the changes to settle.

TEN STEPS TO CORE TRANSFORMATION

When you are familiar with the Core Transformation Process you may choose to use the following abbreviated outline as a brief reminder of each step.

Step 1. CHOOSE A PART TO WORK WITH: Experience it, receive and welcome it.

Step 2. DISCOVER THE PURPOSE/FIRST INTENDED OUTCOME: Ask your part, "What do you want?"

Step 3. DISCOVER THE OUTCOME CHAIN: Ask your part, "If you have [Intended Outcome from previous step], fully and completely, what do you want through having that, that is even more important?" *(Repeat as needed.)*

Step 4. THE CORE STATE: REACHING THE WELLSPRING WITHIN: Take a moment to enjoy your Core State.

Step 5. REVERSE THE OUTCOME CHAIN WITH THE CORE STATE:

a) General: Invite your part to notice, "When you just have [Core State] as a beginning, as a way of being in the world, how does already having [Core State] make things different?"

b) Specific: "How does already having [Core State] as a way of being transform, enrich, radiate through [Intended Outcome]?" *(Do with all Intended Outcomes.)*

c) Transform the Original Context: "How does already having [Core State] as a way of being transform your experience of [the context where you used to X]?"

Step 6. GROW UP THE PART:

Ask your part:

a) "How old are you?"

b) "Do you want to have the benefits that come from evolving forward in time to your current age, with [Core State] fully present?"

c) Evolve forward through time, from whatever age it is, all the way forward to your current age, having [Core State] there through every moment of time.

Step 7. BRING THE PART FULLY INTO YOUR BODY: Notice where your part is located now and allow it to flow fully in and throughout your body, permeating every cell with [Core State].

Step 8. REVERSE THE OUTCOME CHAIN WITH THE GROWN-UP PART fully in your body *(general, specific, original context).*

Step 9. CHECK FOR OBJECTING PARTS: "Is there any part of me that objects to my just having [Core State] now as a way of being in the world?" *(Bring any objecting parts, and any additional parts associated with this issue, through steps 1-8 before going on.)*

Step 10. TIMELINE GENERALIZATION:

a) Envision your timeline and float back over it to just before you were conceived. With your Core State radiating through your being, allow yourself to move forward through time, letting [Core State] color and transform every moment of experience to the present.

b) Envision yourself moving forward on that same trajectory into the future, noticing how that is also colored by having [Core State].

c) Cycle back through the Timeline Generalization several times, faster each time.

—SECTION VI—

PARENTAL TIMELINE REIMPRINTING

Bringing Core States To Your Past, Present and Future

—CHAPTER 20—

INTRODUCTION

PARENTAL TIMELINE REIMPRINTING

Bringing the Core States To Your Past, Present and Future

What lies behind us and what lies before us are tiny matters compared to what lies within us.
—Oliver Wendell Holmes

Once you have discovered something as powerful and transforming as Core States, it makes sense to utilize them in many ways. In this section you will learn how to use these gifts from within to transform and heal your past. You will be giving the gift of the Core States to your inner parents and grandparents through the Parental Timeline Reimprinting Process.

Parental Timeline Reimprinting will also assist you in taking the powerful changes created by experiencing Core States into all life contexts. We want the Core State to be naturally and automatically available to us. This doesn't mean that every moment of the day we feel it as strongly as we feel it when we are doing the process, but that at a deep level the Core State is constantly there, through every moment of our experience. Parental Timeline Reimprinting will strengthen your experience of the Core State through time.

Several years ago Steve and I (Connirae) bought a new couch for our living room. We all loved the couch and immediately rearranged our furniture so that it would fit in and could be used. Over the next several days we found ourselves walking to where the bookcase used to be, and then remembering it was now in a new location. Sometimes we "forgot" that the couch was there and available for us to enjoy. We had to remind ourselves that we had a comfortable new place to sit and read to the boys. Even though the couch was there, our thinking wasn't yet reorganized to make full use of this new resource in our lives. It took some time for it to become a part of our lives that we automatically relied upon, used, and enjoyed.

In the same way, when we gain personal resources by doing the Core Transformation Process, we also need to reorganize our inner programs to automatically live based on the new and wonderful resource now available to us. Parental Timeline Reimprinting can assist you in doing that.

In summary, Parental Timeline Reimprinting will help you:

- Further amplify the Core State.
- Extend the Core State to your inner parents and grandparents.
- Deepen the timeline generalization you already did.
- Make the positive change you've experienced permanent and grounded.

Victoria had difficulties with low self-esteem. Her health problems were aggravated by the stress in her life. She was adopted, and when she was growing up her adoptive parents told her that her biological family was "trash." No matter what Victoria was able to accomplish she always had a lingering feeling that she was bad, because her biological parents were bad. Parental Timeline Reimprinting enabled Victoria to forgive both sets of parents and move on. Before doing this process she had experienced her past and her family history as limitations. Now she experiences them as resources. Because life is less stressful for her now, her health has improved. You will learn more about how Victoria resolved her problems in Chapter 24, "Victoria's Story."

Automatic Learning Transfer

It has been well-documented that patterns of behavior, emotion and relationship operate not only in individuals but also in family systems. Certain traits are said to "run in the family" across many generations. Many people are dismayed to discover, as an adult, that they have embodied some of the traits of one of their parents even though they had sworn they never would.

On the behavioral level our automatic learning from those around us is very obvious. If you grew up in the South, you learned a Southern accent. If you grew up in the Northeast you learned an entirely different accent. If you have observed parents and their children walking down the street, you may have noticed amusing similarities in posture and gait. All of this learning happened *automatically*, without effort.

When one of our sons was three and just learning to speak he observed his father reach into the refrigerator and take out a pottery plate with butter on it. The plate was a bit slippery and fell to the floor with a crash. In surprise and annoyance, my husband let out a swear word, which he doesn't ordinarily do around the children. A few minutes later our son picked up a block, climbed up onto the arm of the couch and carefully let the block drop, uttering the same swear word. Even though he had no idea what the word *meant*, he managed to duplicate the voice tone and expression quite well! We have all observed these immediate and automatic learnings in children. Whether we react in amusement or dismay, it is clear that children learn a great deal, *just by observation and imitation.* Children easily absorb whatever is in their environment.

Most of us recognize how our past has influenced who we are today. Growing up in a particular family environment provides both resources and limitations. If one of our parents was shy, for example, we may have adopted a similar personal style—or we may have become very outgoing in contrast. If a parent was continually worried about the future, that affected us. If a parent constantly criticized or nagged, that made a difference. If a parent ignored us or seemed more interested in other things, that affected how we grew into adults. We have developed many of our beliefs, qualities and habits from our relationship with our parents. We have all learned valuable things from our parents that make us more resourceful, and everyone we know has learned *some* things from their parents that they would like to unlearn.

My mother has a good voice and a good ear for music. While growing up I absorbed these abilities from her. She and my father both sang a lot, and both of them had an exceptional sense of pitch. Since the songs I heard from them were in tune and "in the air" around me, I naturally developed a sensitivity to pitch that I might not have acquired so easily in another family.

My husband Steve grew up in a household that was almost always orderly. His mother was quite poor, so they had few things, but what they did have was well-organized. She was also good at logistical planning. Steve naturally acquired an ability for planning that comes in very handy when we are juggling the activities of our three boys and our two businesses.

This same automatic learning transfer also occurs with Core States. When parents have strong inner states such as inner peace, OKness, beingness, love, and oneness, their children often naturally develop these same inner states over time. There are family systems that, to varying degrees, include these Core States, and they are passed on from generation to generation.

Changing What We Have Learned

Since the way we absorb patterns from our families is so automatic, it is easy to conclude that we are stuck with the unresourceful patterns we learned from them: "I'm that way because my mother is that way. That's just how I am. All the Smiths are stubborn, and I'm a Smith."

However, Parental Timeline Reimprinting offers us methods for changing unuseful behaviors, feelings and responses that have been passed down to us by our parents. In addition, we can easily learn useful things that our parents did *not* teach us. Parental Timeline Reimprinting makes use of our natural tendency to absorb qualities from our parents and from our past history, to make a profound shift *in the direction we want.* It gives us the opportunity many of us wished for, to learn from the kind of parents we wished we had. Think what a difference it would make in your life if you had just absorbed inner peace, love, OKness, oneness and beingness from your parents!

Giving Our Parents Our Core States

The Parental Timeline Reimprinting Process is an experience of giving our inner grandparents and parents our Core States, and then receiving those Core States from our parents. When George did the Parental Timeline Reimprinting Process, he was reluctant at first to give his parents his Core State:

> I was an abused child. From what I understand, my father gave my mother a hard time, and my mother released her anger and frustration on me. I experienced physical beatings and incredibly traumatic experiences that are still hard to talk about. I had forgiven my mother four years ago, because she came to me and asked for forgiveness. However, my dad would never come to me and say, "I'm sorry." That's why I needed to resolve it myself, and I didn't know how to do it.
>
> My dad and I communicated on Thanksgiving, Christmas, New Year's, or a birthday. We only said what we had to. Our communication was from a distance, as if we really didn't mean it. Deep inside we really loved each other, but we didn't want to show it. I didn't want to express my feelings. Any time I talked to him I went back into my memories about the past and thought about what was going on in my life, and I thought, "You are responsible for these problems." But instead of saying that to him I just avoided him, and I got angrier and angrier.
>
> I didn't go into the Parental Timeline Reimprinting process with the idea of forgiving my parents. In fact, I didn't even want to give my parents the Core State at first! I felt it was such a beautiful thing and they didn't deserve it. Then I realized that I was actually giving it to a part of *me,* so I did the process. I just said to

myself, "Well, let's just go along with it and see what happens."

I have learned that people do the best that they can, but when it came to my parents, I didn't agree with that. It touched too close to home. Thinking of all those things that had happened to me I could not come to the realization that they did the best they could. As the process went along, I got a beautiful feeling. I came to an understanding that my dad is the way he is because of *his* parents. They tried to do the best they knew how with *his* upbringing. Realizing that, I gave a different meaning to how they raised me and how they treat me.

There is a big difference in how my dad is with me now. A couple of weeks ago I bought a computer. My dad's an expert on computers, so I went to his home and said, "Can you help me here?" And he was more than helpful. He actually sat down and started teaching me. I wouldn't even have asked him for help in the past. I know my dad hasn't changed the way he communicates with me! The way I am treating him and how I respond to him has changed and is how he's responding back to me. It is just amazing. My behavior was defensive before, and he responded back to me the same way. Now what happens between us is tremendous!

George transformed his relationship with his father by giving his father his Core State. However, it wasn't George's *outer* father who received the Core State, it was his *inner* father. What shifted was how George perceived his father inside of himself. By giving *himself* what he had wanted from his father in the past, George's current relationship with his outer father was automatically changed.

—Chapter 21—

A DEMONSTRATION WITH DAVE

Giving Ourselves A Happy Childhood

It's never too late to have a happy childhood.
— T-Shirt Message

Dave is attending an Aligned Self seminar and has completed the Core Transformation Process, including growing up a part, bringing it fully into the body, and timeline generalization. In this demonstration, as Connirae does the Parental Timeline Reimprinting Process with Dave, she helps him create an experience of his parents' and grandparents' past, present, and future that includes his Core State. As you read this process with Dave you can simply envision him going through each step. You can also invite your own unconscious to go through each step for you, at the same time, with your own Core State.

As in the other demonstrations, commentary that we have added later is in *(italic and parentheses)*.

....

Connirae: Dave, you have a sense of your past—everything you have experienced so far— and a sense of your future, right? *(Dave nods.)* I would like you to envision your whole timeline—past, present and future—on the floor in front of us, in a pathway or line. *(Connirae makes a sweeping gesture along the floor to indicate where Dave's timeline will be.)* Which way is your past and which way is your future?

Dave: Past to the left and future to the right.

Connirae: OK, great. Is the present where you are now?

Dave: It is now!

DIAGRAM #21-a

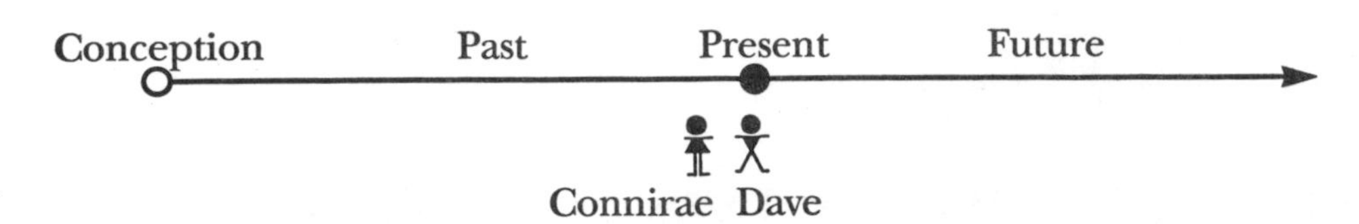

Connirae: OK. So now you can let all of your life experience flow into that configuration on the floor in front of us so that it is all there, even though consciously you aren't aware of all the specific memories. You just have the sense that your whole life is there. Everything that has ever happened in the past stretches out to the left, and everything you envision in your future stretches out to the right. *(Dave nods.)* OK. Now we are going to step off your timeline and walk around it and stand right before the moment of your conception. *(She and Dave walk to the new location.)* Let's stand right over here so we are looking right up your timeline. In front of you is your past, and beyond that is your present and future. *(See diagram #21-b)*

DIAGRAM #21-b

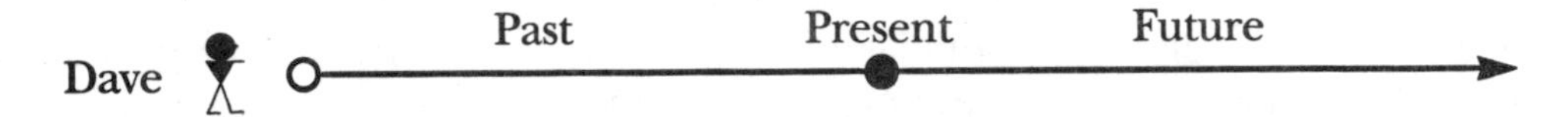

Now, behind you I will invite you to create a space for your parents' timelines. One parent will be on each side. Which parent do you want on your left and which on your right?

Dave: Mother to my left and father to my right.

Connirae: OK. Mother here and father here. *(She gestures where Dave has placed them. See DIAGRAM #21-c below:)*

DIAGRAM #21-c

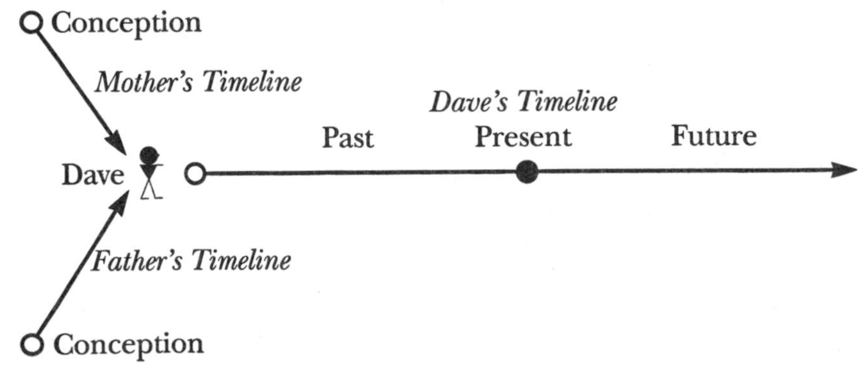

Giving Core States to Father's Side

Connirae: Now we are going to give your Core States from the Core Transformation Process to your grandparents.

Dave: OK.

Connirae: They will appreciate it.

Dave: I am sure they will!

Connirae: So do you remember what those Core States were?

Dave: The first Core State was "beingness," and for the second one the word that came up was "enlighteningness."

Connirae: Enlighteningness, right?

Dave: *(Laughs.)* Right.

Connirae: *(To the group.)* And that is nice, that word characterizes just the quality for him. *(To Dave.)* Great. Which set of grandparents would you like to give these gifts to first?

Dave: My dad's parents.

Connirae: So, on your right. You may want to allow your eyes to close for this so that your unconscious can do this most fully. *(Speaking more slowly.)* Even though you are facing toward *your* timeline, I would like you to have a sense that you can see back behind you to before your father was conceived on his timeline. Before he was conceived, his parents are there, right? *(Dave nods.)* Great. So now you can invite your unconscious to let those resources of beingness and enlighteningness, and all that you know that means, flow into your father's parents before your father was conceived, so you can begin to sense what those two people are like with those resources fully present in them as a way of being in the world, ... just as a part of who they are And I would like you to let me know if at any point you would like me to go faster or slower, or use more words or fewer words, OK?

Dave: OK.

Connirae: That feedback is valuable to me. And are you already seeing, envisioning, sensing them with those resources present? There is a nice ambiguity to the word "present" because it really is a gift. ... You can let me know when your unconscious has added those resources, those states of being, into your father's parents. You may not even have a conscious image or sound of them with those resources, just the unconscious sense and knowing that they *have them now.* ...

Dave: OK.

Connirae: OK, great. With those resources present, you can begin to experience, at the unconscious level, what it is like for your father to be conceived in that nourishing environment. He can absorb those states, even when he is a single cell, because he is right there being bathed in them. And now your father's timeline can unfold *this way,* so that your grandparents and your father move forward with this beingness and enlighteningness in them. ... Begin to sense what that's like, with your father evolving forward on his timeline, having these states there to just absorb because that is what is around him. You can allow that to unfold all the way through to right before the moment of your conception, and you can let me know when that has happened.

Dave: OK.

Connirae: Great. Wonderful.

DIAGRAM 21-d

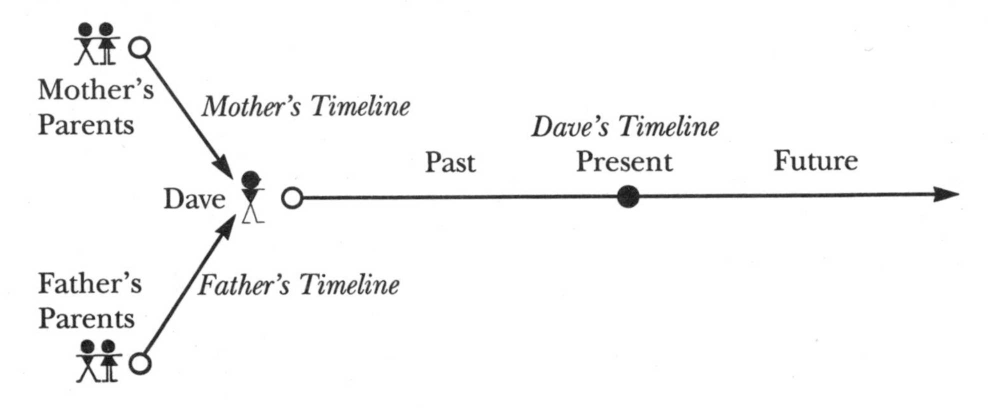

Giving Core States to the Mother's Side

Connirae: And now that your father has grown up with your Core States, we are ready to find out what happens when you give that same gift on your mother's side of the family. Your father can wait here for a moment as we turn to the grandparents on your mother's side, right before the moment of your mother's conception.

Now, letting those states of beingness and enlighteningness, ... that's right, ... flow into them so that they are transformed into the people that they are, with those resources present, with the beingness fully present and the enlighteningness fully there in them. ...

As soon as you are ready and your unconscious is ready, you can allow that to unfold also so that your mother is conceived into that supporting environment. There are those qualities of beingness and enlighteningness around her to be absorbed. ... She is bathed in them, allowing her to develop naturally as she does, having these resources around her, letting that unfold all the way forward to right before the moment of your conception. You can let me know when that is complete.

Dave: ... OK. *(Dave's eyes open.)*

Connirae: OK, excellent. ... Dave, is it all right with you to do this phase again, so that your grandparents and parents will have the Core States even more fully? *(Dave nods.)* Now you can give your grandparents on your father's side even more of that beingness and that enlighteningness, sensing and experiencing them as they are, having even more of those qualities fully in them, and letting the timeline unfold on that side, ... that's right, as your father is conceived in that environment, having even more beingness and enlighteningness to absorb, sensing him as he absorbs those qualities, and his timeline unfolds all the way forward to right before the moment of your conception. ... You may find that the second time through, your unconscious finds it easier to do this more completely and thoroughly by allowing the tempo to move even faster, so that you experience it at a different tempo. It is useful to run different cycles at different tempos because it transforms a different portion of our neurology.

Now that beingness and enlighteningness can sink even more fully into your father, and be there, radiating out. You can let me know when that is complete and he is all the way to the moment right before your conception. ... *(Dave nods.)* Good.

So now, let your unconscious also do that on your mother's side, so that her parents have an even deeper, more enriched, more enlightened, complete sense of that beingness and enlighteningness in them. And if you would like to add even more qualities this time, that is OK. If your unconscious decides to add in a sense of grace, peace, loving, OKness, or worthiness, it is certainly all right to have that also as her timeline unfolds and moves forward, so that as she develops, your unconscious just automatically allows even more of these Core States to be present in her, all the way forward to right before the moment of your conception. Your unconscious can notice those qualities and those states moving through her being and through your father's being, also, from head to toe, all the way through. And you can let me know when that has happened. ... *(Dave nods.)*

Connirae: Would you like to repeat this again, or is your sense that you have already finished this phase?

Dave: I think I need to do it once more.

Connirae: OK. So now, Dave, having this new baseline, you can invite your unconscious to add in anything that you intuitively know will be useful, building from what you now know, building at all levels based on where you are now, because each step we take opens up the door for seeing, hearing, feeling that so much more is possible, that we weren't able to see, hear and feel as possible before, but that now becomes clear. With this new baseline you can allow your grandparents on your father's side to again have even more of those qualities of the beingness and enlighteningness. That's right, and that goes in and deepens even more. Your unconscious can feel invited and free to add in anything else that your unconscious wisdom knows belongs there, a sense of valuing or OKness, anything about a sense of loving, fullness, grace, inner peace, or anything else that your unconscious knows would be a real gift to them. And as that is added in, that can unfold and you may find a different tempo is appropriate now, and that might be even faster, or it might be faster and then slower, and then faster—you can allow your unconscious to just choose its tempo.

Dave: I want it to be faster. You are going to have to talk less.

Connirae: I'll shut my mouth then. *(Laughter.)*

(Dave feels comfortable asking for the kind of assistance he wants from Connirae. Verbal guidance such as you have read so far can often assist in creating the fullest unconscious experience. Others prefer to do the process in their own way, without verbal assistance, especially in the later cycles such as Dave is now in, which are often done faster.)

Dave: I've done the grandparents.

Connirae: Great, so now we will just let it do itself, OK? And, you tell me when you are done.

Dave: *(Nods, and continues to process internally.)* OK.

Connirae: Great. And now your grandparents on your mother's side so that they fully have all those qualities even more completely. *(Dave nods that he is done.)*

(Each time Dave has cycled through this phase, we can see an increase in how fully he experiences the Core States in his grandparents and parents.)

Dave Absorbs His Core States From His Parents

Connirae: So now your parents are both here right before the moment of your conception, as they are, with these resources in them, because they have gotten them from their parents, right? *(Dave nods.)* So with these parents having those states fully present in them, whenever you are ready you can step into this new timeline in which your parents have these resources. It is going to unfold in a new way with these resources. Whenever you are ready you can step into the moment of your conception, feeling what it is like to be bathed in these states just because they are there in your parents, and you couldn't *not* take these states in also, in an even deeper, fuller, more complete way, because it is so easy to absorb what is surrounding us. So are you ready now? *(Dave nods and begins to step forward.)*

DIAGRAM #21-e

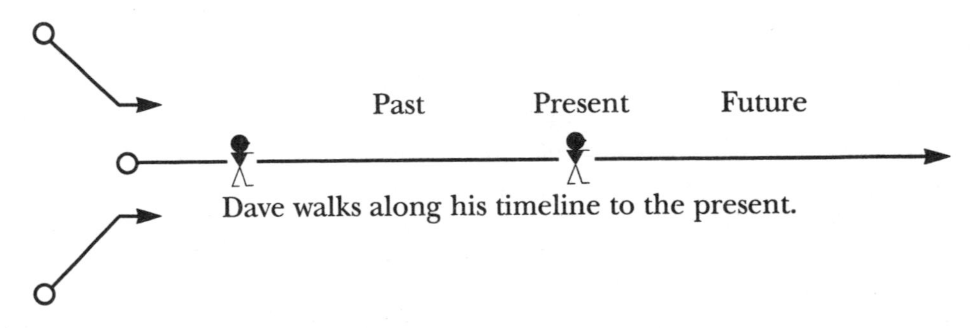

OK, so you can step forward into your conception, feeling what it is like to absorb this beingness and the enlighteningness from your parents because that is just the way it is, that is just the way they are, and that is what is surrounding you. ... And as a single cell, already, you have that beingness and that enlighteningness, and then, as you double in size and you become two cells, of course, those states double, and as you become four cells, of course, those states double again, and you know what happens as you become eight cells, and sixteen cells, and continue to develop your physical being as these Core States intensify. ...

And as you move forward through time, allowing your unconscious, ... that's right, to guide you at the appropriate tempo that will allow your unconscious to experience the transformation that is occurring, that will fully, completely enable the absorbing of these states, noticing what it is like at the unconscious level as your timeline unfolds in a whole new way, ... having these states fully present just because that is what is there to absorb. ...

That's right, all the way forward. And there may be some moments when you're consciously aware of the transformation that is taking place and at other times only the sense of what has happened as you have moved forward along the pathway with these states fully there. ... That's right, all the way forward. And you can let me know when you are in the present.

(As Connirae is speaking, Dave walks forward on his timeline toward the spot that represents his present. As he walks, Connirae observes many signs of unconscious integration. Dave's breathing becomes fuller, and the movement of his breathing extends into his limbs. He flushes and beads of perspiration appear on his forehead.)

Dave: OK.

Connirae: Great. So now, allowing your unconscious to continue that integration as I talk with you, you can let yourself notice and appreciate how your past timeline is now different, as if you had eyes in the back of your head. You can let me know if there are differences that come to consciousness. If the changes are all unconscious, that is OK, too.

(Dave already looks much different. Clearly his Core States of Beingness and Enlighteningness have become much fuller. These nonverbal shifts are a more important indication to Connirae than his verbal report.)

Dave: Consciously, I am aware of a shift in the darkness that was along the line. It is a lot lighter, especially in situations involving my parents.

Connirae: Great. So now, having that sense of what has just happened on that trajectory, *(Connirae gestures from Dave's past to his present.)* you can stay here in the present and just allow your unconscious to let that trajectory continue on into the future, seeing how your future now unfolds with that beingness and enlighteningness present, letting your unconscious re-sort, re-code, re-color the future, ... and you can let me know when you sense that your unconscious has done that.

Dave: ... OK.

Connirae: OK, great. Now, Dave has a new level of this beingness, enlighteningness that comes from having these Core States absorbed from his parents throughout his timeline.

Repeating the Process

Connirae: Now that you have experienced this level of beingness and enlighteningness, we are going to do this again, this time beginning with the *new* level of beingness and enlighteningness you have *now.* The level of beingness and enlighteningness you have now is your new baseline, Dave. So now we get to go back to the moment right before your conception. *(They walk back to the beginning of his timeline again and Dave stands waiting.)* You can again allow your eyes to close, feeling this new baseline, this new level of beingness and enlighteningness that you feel in your body and in your cells—in your unconscious as well as your conscious awareness. You can let that guide you to an even deeper and richer experience ... *(Dave begins walking his timeline and then pauses. His face looks like he is experiencing some strong emotion.)* ... and what is happening now? Is there something you want me to know about?

Dave: Well, the emotion doesn't feel like hurt. It is kind of the feeling I get with the enlighteningness. It feels really nurturing.

Connirae: Wonderful. So you can allow that to continue and to deepen even more, just as you are already doing, so that your unconscious and your conscious use that as the basis for an even deeper, richer experience. Then, when you are ready, you can step forward into the moment of your conception, having these parents now at this new level of beingness and enlighteningness, with those states there, to be even more absorbed by you, automatically, just because you are there. *(Dave steps forward.)* That's right. ... Sometimes a different tempo will enable the Core States to wash through a different set of memories. ... Again, feeling that multiply as you move along this trajectory, because things do build upon themselves, as you move forward in time, having even more richness and completeness. ... That's right, as even more becomes transformed most completely, all the way forward through to the present. You can let me know when you are there. *(Dave is walking faster on his timeline, and now he takes a deep breath.)* That's right, breathing in all of the transformation that is occurring at the unconscious level. That's right, all the way forward to the present. All right.

Dave: I am here. *(Dave is standing in his "present" on the timeline.)*

Connirae: Wonderful, and once again it is time to just let yourself sense and appreciate that trajectory you just moved along. Notice again the additional transformation that happened that time, and you can let us know if there is anything additional you sense at the conscious level.

(Speaking to the group.) We obviously noticed the deepening of the state in his physiology, right? Beginning with that new baseline, we get a tremendous deepening the second time through.

Dave: I noticed some things that I reclaimed for myself when you had me go out into the future, when I was creating the first baseline. With the personal work I have done in the last year I have had the sense of there being a light that I was being drawn towards—out on my future timeline, at the end. This has changed to a sense that light was reflecting back what was shining out from me.

Connirae: Great.

Dave: That came up for me the first time you had me go out into the future. This time, as I saw myself going onto my future timeline, I was shining the light out into other people. *(Dave is moved to tears.)* And so now I can feel the light of my grandparents coming through them and through me and shining out into the future.

Connirae: That is wonderful. You can invite your unconscious to fully take that too. *(Dave nods and smiles.)* OK, that is wonderful. So you can let yourself appreciate and absorb that even more, in whatever ways you intuitively and unconsciously know to be an even fuller representation of that experience. ... That's right. You have already begun the next step, which is moving into the future, letting these qualities continue on that same trajectory from the past into the future, with even more light reflecting in so many directions now that you may not be able to track it or even want to. *(Dave nods.)* OK. Whenever you are ready, I would like you to let me know. *(Dave nods again.)* Wonderful, OK.

You got a nice deepening from doing the process a second time. Would you like one more time through to be sure that it is totally full and complete?

Dave: *(Nods and laughs.)* I don't think we are done.

Connirae: *(Laughs.)* I think we have more to go, we are on a roll.

Dave: There is one thing that was really weird the first time we went down my timeline. My body got really hot. It felt like I had a cleansing fever or my body was burning off toxins.

Connirae: I'm not surprised, because you were really sweating. *(To the group.)* Did you see the sweat?

Dave: What will my future do this time? *(Laughs with the group.)*

Connirae: There's one way to find out! *(They walk back to the point just before Dave's conception.)*

OK. And now you can step forward into the moment of your conception, this time letting yourself move forward at the tempo that's most useful *(Dave walks forward on his timeline more rapidly.)*, that's right, so that your unconscious can allow this beingness and enlighteningness to seep into any memories or neurons or cells that they hadn't yet fully manifested themselves in yet. ... That's right, all the way forward to the present *(Dave reaches the present and stands at that point on his timeline.)* and on into the future, enlightening that also even more. That's right. Great.

Dave: OK.

Connirae: OK. Do you want to do this even more?

Dave: *(Laughs.)* I think I am done for now.

Connirae: OK. Often three times works really well. *(To the group.)* There are a few people who do this once and they're done. I can usually tell when that happens because the person goes through a massive reorganization the first time that is easy to see from the outside. They've done it all, and they don't want to cycle through again. Occasionally, it takes more than three times. I have done it up to seven times. If someone wants it that many times, it starts going really fast—you can almost run up the timeline, so it actually doesn't take much extra time, but each time gets a deepening. You can use this question as a guide: "Are you still getting change?" Once you've reached a plateau and a further repetition doesn't deepen the Core States any more, you are finished with this phase. As long as you are getting more light, more color and often a broadening of the timeline, you keep going. *(To Dave.)* What are you aware of in your future? How has that changed, Dave?

Dave: *(Laughs.)* There isn't any future. ... Well, there is, but it is really weird! I feel like that Core State has gone to the point of encompassing what I know of as reality. My sense was that not only am I shining this light off of something in the future, but I felt there is no future—it is a mirror. When the light was shining back into me, it was my own light all the way around. There was only a loop—there isn't any time.

Connirae: I was beginning to get that sense from you, too. That is interesting and from the expression on your face, I can tell it is wonderful. OK. Most people who do this find that the future opens up—it literally gets wider, and usually brighter as well. A few people describe something like Dave is experiencing. His future opened up totally. The light now has an all-encompassing timeless quality. OK.

Grounding Dave's New Core States

Connirae: Now there is one more phase of this. Having this state with you, the next step will create even more grounding and deepening of this state.

(To Dave and the group.) My sense is that people who have these Core States naturally, got them from having grown up in an environment where their parents had those Core States. So they got to absorb it, just as we have created that for Dave in his timeline.

Now, the people who really have those Core States deeply and fully in them are not those who had a perfect life. They are not the ones for whom every moment was totally wonderful and everyone was super kind and always nice and loving. People who had no challenges or obstacles in life end up being shallow. They don't have what is known as "character." They don't have a depth to their resourcefulness, because they have never gone through any challenges.

The people who have a deep resilience and inner strength are usually the ones who began by receiving these Core States from their parents, and then experienced some challenges. When you already have these Core States *in* you, a challenge in life doesn't take away from the Core State at all; it is actually the experience that *deepens* these states within us. Then when we are in a situation that is challenging, it becomes not a difficulty but a deepening of the inner resourcefulness that is already there. It becomes a stronger resourcefulness that then moves forward to the next challenge. Does that make sense to you, Dave?

Dave: Yes.

Connirae: Good. Now you have already experienced absorbing the Core States from the outside. So now we are going to take what you have thought of as your past, and treat it as that moment of difficulty, which deepens and strengthens. Do you know what I mean?

Dave: Yes.

Connirae: So with these Core States fully here in your core and your whole body, let's go back and stand right before the moment of your conception. *(They walk back to the beginning of his timeline.)* So that this experience becomes completely grounded, you can let yourself feel these Core States fully, the beingness and enlighteningness. ... And those words may not even be adequate anymore, but you know the state. Now you have this state in you from what we just did. Sometimes people experience it at this point as if it's from a spiritual parent or a spiritual source. However it got there, it is in you as you move forward this time through your life the way you think that it went, letting that all be transformed also by this Core State. Do you know what I am asking? This time you are going to have your parents acting the way you remember them, and that is going to be transformed by you having these states. Do you know what I mean?

Dave: OK, so I still have the Core States inside of me but my history basically looks however I remember it.

Connirae: Yes, except that you can allow your history to change as it naturally does by you having these Core States *within* you, radiating out. You will experience your history *very differently*. Even if an event is factually the same, your sense of it will be completely different.

Dave: I think I was already starting to do that.

Connirae: Great, I thought so. Please go ahead and do it again.

Dave: Just start from my conception or start before my conception, with my grandparents?

Connirae: Start from your conception, having the resources fully there, that's right, in you ... and it is often easier to let your unconscious do it *(Dave begins to walk up his timeline.)* ... so that you can move through fairly quickly and easily, as your unconscious allows that to all be transformed also ... because that is what lets us know at a very deep level what it is like to have resources fully there, even in situations where others aren't yet aware of the resources that are within them. That's right, all the way forward to the present.

(Dave reaches the present and stands there.) ....and then letting that flow out into the future or whatever kind of time now makes sense to you. *(Dave breathes deeply, sighs and nods.)* Great. Now it looks like you went through that fairly completely. Do you sense that is complete or do you want to go through it one more time?

Dave: One more time.

Connirae: Great. *(They walk back to the beginning of his timeline.)* And once again, taking the new level of these Core States *(Dave begins walking up his timeline.)*, and again, that's right, moving forward with every step deepening these states *(Dave reaches the present.)* to the present and on through time.

Great. So that is the process *(Very softly spoken.)* and if you would like to let your unconscious do any more absorbing, or generalizing, or letting that light flow and deepen in any other ways, that is fine. The integration can continue in whatever ways are appropriate and right and fitting, and natural and automatic, even after we finish, because this kind of shift and integration often does continue and it is a nice thing to acknowledge that happening. So whenever you are ready you can just let yourself consciously return to us in this room, as the integration continues unconsciously. Thank you.

(Dave hugs Connirae.)

....

—CHAPTER 22—

PARENTAL TIMELINE REIMPRINTING

Understanding the Structure

Life can only be understood backwards,
but it must be lived forwards.
—Soren Kierkegaard

Parental Timeline Reimprinting is a three-phase process:

Phase I: Giving our grandparents our Core States and then letting our parents fully absorb the Core States from our grandparents as they grow up.

Phase II: Absorbing the Core States from our parents as we grow up.

Phase III: Grounding our Core States by going through our timeline with them already there within us, to transform our sense of all that "really" happened to us.

Here is a brief description of each of these phases and their purposes. If you prefer to just do the process yourself and discover the structure through your own experience, feel free to turn to the next chapter for the exercise.

Phase I: Giving Core States to Our Grandparents & Through Them to Our Parents

Our past colors how we experience ourselves. No one is more influential than those who raised us. For most of us that is our parents. Our Core States can transform our past very easily when we go back far enough in time and start by having the Core States present in those who influenced us. For most of us, giving the Core States to our grandparents is much easier than giving them to our parents directly. Our ideas about who and what our parents are tend to be more fixed and rigid than our ideas about our grandparents. If giving the Core States to our grandparents is not easy enough, it is always possible to go back still further in time and give the Core States to our great grandparents. One person needed to go back to Adam and Eve, and give the Core States to them. In a matter of seconds, this person let the Core States travel forward from Adam and Eve through all his ancestors, up through his parents.

If you had adoptive parents, we encourage you to give the Core States to both your adoptive and biological parents. Even if you didn't know your biological parents while you were growing up, you probably have some sense of who they are. It doesn't really matter if your sense of your biological parents is accurate. It is your *ideas* of your parents that will be transformed by the Core States.

Phase II: Absorbing Core States From Parents & Experiencing Them Through Time

This phase offers yet another way to experience just having the Core State that our inner part wants. Most people feel very deeply nourished and loved when they have the experience of absorbing the Core States from parents who already have them.

Phase III: Grounding Our Core States by Transforming What "Really" Happened

It is wonderful to experience our past with "super deluxe" parents who have Core States. But if we only experience our past with these super deluxe parents we may not be prepared for encountering our real parents, or people like them. We want to make sure we can have our Core States even when those around us don't have full access to theirs. This phase grounds our Core States even more strongly within us. The Core States are already strongly present and in this phase they radiate through all of our past experiences, including times when our parents clearly did not have access to their own Core States. Since we now have our Core States as we move through our timeline, times that may have been traumatic when we went through them in "real life" actually become important and positive resources.

Cycling Through Several Times

It is difficult to convey in words the intensity of the state people usually go into when they do this process. This is because the Core States are themselves very powerful. Then, the process of moving quickly through time—through past, present, and future—amplifies the experience. Cycling through our timeline again, several times, makes our Core States increasingly intense. Dave began the Parental Timeline Reimprinting process with very intense Core States, and yet he shared with us that the intensity with which he felt them at least tripled by going through this process.

Encouraging Unconscious Processing

In the demonstration with Dave, Connirae encourages him to allow the process to happen at unconscious levels. She is watching him closely as she guides him in each step, noticing what amplifies his unconscious processing and recoding of events with the Core States present.

As you do this process with yourself, you will become increasingly in tune with what makes it easy for you to "turn your inner mind loose" with each step, allowing the shifts to just happen in ways that you don't need to completely understand. As you allow your unconscious to transform your experience in ways that truly fit for you, you will sense shifts taking place without knowing exactly what those shifts are.

The Results of Parental Timeline Reimprinting

Many people comment that they feel their Core States are more grounded: fuller and richer, and more a part of the ongoing stream of living. The Core States don't seem like just a "high," but are experienced as daily reality. Phase III of the Parental Timeline Reimprinting process, "Grounding Our Core States by Transforming What 'Really' Happened" is very important in getting this result. We don't just have a Core State that is separate from our daily living, we have a state that radiates into all our memories and our sense of the present and future.

Several other results are common and you may experience some or all of these. Frequently people report that their past becomes a much greater resource. Even those times that were difficult are experienced as somehow a blessing. Sometimes memories emerge that were previously too painful to remember, but are now experienced as OK in a deep sense, even though they were very traumatic at the time. It is not that we now like it that bad things happened to us; it is that on a deeper level we no longer judge that experience, ourselves or the others involved, as wrong. As the Core States wash through those experiences they are healed.

Another result is that we feel free of constraints we may have thought our past imposed upon us. If we felt limited by our past before—"I don't have any choice because I had X, Y, Z experiences as a child,"—we feel a sense of freedom to live from our Core States, no matter what past we had.

After doing this process we usually gain a sense of openness about the future. Many people notice their future becoming literally brighter and more expansive. If you want to, notice how your future appears to you when you begin. How dark or bright is it? How narrow or wide? These dimensions are likely to become literally different, and along with it, people describe a corresponding shift in their feelings about the future. A few people have cycled through past, present and future with their Core States and experienced their sense of time "pop," moving them into an experience of simultaneous reality such as Dave experienced with his future. This results from the quality of oneness that permeates most Core States. One way to experience oneness is that I am everything, at this moment in time. Another way to experience oneness is that I am one with every moment in time, also.

Summary

When we are finished with all three phases of Parental Timeline Reimprinting we have experienced our desired Core States in many different ways, and have allowed the Core States to transform different aspects of our memories and experience. Each phase literally transforms and reorganizes different portions of our neurology.

By approaching Core States from so many different angles, it is like experiencing a sculpture from all sides. If we only approach the sculpture from one side, we only experience once facet of it. If we approach the sculpture from all sides, we can see all of it. If we touch the sculpture with one hand, we will not experience as much of it as we will if we touch it with two hands.

—CHAPTER 23—

DOING IT!

THE PARENTAL TIMELINE REIMPRINTING EXERCISE

Giving the Gift of Core States to Yourself and Your Inner Family

Misery Is Optional
—T-shirt message

Parental Timeline Reimprinting deepens and amplifies the Core States that were identified during the Core Transformation Process. To do this process easily and effectively you need to have completed the full Core Transformation Process, including growing up a part, bringing the Core State fully into the body, and timeline generalization. If you can, have somebody read this exercise to you in a slow, soft voice. Tell them the names of your Core States before you begin. If you are doing the exercise on your own, it will work best to read it through once before doing the exercise. If you are reading these instructions as a guide for someone else, parts that are italicized do not need to be read aloud. As the guide, your partner will gain the most if you are coming from one of your own favorite Core States.

....

LAYING OUT YOUR TIMELINE

1. Lay your timeline out on the floor the same way Connirae and Dave did in the demonstration. First, sense your past, your present and

your future. Put them out there on the floor in a sweeping, straight line or path, so that your lifetime fits into the available space. *If you can, find a space that is long enough for your timeline. If not, it is OK to temporarily "condense" your timeline for this process.*

2. Now walk beside your timeline to the point just before your conception. At this point, turn and look down your timeline. *(see diagram #23-a)*

DIAGRAM #23-a

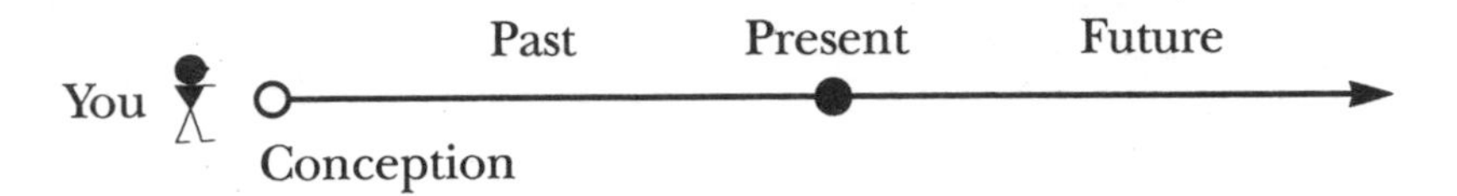

3. As you stand before your conception, facing toward your timeline, you can imagine two timelines, one for your mother and one for your father, coming together before your conception. Which side is your mother's and which side is your father's? Who do you want to give your Core States to first—your mother or your father?

DIAGRAM #23-b

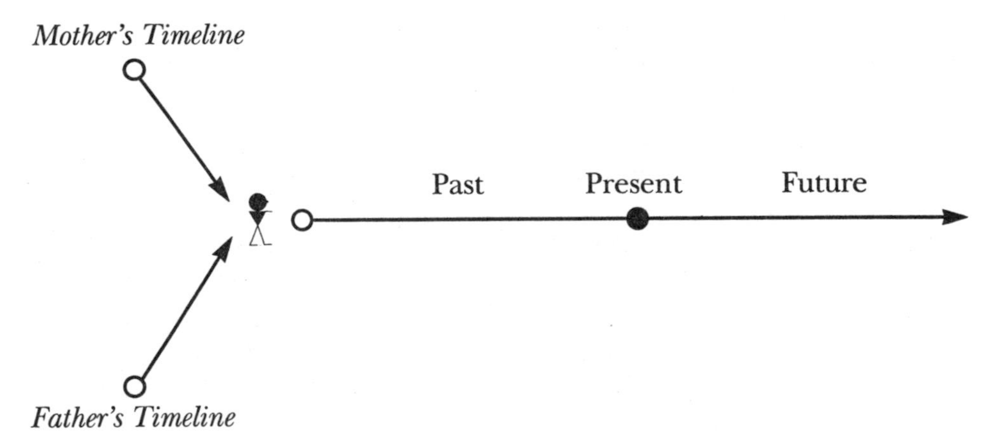

GIVING CORE STATES TO YOUR GRANDPARENTS' AND PARENTS' TIMELINES

4. Look down your mother/father's timeline, all the way back to just before his/her conception. See your grandparents standing there, before your mother/father was conceived. About how old are they at this time? (It is OK to make this up, if you don't know.)

5. Now, allow [Core States] to flow into your grandparents until they are completely filled up with [Core States].

6. Now imagine your mother/father being conceived into this environment, just absorbing [Core States] from his/her parents. Allow your mother's/father's timeline to unfold as it does, with these Core States available. Notice how as s/he develops, s/he absorbs these Core States even more fully. Allow his/her timeline to unfold until right before your conception.

7. *Repeat steps 4-6 with the other parent. (Repeat Phase I (steps 4-6) until both parents are completely filled with the Core States before going on.)*

ABSORBING CORE STATES FROM YOUR PARENTS

8. Now step into the moment of your conception, so you can experience being totally surrounded with [Core States]. You are now just a single cell, in a universe that is filled with [Core States]. You can completely absorb [Core States] because that is what you are immersed in. When you divide into two cells, [Core States] can double. When you divide into four cells, [Core States] double again. You can continue developing, as [Core States] develop with you, and you continue absorbing even more from what's around you.

When you're ready, take a half-step forward into the moment of your birth, being born into a family that has [Core States]. As you are held by your parents for the first time, you can absorb even more [Core States] from them.

At your own speed, slowly or quickly, allow yourself to move forward through time, allowing [Core States] to grow within you as you continue to absorb them, until you have reached the present. Your unconscious can notice how having [Core States] in each of your experiences transforms everything in powerfully resourceful ways.

9. Now that you have reached the present, sense yourself moving on into the future with [Core States] building even more, fully available to you in all situations. (*Repeat steps 8-9 as many times as desired, for you to have all the benefit from this phase. Vary the speed, from a couple of minutes to a few seconds. If you are reading this to someone else who is going quickly, you won't have time to read all the words in this script. Just read whatever you have time for. For example, you may only need to say, "That's right, transforming past, present and future, <u>even more.</u>"*)

GROUNDING YOUR CORE STATES

10. In a moment you can go back to your conception and up through your past again. This time, with your parents acting the way you remember them in "real life," you already have [Core States] coming from inside you, and you'll find out how *that* transforms your entire past. Do this quickly, so that the new connections can take place most easily and fully on an unconscious level. When you reach the present, sense [Core States] also radiating out into the future, allowing everything that will happen to be transformed by [Core States] already being there. (*Repeat step 10 as many times as desired, to strengthen the grounding. Again, you can vary the tempo.)*

11. Now that your past, present and future are transformed with these [Core States], you can let your new timeline flow back around you in the way that most fits you now, so that it is there with you as you go into the future. The more [Core States] fill your past and future, the more strongly you can experience them here and now.

....

Handling Objections

Most of the time, after doing the Core Transformation Process, we are immediately ready to move into Parental Timeline Reimprinting. It is very unusual to have any objections to this process. If an objection does come up, it is very important to honor it and satisfy your concern. The most important guideline is to proceed gently with these processes. Remember that each step of the process is an invitation for us to do something that can help us learn and grow. We always respond to the concern within an objection before proceeding. An objection often reflects a way in which we don't quite understand the process or the purpose of doing the process.

Here are the three most common objections that occur to the process, and how you can honor them in a way that enables you to move forward:

Objection #1: "If I give my parents these Core States it is not real. My parents didn't really have those resources."

That's right, they didn't. You aren't adding these Core States to your *real* parents, you are adding them to the parents you carry around inside of you. You aren't really changing the past, you are giving *yourself* the chance to experience what it is like to have had parents with those resources, so that *you* can benefit from that here and now. We first do this with 'enriched' parents who are more resourceful than the parents you remember, because you have given them these Core States. Then you will walk through your timeline with your parents the way you actually remember them. Usually when this objection arises, we just need to know that we will still be able to remember what happened in our life.

Objection #2: "I hate my parents and don't want to give them resources. They don't deserve them."

Because you are giving these resources to the parents you carry around inside of you, you are really giving them to yourself. You are giving *yourself* the kind of inner parents you deserved to have had on the outside. Sometimes it is also helpful to gently remind yourself that your parents learned how to be a parent from *their* parents. If you invite yourself to think of your parents as they were when they were babies who needed nurturing and love, it typically becomes easier to give them resources.

Objection #3: "I don't think the changes will last."

In this case you need to find out if the part that is concerned has an *objection* to the changes lasting. Usually the part really wants the changes to last and is concerned they might not. If you have this concern, turn within and ask the part of you that has this concern:

"Is it OK with you if the changes *do* last?"

"Are you interested in doing the process to find out if they last?"

"Do you want to be a part that helps make *sure* the changes last?"

"Do you want to be a part that alerts us if the changes don't last?"

If the part that is concerned is a younger part, it will probably be useful to do the full Core Transformation Process with this part, to reintegrate this part back into you.

When You Don't Have the Core State

If any other difficulty occurs (other than the above three objections), most likely it simply means that you don't have the *Core State* for the part you have been working with. What you probably have is an intended outcome that is very close to the Core State.

Reed did the Core Transformation Process at an Aligned Self seminar with a part of him that felt compelled to blame others. The Outcome Chain he had discovered went as follows:

Blame —> Revenge —> Knowing I'm Right —> Satisfaction —> Strong Sense of Self

Reed thought "strong sense of self" was his Core State, yet when he did the Parental Timeline Reimprinting process, he felt very ambivalent. He and his partner came to me for assistance. When I watched what Reed looked like in this state, it was clear this wasn't a Core State. It didn't have the needed qualities to transform his timeline in a fully satisfying way. Together we simply turned back to Reed's part and asked, "And if you *have* this strong sense of self, what do you want, through having that, that is even more important?" Reed discovered two more steps in his Outcome Chain. After strong sense of self came "bursting presence," and then a sense of oneness. When Reed completed the Core Transformation process with oneness, and did Parental Timeline Reimprinting with oneness, there were no objections. He commented afterwards, "That really cleaned something out that's been inside me for a long time. I feel a directness in me now. It's way beyond that—it's more like this oneness goes through everything. I never wanted to do this blame thing, but I didn't know what else to do."

—CHAPTER 24—

VICTORIA'S STORY

The Gifts of Taking Core States Through Time

"...It was as if each of the sparkling dots [now in my timeline] was a healing, and no matter how tragic these circumstances were for me, I had taken some gift from them."
—Victoria

Victoria attended an Aligned Self seminar. For her the Parental Timeline Reimprinting Process was particularly powerful. A year later she is still very excited about the changes she experienced as a result of doing the process. Here is her story:

> Parental Timeline Reimprinting was a really wonderful thing for me. I have gone to church, and heard all this stuff about what God is, and about forgiveness and unconditional love and healing. Academically, I said to myself, "Yes, I believe in that. That's what I want to do!" And yet the process of unconditional love and forgiveness was never clear to me until I did the Parental Timeline Reimprinting.
>
> I said, "This is it! This is the process that they all talk about, but no one ever teaches you how to do it!" It is amazing to me that anyone ever comes upon unconditional love without having something like this process.
>
> I was adopted, and I was told by my adoptive parents that what I had come from was trash. I don't think they ever understood the impact that those words had on my life. It affected my self-esteem at a very deep level. No matter how good I was, I

believed that what I came from was not good, so therefore a part of me wasn't any good. The process was a real healing in terms of forgiveness. I began to understand on a deep level that my natural parents had things happen to them which were not my responsibility. I began to have choice about how I thought about myself, and that took a great deal of pressure off of my heart.

I have had diabetes for years. My health has improved since that workshop, and I attribute a large part of that to the Parental Timeline Reimprinting. There was a place inside of me that was like a volcano, or a pressure cooker. And I didn't know what all the intensity was about! It only took a voice tone to trigger an intense reaction in me. I was bewildered by the intensity of the anger or pain I felt. I didn't understand how a little thing that someone did could trigger such an insurmountable reaction in me. When I did the Parental Timeline Reimprinting I became aware of how much pain was back in my past and how much I had overcome in my life. I became aware that the thought patterns and beliefs I had formed from those early experiences were creating my everyday life. And many of those beliefs and thought patterns were not healthy.

As a diabetic I risk having my blood sugar bounce between extremes. Without taking insulin, my blood sugar is too high, and I could go into diabetic coma. When I take insulin, my blood sugar goes down. If I take too much insulin, it goes down too far, and I could go into insulin shock. Adrenaline, which is useful in a situation of immediate physical danger, is very detrimental to the body if it is constantly dumped into your system. In my own mind, I feel that the adrenaline and other physical responses from the constant fight-or-flight reaction that I have lived in all my life is what damaged my pancreas. It causes blood flow restrictions and heart palpitations. I experience it as a feeling that I am in terrible, terrible danger. And I reacted that way when somebody looked at me the wrong way. When I go into my fight-or-flight response and adrenaline is dumped into my system, my blood sugar level goes crazy and it is very difficult to know how much insulin to take. Therefore, when my emotions were so out of balance on a regular basis, I had a tendency to yo-yo, with my blood sugar swinging from too high to too low instead of keeping a nice even middle line.

When I'm not in that fight-or-flight response, I can digest food better and I can metabolize sugars more evenly. As the results of the Parental Timeline Reimprinting became more and more pervasive in my life, my emotions became more balanced and stable, so my blood sugar levels became more stable.

I had an especially difficult time with feelings of abandonment. When something triggered my fear of being abandoned I felt fragmented. When I felt separated from someone, I felt extremely fearful. On the outside people may have seen my behavior as arrogance, immaturity, or something else. But inside I was feeling the stark raving terror of abandonment. It was often a tonality in someone's voice that triggered this terrible fear.

I had a lot of intellectual knowledge that my thought patterns are like seeds, producing the results that I have in life. I understood that, but I didn't know what the thought patterns were. The timeline work made me aware that when I responded to someone so strongly, their tonality was similar to one my parents used, and so it triggered the old reaction even though the subject matter was totally different. Now, when someone uses that tonality, I have this sweet little voice in my ear that tells me, "This is not about you!" I no longer have adrenaline constantly flowing through my system.

I used to judge everything someone said as meaning something about me, when in fact it usually has nothing to do with me, and everything to do with them! It was low self-esteem behavior to the extreme!

When I first put my timeline on the ground and I was going to walk into my past, there was a part of me that would not walk back into it. My guide suggested that I back up into it. As I backed up, I hit metaphorical bumps in the road. I felt there were big black things there, like black holes, and then I thought about it and a picture of an incident came up that went with the feeling. I had suppressed those black holes so deeply for so long, I didn't even know they were there. I was not ever allowed to talk about this stuff with my adoptive family. We were very neglected kids.

I did the Parental Timeline Reimprinting process twice with someone guiding me, and then once on my own. Since I had both natural parents and adoptive parents, I did the process with all four of them. It was a real integration process. The third time I did it, I could swing my past timeline to the left of me where I could see it, and I realized that those places that had been black holes were now sparkling dots! I felt so much better. It was as if each of those sparkling dots was a healing, and no matter how tragic those circumstances were for me, I had taken some gift from them.

Someone told me once that my relationship with God was very solid, but my relationship with myself was in great jeopardy, and that was what caused my health problems. Now, each of those sparkling dots is a healing, a piece of myself that I had previously splintered from and that I can now reconnect with.

I sent back a sense of love to my parents. My mother, in particular, needed to have enough love inside her to be able to give it. In addition, I sent back the ability to be compassionate and understanding.

When I stood in the present and looked toward the future I had the sense that things were going to be much better than I ever could have imagined. I remember walking into the future and looking back into my past, and there was a quality of light whereas before there was darkness. That was very important to me. The further into the future I went, the brighter my past got, and the more I realized how important my past was in making me the person that I was in the future. It was wonderful to experience my past as having a real purpose in building the character of the person I am! For instance, I had a foster parent who tried to drown me more than once. It might sound weird, but knowing I survived those incidents is now a resource to me.

I found the process to be highly valuable in terms of my own personal well-being. I feel that the cause of my health problems is in my identity, in things in my head that I didn't even know I had there. It was, to me, the most spiritual piece of work I have ever done. Learning how to really forgive someone is a gift that, for me, is of the highest spiritual nature. And I revere it in that way when I do the process with people. I think it helps people find the gift in their lives. No matter what has happened to them, there is something positive that they have walked away with that has made them the person that they are.

Every time I do this process with someone else, I feel honored and I feel like I walk away with a gift. I feel as if another piece of *me* gets healed, too! I think that's because so many of us have things in common, and my unconscious mind finds something similar to their experience and heals it along with them.

—SECTION VII—

ENHANCING YOUR RESULTS

Making a Good Thing Even Better

—CHAPTER 25—

INTRODUCTION

ENHANCING YOUR RESULTS

Making A Good Thing Even Better

You use your senses
to seek the answer
outside yourselves,
not seeing
it is within you
all the time.
—*Huang Po,* c. 850

There are many ways to use the Core Transformation Process in more depth to create more pervasive levels of change in your life. In this section we will give you many ways to enhance and deepen the changes you have experienced already. We will give you ways to discover more parts and share some ideas about how those parts were formed. We will give examples of some basic personality patterns that don't serve us, and how to work with them, using the Core Transformation Process. Working with illness and other major life crises is also covered in this section, along with accounts of people who have used the process with illness. You will learn an exercise called "Generalizing the Core Transformation Process," which takes groups of parts through the process all at once.

In the last two chapters of the book we will talk about Core Transformation and spirituality, and how to use the process in an ongoing way.

—CHAPTER 26—

FINDING MORE PARTS TO TRANSFORM

Tapping Into Greater Inner Blessings

There is only The One Mind
and not a particle
of anything else.

All phenomena, from the
tiniest atom to the great
chiliocosms, are no more
than bubbles and foam,
patterns of thought
in a great dream.
—*Huang Po,* c. 850

Most of us are accustomed to *disliking* our limitations and trying not to have them. As we use the Core Transformation Process over time a real shift happens—we develop the attitude of welcoming, receiving, loving and accepting our limitations and bad habits, our quirks and foibles, our compulsions and weaknesses. This attitude of welcoming and accepting all parts of ourselves is a tremendous gift, over and above the specific changes we get through doing the process.

When you first start using the Core Transformation Process you will most likely have a list of feelings that are off-balance, or habits and behaviors you want to change. This is a good place to begin and provides significant benefits. However, some of the most important changes come when we work with parts that aren't obvious at first. Each of us has the opportunity to discover and transform many inner parts, leading to greater wholeness. This chapter is designed to assist you in discovering more opportunities for tapping into inner blessings.

WORKING WITH PARTS THAT ARE ANGRY

Before Working With Angry Parts, We Are Likely To Speak in "You" Statements:

You shouldn't ...
You shouldn't have ever...
It was very *wrong* for *you* to ...

When Our Anger is Clean We Are More Likely to Speak in "I" Statements:

I am angry at ...
I feel frustrated about ...

Working With Anger

Issues about anger are very common in our culture. Doing the Core Transformation Process with parts that are angry can be a wonderfully rewarding experience. Getting angry sometimes is a part of being human. The goal in working with angry parts is not to eliminate our anger, but to become clean both in how we feel anger and how we express it. Any time your anger is not clean it is something you can work with.

Anger is clean when my goal in being angry is to *express* my feelings and thoughts. If I am owning my feelings as mine rather than saying it is right that I am angry, then my anger is clean.

If I am using my anger to try to intimidate or coerce someone else into changing or doing things my way, my anger is not clean. Art was a small business owner and accustomed to making the rules. At home however, Art's wife Rosemary didn't always respond with the willingness to do it his way that he could count on from his employees. When Rosemary started hand-digging their garden instead of waiting for Art to rototill it, as he wanted to do, he began yelling at her. Art realized he wasn't just expressing his feelings to his wife. A part of him wanted to "get her to do it my way." Working with this part made a difference for Art.

If I am using my anger to make someone wrong or blame someone, my anger is not clean. If my anger is extreme, like rage, I am probably reacting based on the experiences of a younger part of myself rather than from current time. This can be "updated" by working with the part of me that is enraged.

Anger is clean when it is not used to mask another emotion. Jan felt very hurt because her husband forgot their anniversary, but thought it was weak to admit it. She had an easy time getting angry, so the next day she got very angry with him over a seemingly small thing. Jan was really both hurt and angry. She had several parts she could work with: the part that was angry, the part that felt hurt, and the part that judged being hurt and prevented its expresssion.

Any time you are feeling angry you can do the Core Transformation Process with the part that is feeling angry. Sometimes your anger will melt away completely and be replaced by compassion and understanding. When Julianne (in Chapter 9), did the Core Transformation Process, her feelings of anger became an inner laugh. Once your feelings are acknowledged, then they can begin to melt and transform.

At other times you will still feel angry but your anger will have a different quality. It will have greater strength, yet be less intense. You will become clearer about what you don't like, how you want things to be, and what you are and are not willing to live with. You will experience a greater ability to express your anger clearly, without judgments or coercion.

Primary and Secondary Emotions

Some emotions naturally fade away or are completely transformed after you have worked with them through this process. If your emotion fades or is transformed, it was what we call a *secondary emotion.* Secondary emotions seem to be produced because we have separated from our Core States. As we return to having the Core States wanted by these parts, these emotions dissolve. The secondary emotions include rage, jealousy, revenge, guilt, and resentment. As these fade away we can more clearly express our *primary emotions,* including anger, sadness, hurt, love, gratitude, compassion and joy. You will experience these emotions in a cleaner way, and they will be more aligned with your Core State.

Experiencing all emotions is a natural part of living. Each of us needs this range of feelings to be a full human being. At the same time, whenever you are feeling a strong emotion you will most likely gain value from doing the Core Transformation Process with that part.

Welcoming Emotions

When we do the Core Transformation Process with intense emotional parts, our emotions tend to come into greater balance and be less intense. When we first notice an unpleasant emotion we tend to want to get rid of it in some way so we don't feel it. If, instead, we acknowledge and work with these parts, each pain or discomfort will lead to a deeper connection with ourselves. Emotions can become blessings that assist and direct us in our lives. One of my workshop participants had a whole series of parts emerge that she at first experienced as "painful" or "awful." These parts felt extremely needy, unworthy and not OK, yet each wanted an important Core

State. After including four of these parts she said, "I'm getting it now—I'm realizing that there is *nothing* I can find in myself that is really awful."

If you have suppressed or shoved aside many of your feelings up until now, as you become more accepting of yourself you may go through a phase of experiencing your emotions *more* intensely. One of my clients who did the Core Transformation Process was concerned because the first result was that she was feeling *stronger* emotions. She had been accustomed to thinking of emotions as dangerous and bad. Actually, her feelings had always been strong, but she had been used to just shifting them out of her awareness and not noticing them. As she did the Core Transformation Process with each emotional part, she gained a new sense of comfort with, and appreciation for her emotions. Within a few months she found her life naturally becoming more emotionally balanced and on track.

What Do I Judge In Myself or Others?

Asking yourself, "What do I judge or criticize in myself or others?" can bring forward important parts to work with. Things we criticize in ourselves or others can point the way to parts with inner gifts to offer through this process. Often, what we criticize and judge most strongly in others is also, unconsciously, what we criticize and judge in ourselves.

I (Connirae) noticed I had been critical for years of a woman I thought was arrogant. I decided to explore my relationship to this. I noticed one part of myself that felt intimidated by her—that wilted around her. Then I searched for a part within me that was arrogant. At first I didn't want to notice this, because I wanted to think I was very different from her. After all, arrogance was something I didn't like. Yet when I searched, I discovered a part within me that also felt arrogant. This was a part that wanted to feel superior to her. When I welcomed this part in, and did the Core Transformation Process with it, I found it had something wonderful to offer me. Afterwards, I noticed that I no longer felt so "different" from people who act arrogantly. I no longer needed to hold myself separate. I still don't enjoy arrogance—either in myself or in someone else—yet I don't judge or criticize it in the same way I did before. I feel a greater sense of compassion for those arrogant parts within others and within me.

As I have searched for other inner parts that are like what I criticize in other people, I have noticed myself feeling less judgmental. I have always considered myself to be an accepting person. I have been a therapist for a long time, and have always been willing to accept any quality in my clients that could emerge. Now I notice a different quality to my acceptance. Before I accepted others in a more "mental" way—I was still holding myself as separate and different from them. Now I experience myself as the same as each person I work with, in a much deeper way than before.

Another example may help you discover the critical or judgmental parts in yourself. When my husband was using this approach, he noticed that he criticized others for being irresponsible. That was something that pushed his buttons. He found several parts to work with. One was the part that became angry when others didn't do their share. Another was the part within him that wanted to be free of responsibilities. As a young child, circumstances had forced him to become very responsible very quickly. He was born in Hawaii, and was six years old when Pearl Harbor was bombed. He was taken to the mainland with his mother along with many women and children who were evacuated. His father died four years later, so his mother was on her own with a young son and an older daughter, and needed him to grow up quickly. Times were tough economically for his mother, and Steve stepped in at a very young age to help with grown-up responsibilities. Then, because of his mother's health problems, he supported both his mother and himself while putting himself through college. Clearly this part within that wanted to be free of responsibility had been shoved aside for good reasons at a much earlier time.

We have covered three main aspects of working with our inner parts that judge and criticize: 1) Our inner parts that judge and criticize—either ourselves or others; 2) Our inner parts that respond unresourcefully when others do things we criticize; and 3) The inner parts of ourselves that are *like* what we criticize in others.

As we reclaim each of these parts within ourselves we become better able to accept a wide range of behaviors and responses from others. As we become less judgmental and reactive, we are better able to clearly observe and identify both our own and others' behaviors such as arrogance, jealousy, wimpiness, nervousness, competitiveness, frivolousness, laziness, and the need to control or be the center of attention. This doesn't mean we *like* these behaviors, it means we don't *judge* them as wrong or bad, and our buttons don't get pushed by them anymore. We can observe them with neutrality and compassion. (For more on working with self-judgment, see Chapter 18, "How to Recognize Parts That Need to Be Included.")

What Do Others Criticize in Me?

Another way to find parts is asking ourselves, "What do others criticize in me?" When another person criticizes us it can be tempting to shove the message aside, or decide the other person "just doesn't understand," or is projecting their own issues onto us.

I find it easiest to work with this area when I bypass the issue of whether the criticism of me is true or not. The criticism may actually be more true of the person making it than of me, yet I often can use a criticism to find a part within me that is worth working with. This is particularly true of a criticism that has come up more than once.

Tom complained that his wife, Betty, was moody and unpredictable in her emotional ups and downs. While Betty acknowledged that this was sometimes true of her, she felt it was a small part of their life together and was more Tom's issue than hers because he felt so strongly about it. However, she decided to do the Core Transformation Process with the part of her that was moody and emotionally unpredictable, and discovered a cluster of parts with very strong feelings such as hurt, rejection and sadness, that felt pushed away and ignored. As she did the process with each part, she discovered they all had a Core State of "communion with all." Some time later Betty reported back to us that her periods of moodiness were much less intense, and that she had started acknowledging her feelings of hurt and sadness to Tom and to herself. Tom reported that when Betty was moody it was no longer a big issue for him, and that as Betty had started to share her feelings with him, he had been inspired to work with his own feelings of hurt and sadness.

Parts We Avoid

Here are some good questions you can ask yourself when you are looking for parts. Whatever first comes to mind as you read these questions will probably offer you good material to work with.

What are the things I'm sure are not true of me?

What do I most *not* want to work with?

What don't I want to be true of myself?

Most, if not all of us, have some inner qualities we would rather deny altogether. When I asked myself the above questions I discovered a "set" of qualities I had denied in myself. One of those qualities was pride. I grew up in a church community where pride was not considered a virtue. I learned to be humble very early, and did a good job of it. I thought of myself as a humble person, and acting humble certainly gained me more respect from those around me. Discovering the part of me that felt proud, reaching its Core State, and welcoming it back in was a useful step for me in becoming more whole.

Similarly, as a child I learned that being nice and kind were very important qualities. In church and in our community these qualities were praised. I became accustomed to pushing my own "mean" thoughts and feelings so far out of the way that I didn't even notice them. It has been important for me to recognize and include the parts of myself that think unkind thoughts or impulsively want to do something I would have judged as mean.

As we acknowledge and work with these parts of ourselves with the Core Transformation Process, we don't become "meaner," we become more whole and balanced. We are more likely to speak for ourselves more clearly and strongly. Out of being more whole and including all of ourselves, we become more truly kind, from the core of our being, rather than just having a kind "act."

In reclaiming these parts you may find it helpful to work with any inkling of a part that emerges when you ask the above questions. At first it is a big shift to even consider that we may have a quality we feel it is important not to have. These inner parts have been banished by us and may need some extra welcoming. Keep in mind that if you discover a "greedy" part, or a part that wants to control, or anything else you don't like, this doesn't mean that you are a controlling or greedy person—you may in fact be the opposite most of the time. It just means that this is one of your many facets, and a source of energy that you may now reclaim. Whenever we don't want something to be true of us we narrow our inner range; our being becomes constrained in some way. As we welcome these banished parts of ourselves back in, we move toward wholeness.

After working with many others and with myself it has become clear that the further away we try to shove inner parts of ourselves, the more distorted and garish they become. Whatever I try to disown as "not me" becomes more extreme and unbalanced. When we welcome back our lost parts we become more balanced.

Abigail tried to control her desire to take a break and have time for herself. She considered that laziness and thought she should always be working hard. She did work hard most of the time, but it was always a struggle. As she forced herself to keep going she found herself frequently distracted by thoughts of the "idle life." Abigail thought she was being very immature to keep getting lost in dreams of just dropping everything. She wanted to do something about it because she began to feel tired so often that it interfered with her work.

Abigail needed to reclaim the part of her that wanted to drop everything. She needed to include it, rather than fight against it. She also had a part that judged herself when she enjoyed herself. When she got to the Core State of these two parts, they were the same; inner peace. After reclaiming both parts at the level of their Core States, Abigail felt herself living out of a new sense of ease. She enjoyed working for the first time she could recall, and found it natural to include time for herself as well.

As you seek to include your own denied parts, one way to allow them to surface is to welcome any "possible" part, pretend it is part of you, and work with it. As Abigail did, you can also work with the part of you that judges these parts to be bad.

The Body Scan

Doing a "body scan" can be another abundant source of parts to work with. We tend to carry leftover emotions in different parts of our bodies. We can become aware of these by checking for any sensations that stand out to us. We may notice feelings of heaviness, extra warmth, minor and major aches and pains, feelings of weakness, or sensations that can't quite be described. As I (Connirae) check through my body, I feel for these kinds of signals. The signal of an ache or pain in a body area may be the introduction to a part. I have often started with feelings I couldn't really put into words, but I could sense them somewhere in my body. Once I did a body scan and noticed some slight tingling, warm sensations in the left part of my stomach. I turned within and asked that sensation, "What do you want?" I got the immediate response, "I want love." I had my first answer, and was ready to get the full Outcome Chain. I never did learn what early or current experiences this part had to do with; I didn't need to know in order to get benefit through the Core Transformation Process.

Attachment

Attachment defines another area for finding parts. By attachment we mean that we need ourselves or others to *be* a certain way or *do* a certain thing.

When it is important to me that things go a certain way, I am attached. Attachments to things that are positive—like success, intelligence, appearance, other people, jobs— are the most likely to be overlooked. If I think I am stupid, I will probably notice this as a problem. Yet if it is important to me to be intelligent, this subtle judgment can also get in my way. I may have a harder time noticing, acknowledging and truly accepting my mistakes. I may become tense over the effort to act intelligent. I may act superior to others, and be less ready to embrace the wisdom in each person. By working with both my negative and positive attachments, I can balance myself and be able to observe and appreciate whatever *is*.

If you want to discover what positive qualities you are attached to having, try making a list describing your positive attributes. Then check for a part that takes pride in being that way. The parts we deny in ourselves are usually the *opposite* of what we recognize in ourselves. If I have, "I am a generous person," on my list of positive qualities, I can seek a part that wants to keep everything. If I have "I am tolerant and give in to what other people want," I can look for a part that wants to have my way. If I have, "I am kind" on my list, I can look for a part that is unkind. When I work with both parts—the part that is kind and loves being kind, plus the part that wants to be unkind—I will move the furthest toward wholeness. When I reclaim both parts *at the level of their Core States,* I become less attached to being kind, and more compassionate and neutral toward unkindness in myself and others.

Thinking about "What am I attached to?" has helped me (Connirae) notice my responses in my family and in my work that have been off-balance. For example, with my children I have sometimes noticed that I "need" them to respond a certain way. If one of them comes home from school feeling unhappy about something, I naturally want him to feel better. But sometimes I have noticed I am *attached* to having him feel better, and I become upset when he doesn't. This kind of attachment can make it difficult for my children to accept their unhappiness and move through it in their own way and their own timing. After working with the part of me that is attached to my children feeling better, I feel much more able to receive them fully as they are—happy or unhappy. I feel more able to support them in developing in their own way.

When my children struggle with a subject in school, again, I have felt my own need for them to learn it comfortably and easily. As I have worked with the part of me that needs them to learn it easily, I have become more deeply accepting of however it goes for them. I still want them to learn it easily, and I still think of creative and resourceful ways I can assist them with this, yet I feel less attachment to the results, and more accepting of however my children respond.

I have also noticed times when I've had a strong opinion about how to parent our children and felt the need for my husband to see it my way. Working with the part of me that was "attached" to having him agree with me helped me share my concerns and ideas out of an attitude of wanting the "truth" to emerge, rather than wanting to convince him.

Last month I (Tamara) woke up one morning with the flu, and I desperately wanted to be well, so I went inside to communicate with the part of me that was creating the flu. As I was focusing inside myself, I did not get a response from the part of me that was creating the flu. I began to feel more and more unhappy about not getting the responses I wanted! I realized there was a part of me that was very attached to getting well, and so I shifted gears to work with that part. Through the Core Transformation Process, I got a sense of profound inner peace. Although I still wanted to get well quickly, I no longer felt attached to it. I rested much more peacefully, and within a few days I fully recovered.

Another way to look at attachments is as "shoulds." Any time I'm telling myself or someone else that something "should" be done a certain way, that's a good signal that a part is in there that's attached to an outcome and that it would benefit from the Core Transformation Process.

Noticing what I am attached to can help me notice the subtle ways in which I am not yet whole. When I need something from outside of myself, it is a sign that I am not recognizing how I am already whole within. When I need myself to be a certain way, it means I am not yet recognizing how I am already complete in a much deeper way.

Using these methods to find inner parts, and working with them, helps us go far beyond remedial change. Remedial change is "fixing what is broken." The level of change we get through this kind of process is more like what happens when the metal of an ore, such as iron, is fired. There is nothing "wrong" with the original iron. Yet when it is fired it becomes increasingly purified and it is possible to use it in many other ways.

Am I Leaving Anything Out?

When I teach this process in workshops I notice that people are frequently shocked (at first) to discover and work with their own inner parts that are the most negative or hateful. For example, they are shocked if they discover that one of their parts wants to kill someone. However, these are the parts that most need attention, and they have much to give us. Once people feel safe enough to work with them, these parts feel free to change.

The Core Transformation Process gives us a way to reclaim hateful and even "murderous" inclinations in a way that paradoxically just expands and enlarges our ability to love and be compassionate. If we have not found any parts that want revenge, want to control, or even want to murder, then we are probably leaving something out. It is worth going on a search for parts like this, and for those parts of us that judge these qualities as bad. When we find a part that wants these negative things, through this process, even the most negative or hateful urges imaginable always flip to the positive at some point. Having a part that wants to destroy doesn't mean that *I* would destroy. This is only one aspect of my being. In fact, if I integrate this part and its Core State, I become much less likely to actually act destructively. If you have any concern about negative impulses spilling out into behavior, we encourage you to get assistance from someone trained in the process.

Reclaiming our most negative facets is perhaps the most touching and awe-inspiring work in this process. Working with negative impulses helps us reclaim vitality and energy. By allowing the part to *pretend* fully that it gets what it wants—revenge, destruction, or whatever it may be— that impulse gets to play through our system. It is this reclaiming of the impulse that we need, not doing the behavior. However, this process goes far beyond simple catharsis. We let the impulse play through our system so that we can ask, "What do you want through this that is beyond this?" Sometimes there are several layers of very "negative" impulses our parts need to go through and reclaim before they discover themselves in the positive.

As we experience these negative facets leading directly to Core States, the message that we begin to feel is this: *No matter what I find within myself, no matter how awful it seems, it has something tremendously wonderful within it.* As we experience this within ourselves we begin to know this about others also.

After doing the Core Transformation Process with my own inner parts literally hundreds of times, I have gradually come to a different way of experiencing myself. Over time I have found parts in myself that are like every part I have ever encountered in someone else. Discovering this has given me a much deeper sense of being like every other person, and a reverence and respect for each of us. Each of us is in some sense a complete mirror for everyone else. In other words, I am a mirror for you and every other person. I have facets within me that mirror all the qualities that are possible for a human being. You have this within you, also. When I recognize and include all my facets, and the Core States within them, I am whole. If I discover some of my parts and say, "That's not me, I have nothing in me like that," in some way I then sap my own strength.

This way of thinking about humanity is much like a hologram. One unusual characteristic of a holographic image is that when you cut one piece out of the whole image, that small portion of the image can still create the entire image, though less clearly. Each of us has within us the "whole picture" that is all of humanity.

—CHAPTER 27—

HOW PARTS ARE FORMED

Splitting Off and Separating Aspects of Ourselves

"You must never feel badly about making mistakes," explained Reason quietly, "as long as you take the trouble to learn from them. For you often learn more by being wrong for the right reasons than you do by being right for the wrong reasons."
—*Norton Juster,* The Phantom Toll Booth

As we welcome and reintegrate our inner parts, it can help to have an idea of how we created them to begin with. You have read some examples of how parts are formed in the personal examples and stories throughout this book. Here we share several more specific examples of how this can happen.

Not Getting What We Want and Need

Sara was feeling sad and depressed, and decided to work with it using the Core Transformation Process. She discovered that the outcomes her part wanted were as follows:

wanting to be taken care of —> rest and warmth —> peace and comfort —> bliss —> being

When we do the Core Transformation Process we usually don't learn how our inner part was formed. The process guides us in simply healing what is there. However, when Sara asked her part "How old are you?" she got the answer, "three months old," and was immersed in a memory. Sara experienced being an infant, lying in her crib, with her parents arguing loudly nearby and not taking care of her. After completing the process Sara immediately felt better. She was pleased that in addition to having her depression lift, wanting to be taken care of was no longer an issue in her relationship with her boyfriend.

When Ruth was about four years old, her mother left her at a summer camp for three months. Her mother explained that she would come back for Ruth and take her home again, but Ruth was too young to really understand what that meant. She assumed she would never see her mother again. Ruth felt devastated and alone. The part of Ruth that felt devastated became "frozen in time" at that younger age. This part concluded that Ruth would never get the security and love she wanted, and that in some way she must be unworthy. As an adult, Ruth noticed that she felt uncomfortable asking for what she wanted. It was as if some part of her thought she didn't deserve it.

When Joe was six months old his mother became seriously ill. She was completely bedridden for two months. With his father spending his days at work, and his mother ill, Joe was left to lie alone in his bed most of the day. He wanted the human warmth and holding he was accustomed to, but wasn't getting it. Soon Joe's soft cry turned into a desperate wail. It was as if a part of him concluded that he could no longer get what he wanted and needed. The part of him that wanted physical nurturing became separate, and continued to function as a six-month-old infant.

One way to think about inner parts is that when we were young we separated or "split off" a part of ourselves in a time of difficulty or crisis. Once a part has split off it tends to persist in the behaviors it chose as a young child. Since it is separate from us the part doesn't have access to other information and choices we learn as we grow up. In a sense this part remains frozen in time. This part of Joe may feel like "wailing" as an adult, even if he tries to suppress it. Ruth felt childlike feelings of abandonment as an adult. Sara experienced the need to be taken care of in a way that was out of proportion to her resourcefulness as an adult.

Judgment, Criticism and Unaccepted Feelings, Actions, or Thoughts

Ron complained of feeling held back. He didn't feel in control of his own life and often got angry thinking others were trying to control him. When Ron treated the feeling of being held back as a part, he went back to a time of being a small toddler, sitting in a baby chair attached to a table. He was happily banging on the table, making a lot of noise. Then his mother came along and firmly held his hands down. Out of this experience, Ron formed an unconscious belief that he wasn't in control of his life.

Karen grew up on a farm, and there was often a litter of kittens to play with in the barn. She loved and cared for them as if they were her own children. She remembers vividly the first time one of them got killed. Someone had run over it, and she was very sad and confused that someone would do this to a kitten. She picked up the kitten and carried its little body in to her mother. Karen's mother acted annoyed about being bothered, and abruptly took the kitten and threw it in the trash can. Karen was shocked that something she loved would be discarded in that way. She felt a part of her had been thrown in the trash along with the kitten. She began a pattern of throwing her own feelings away.

Frank's father panicked whenever Frank experienced pain and cried. As a little boy, when Frank stubbed his toe or scraped his knee and began to cry, his father would rush to him, insist that the injury was getting better already, and started making jokes. If Frank continued to cry, his father told him he was being a baby, and that big boys didn't cry. Soon he didn't even feel the pain himself. Frequently he got scrapes or cuts that he literally didn't feel, and wasn't sure how he had gotten them. As an adult Frank was unemotional and didn't think he got as much joy out of life as others.

When we are young, parts may split off when we have strong feelings that are not acknowledged. The part of Frank that felt pain and wanted to cry was not acceptable to his father, so he shoved this part of himself aside. When Karen's feelings of loss and sadness for her kitten were met with annoyance and disregard by her mother, a part of her began treating her feelings with the same kind of disregard. When Ron happily expressed his feelings as a toddler his mother "controlled" his feelings by holding his hands down, and a part of him made a decision that he was not in control of his own feelings.

Judgment and criticism from those around us frequently results in parts splitting off. If a child is excited and enthusiastic about going somewhere, and is angrily told to calm down and be quiet, the part of him that is enthusiastic may shut down. As he matures, he may be unable to express or even feel enthusiasm. We can all think of times in our childhood when we felt judged, criticized, or not accepted. It may have been our dirty diapers, our messy eating, our inability to learn something, our unwillingness to stop what we were doing, our unwillingness to hurry, not understanding instructions, exploring our own or someone else's genitals, being afraid of something, crying, yelling, hurting a sibling, or not wanting to share toys. When we judge any of these kinds of thoughts, feelings or actions as wrong, we are likely to try to separate them from ourselves. We unconsciously push them away and pretend they are not us. Judgment of some kind is often the basis for splitting off parts of ourselves.

Jon was a salesman, but his reluctance to make cold calls was a block to his career development. When he even thought about making a call he immediately felt afraid, cold and tight in his chest. Jon discovered this part's outcome chain was:

—> protection —> be safe —> freedom —> have fun and play —> be happy —> peace —> deeper peace —> death —> silence —> peace and relaxation —> eternity

This part was nine months old, and an experience emerged that Jon guessed had created this part. He described it this way: "I'm in my crib and I see Mom's face. It's angry. I'd better not make a sound. She has all the power and I don't. She's right and I'm wrong. Maybe she's mad at me for crying." After completing the Core Transformation Process with this part, Jon's part felt the Core State, eternity, even in this situation with his mother.

Even though this made a dramatic difference in Jon's feelings about making cold calls, he didn't feel finished. When he explored further he noticed inner images of a whole bunch of children—himself at younger ages. He sensed that these represented numerous times when adults had responded to him in ways that made him feel hurt, afraid or separate. After doing the Core Transformation Process simultaneously with all of these parts (See Chapter 30, "Generalizing the Core Transformation Process"), Jon was able to make cold calls without feeling afraid.

In addition to splitting off the parts that are "unacceptable," we often form parts that are like a judge. These parts take over the role of judge and continue judging us and others, even when our parents, or whoever "judged" us, are not around. For example, if we were told we shouldn't be afraid, we may have tried to get rid of the part that was afraid. In addition, another part became critical of having fear, and that part is likely to judge both ourselves and others who act fearful.

Parts That Protect Us from Trauma

When Alice was about nine years old her parents asked her and her brothers to get dressed to go to the train station. Even though her parents were quiet and stern, Alice didn't realize anything was unusual. When they arrived at the train station Alice's mother turned to the children and told them, "Say good-bye to your Dad, you are never going to see him again." Alice was stunned. A part of her didn't want to see what was going on. When she thought back to that memory, she literally saw the event up to the train station clearly in her mind's eye. When she thought of driving away from the train station, her memory was blurred. Soon after that experience she needed glasses. The part of Alice that made her vision blurry wanted to protect her from that very unpleasant experience.

Rose couldn't remember much of her childhood, and several years were completely blanked out. She had been severely abused as a child. Fairly early, an inner part was formed that tried to protect her from this trauma. This part noticed that if she thought of the horrible things that had happened to her, she felt bad all over again. At an unconscious level this part did the best it could to protect Rose by blanking out her memory.

When we experience something we don't know how to assimilate, like Rose and Alice did, usually a part of us tries to shut this experience out. This is the best way we know at the time to protect ourselves from something we don't have a way of integrating into our world.

Jean had a part that felt the need to be perfect. If she couldn't do something perfectly she didn't even want to try. This kept her from doing some of the things she wanted to do in her life. As Jean began working with this inner part it became clear how it was formed. When she was growing up her mother frequently yelled at her. While her Mom's yelling had more to do with her own moods and the challenges in her own life, the young Jean took it personally and felt very hurt. At about the age of nine, a part of Jean came to the conclusion that if she could just be perfect, her mother wouldn't yell at her any more. From that day forward this inner part felt compelled to do everything perfectly.

Accepting All Parts

What we know about how inner splits take place gives us indications about how we can raise our children to be more whole. Here is an example:

Anne comes home from school crying. Mom says, "Anne, what's the matter?"

"They made fun of me! They called me Annie Fanny!" Anne exclaims tearfully. Mom wants the best for her child and remembers when she was made fun of as a child. She doesn't want Anne to have this experience. Mom stiffens a bit and forces a smile and a cheerful voice. "Oh, Anne, it's really no big deal. Don't let a little thing like that bother you," Mom says briskly.

Anne's mother has good intentions, but does not realize that she is giving Anne the message that something is wrong with her experience. Anne will do better if her mother begins with the inner attitude that whatever experience her daughter is having right now is just fine in the largest sense. It is a sign of Anne's wholeness that she is able to feel bad when something unpleasant happens. Anne's mother is then more likely to begin with just empathizing: "Oh Anne, I'm sorry," says Mom, reaching out to comfort her. "You really didn't like being teased, did you?" Anne's mother is then giving her daughter the message that her feelings can be included. It is OK for Anne to have them. She does not need to shove aside that part of herself and pretend that it doesn't bother her.

Setting Limits Without Judgment

Raising our children to be whole does not mean just letting them do whatever they want so they won't be suppressed. Part of growing up healthy, happy and whole is learning to include the needs of others and the situation. Setting boundaries and limits is very important, and children who don't have adequate limits set tend to be unhappy and incapable of relating well to others.

When children are given clear limits without the message that any of their thoughts, feelings or actions are bad or wrong, they do not need to split off inner parts. It is when they are made wrong that children try to get rid of part of themselves. If the parent sets limits while accepting the child's feelings and behaviors as natural and OK, the child does not need to split off a part.

Here is a simplified example: Four-year-old Andy is playing at the neighbor's house and it is time to go home. "No!" Andy shouts, "I'm staying!" Andy's mother has a whole range of choices about how to stick with the plan that works for her (it's time to leave), while acknowledging Andy's response as true for him. She can say, "You're having lots of fun here, aren't you? We do need to go now, Andy. You can come back and play tomorrow," as she scoops him up in her arms. Or she can say, "You'd really like to play longer, wouldn't you? We need to go home now so I can make dinner for everyone. Do you want to say 'bye to your friend?"

Splitting Off and Welcoming Back

We split off many of our parts because we unconsciously concluded that in order to be loved, approved of, protected, smiled at, cuddled, fed, and played with, these parts that "misbehave" need to be "elsewhere." We put these parts outside of ourselves to distance ourselves from them, but the results of doing this are not what we intended. These parts are split off enough from us that they don't grow up and mature with us, so they keep running these "misbehaviors" even when we are adults. Sometimes these parts run these behaviors by projecting them onto other people. For example, if we have an angry part that we have pushed away, it may show up when we are adults as judgment of people who are angry.

Parts always form as our best effort to deal with difficulty. Regardless of how or why our parts have split off from us, we can welcome them back within us and transform them with the Core Transformation Process. You do not have to know how your own parts were formed to discover and work with them. Most people don't. All you need is a feeling, behavior, or thought pattern you want to change. Your beginning point for this work is always your experience now.

—CHAPTER 28—

WHO IS IN THE DRIVER'S SEAT?

Transforming Basic Personality Patterns That Don't Serve Us

Please call me by my true names, so I can wake up and so the door of my heart can be left open, the door of compassion.
—Thich Nhat Hanh

There is a tremendous difference between doing something because you *want* to and doing something because you *have* to. When we act because we have to we are in a state that can be called "driven." Obsessions, compulsions and addictions are what we call some of the more obvious driven states. However, there are many more. We are in a driven state when we are attached to our Intended Outcomes. These can include positive personal goals such as safety, success, wealth, fame, respect, power, security and wanting love from someone. Our attachment to these Intended Outcomes is usually out of our awareness; it is unconscious. In contrast to being driven, when we are moving toward our goals from a Core State, without attachment, then we have a sense of well-being and wholeness whether or not we achieve our goals.

Driven Toward Doing and Getting

A Driven State pushes us to *do* or *get* our Intended Outcomes. Carrie has a belief that if only she *does* enough, she will *be* OK. As a child she remembers only being praised for things she *did,* such as getting good grades, being nice to her relatives, or wearing attractive clothes. She doesn't remember feeling loved and accepted just for who she *was.* She even remembers being told, "You got really good grades, so you are a good girl."

As an adult Carrie finds herself driven to do, do, do, but nothing she does is ever enough. She always feels as if she needs to do more. She does so much that she has thrown her life out of balance, yet she has never gotten to the point of doing enough to feel OK about herself.

Carrie gives us one example of a very common pattern in American culture: most of our lives are organized around doing and getting. For example, we *do* things to *get* achievement, success, security, love, or approval. Goals like success and love are valuable; but when we are *driven* to get them, we lose our ability to choose our behaviors and feelings. We all need to eat. For many of us, eating is not a problem. However, if we are driven to damage our health by eating beyond what our body needs, overindulging in junk food, or avoiding food, that is a problem. When we act from Driven States, our actions have a needy or desperate quality, rather than a sense of wholeness or completion.

It is possible to be driven to do or get anything, but there are some general categories that are familiar to most of us in this culture:

1. Driven By Success
2. Driven By Love and Approval
3. Driven By Strong Emotions
4. Driven By Money and Things
5. Driven By Control and Power

As you read about each of these, we invite you to notice if any of them remind you of behaviors, feelings or responses in yourself. Most of us have some driven behaviors, feelings or responses within each category, whether they are extreme or subtle. Often we're not even aware of the ways we're driven to do or to get, because they fall within our day-to-day experience. We have no experience that things could be different. Just as the fish is the last to notice water, we take our most basic patterns for granted, as "the way things are." Reading about these Driven States can give you the opportunity to begin sensitizing yourself to your own behaviors, feelings or responses that have some quality of being driven.

Driven By Success

> Ted was a very successful businessman. Throughout his fifteen-year career in financial planning, one success led right to another. He was much admired by his colleagues, and everyone thought he really had it together. Because he worked sixteen hours a day, he rarely spent time with his wife and two children. Still, he made sure they benefited from the rewards of his success. He hadn't had a vacation in five years, but he told himself

that work was really more important to him anyway. Besides, the last time he took a vacation, he couldn't enjoy himself. He had a nagging, empty feeling inside, and he hardly knew what to do with himself. When Ted woke up each morning, he was immediately driven to go to work and make sure that this month would be more successful than last month. Nevertheless, his successes were beginning to mean less and less to him. Somehow, even when he did succeed in a big way, he still felt unfulfilled. When Ted was young, his parents had been very busy and didn't pay much attention to him, except when he won an award or brought home good grades.

Margaret was a very talented writer with very little money. Almost everyone who read her stories loved them, and suggested she get them published. But Margaret never contacted a publisher. One of her friends even borrowed some of her work and showed it to a local magazine editor who was very interested. But Margaret never managed to keep an appointment with the editor and he finally gave up on her. Whenever she began doing something to further her career Margaret had this peculiar, empty feeling inside, almost as if she disappeared. When a big opportunity came her way she got excited about it for awhile, but then the excitement turned into anxiety. She read self-help books that talked about "self-sabotage," and she recognized that she was getting in her own way. But she couldn't stop. Margaret's parents had been very successful, but in her opinion they were very shallow, cold people.

Ted and Margaret have something in common: they are both driven to have a certain level of success. Ted is driven toward success and Margaret is driven away from success. In some way they identify with their level of achievement. Ted tries to have a sense of self through high achievement; as soon as he slows down, he is aware of lacking a sense of self. In contrast, Margaret, a warm and sincere person, loses her sense of self when she begins to succeed because she equates success with being cold and shallow. Her perception of "success" clashes with her sense of who she is. Both are attached to, and driven by, this thing called success.

Driven By Love and Approval

Sarah is one of the nicest people you could meet. She would do anything for a friend: help in a crisis, organize a surprise party, pick up the dry cleaning on her way over for a visit, or bring little gifts of food. This weekend, while she's baby-sitting for her sister and one of her neighbors she will try to sneak in a few minutes at nap time to work on a quilt for her boss's wife. Then she will have to pack the kids in the car to go check up on her ex-husband's house while he is out of town. Once the kids are all back with their parents she will spend the rest of her evening jogging and reading books about sports. She hates jogging and sports, but she recently read in a magazine article that men like women who are fit and share their interests.

Sarah counts her value, in part, by how many people love her. She feels an emotional void when she is in a new place where she knows no one. She quickly befriends those around her so that she can feel secure. Sarah has been working so hard to get everyone else's approval that she doesn't even know what she wants for herself! Although most people like Sarah, she is still somehow unfulfilled, and continues to worry that people might not like her. She is devastated whenever someone criticizes her. Her life is far from easy, because it's so difficult to please everyone, especially nowadays, when some of her friends disapprove of the fact that she doesn't ever do things just for herself!

Gail has two good friends, but other than that, she keeps to herself. When she was in high school she usually went to the library to read at lunch time because she was terrified of being with her classmates. Now she is in her thirties, and still is afraid to go into a restaurant alone.

Gail works as a lab technician. She stays very busy and doesn't really have time to interact with her co-workers. She likes and admires Gary, one of her co-workers, a great deal, but she doesn't think she will ever muster up the courage to talk to him. She can't bear the idea that he might not like her.

Vic is sometimes driven to do things that others *dis*approve of. He will be loud in a group of people that are being quiet, break minor rules such as smoking in a "no smoking" area, or go into a restaurant with no shirt on. This is an example of being driven by love and approval, because he does not have a sense of well-being that is independent of the love and approval of other people.

Sarah is driven to please others. It's as if her whole sense of well-being is dependent on other people's love and approval. Moreover, she's never quite satisfied that people really do approve of her, and she never really gets to experience a full sense of well-being. Many people who spend their lives driven to please others at the expense of their own needs end up bitter and resentful, because they've done so much for others and yet they still feel unfulfilled.

Although Gail's behavior is very different from Sarah's, what is driving it is, paradoxically, quite similar. She also wants the approval of others, but her fear of not getting that approval is so strong that, in avoiding rejection, she rejects people altogether. Avoiding people protects her from getting hurt, but she still feels driven because she is avoiding just the things she most wants: the love and approval of others.

Vic is driven to get disapproval from others by doing things he knows will get people's attention in a negative way.

Most of us want to get responses like acceptance, love, respect, understanding, admiration, or appreciation from others. Sometimes we're aware of these goals and intentionally seek this from others in our lives. At other times we act more unconsciously, out of a feeling that we'll never be satisfied unless we can get all those positive qualities from others.

We all seek love and approval in different ways. I might dress a certain way, hoping my husband will find me attractive. Or I might buy many presents for my family and friends, hoping they'll love me in return. I could do everything my children ask for, hoping they'll like me, or I could "take charge" at work, thinking this will earn me respect.

Driven By Strong Emotions

Whatever is happening, Helena has strong feelings about it. When things are going well for her she has a vivid imagination and is able to express herself creatively and artistically. However, when things are not going so well, which is most of the time, she gets lost in her own emotions and fantasies. For Helena life is full of pain, loss, anger and sadness. It is always something. One day she was distraught because the store did not accept a pair of torn blue jeans for a refund. She took that as a personal insult—they must not have trusted her. Everyone who came within earshot of Helena that day found out how concerned and distraught she was. The next day she was caught up in sadness over a picture of starving children on TV. She cried and cried. It was as if the whole world was falling apart. She couldn't focus on anything else that whole day. The next day, Helena was consumed with envy about people who seemed to have such an easy life compared to hers. She suddenly hated everyone in her apartment building who had a good credit rating.

Although having such strong emotions makes her life like a roller-coaster, Helena thrives on her feelings. Feeling something strongly lets her know she is alive! Even though her emotions are often excruciatingly painful, for her they are better than the nothingness and emptiness that is there when her emotions have subsided, so she always finds something else to feel strongly about.

Barry's mother died when he was four years old. On that day his father told him that he was a man and needed to be strong. To Barry's father "being strong" meant never crying or showing emotions. Ever since then Barry has kept a stiff upper lip. No matter what is going on in his life he pushes his emotions aside. In fact he has not shed a single tear since he was four. Whenever he's with someone who expresses emotions, Barry begins to get uncomfortable.

From time to time we all have unpleasant emotions. They are part of what makes us human, and every emotion has a positive value. However, at times we get stuck in emotional patterns in a way that does not serve us. At those times we are driven to experience that emotion, often over and over again, and we get caught up in it even though we know it isn't working for us. Sometimes it seems as if we manage to organize our lives to create the same emotional response in ourselves again and again.

Helena is an extreme example of someone who is driven by strong emotions. Some of us get caught up in strong emotions in more subtle ways, and others, like Barry, are driven to *not* have strong emotions. Although few of us push away emotions as much as Barry, most of us can remember times when we have pushed an emotion aside, perhaps blinking back tears while we tried to keep our thoughts on a rational level. In our culture boys are taught that emotions are unacceptable more often than girls are. As a result, there are many more men who are driven away from emotions.

Driven By Money and Things

The Buddha said that desire is the source of all suffering.
It is also the source of all shopping. Advertising doesn't
make you buy stuff. Other people's expectations don't
make you buy stuff. Television doesn't make you buy stuff.
Your thoughts *make you buy stuff. Watch those suckers.*
— Your Money or Your Life,
by Joe Dominguez and Vicki Robin

Greta is addicted to things. Her attraction to various material things goes far beyond a deep appreciation for quality and beauty. No matter how much she gets, she always craves more. Although her husband made an upper middle class income, she always complained that he didn't make enough. She felt very envious of her sister, who had so much more than she had.

Three years ago Greta's husband divorced her. In dividing up their property both of them gave up things they enjoyed; for Greta, each thing that she gave up felt like a piece of herself being cut out of her. So, even though she needed to save her assets, she was compelled to buy expensive furniture, crystal and silver to replace the items her husband had gotten. Every few days she had an empty feeling inside, and to help herself feel better, she bought something else. This would help her feel better for a little while, but it didn't last. Finally, she was broke, and she used credit cards to buy things to get that temporary "high."

Greta met with a financial planner to learn how to save money and invest for her retirement. However, driving home from her appointment with the financial planner, she felt discouraged about all the sacrifices she would have to make in order to put her finances in order. In order to cheer herself up, she decided to stop at a fur sale. That was the end of financial planning for Greta.

Felicia had been raised by her parents' servants, and was sent away to boarding schools and summer camps at a young age. As a result of this experience she decided that money and things were bad, so she embraced a principle of austerity. She lived with as few things and as little money as she could. She was tremendously angry at people who had money and things, and tended to judge them as selfish and shallow. Felicia lives with a man named Gary, who avoids accumulating money and things because he believes they drag him down with too much responsibility.

Our culture has a very strong emphasis on material things. Many people organize much of their lives around "keeping up with the Joneses" in terms of money and possessions. The *Peanuts* comic strip character Linus, attached to his security blanket, is a symbol of being driven by things. Although we may not be as extreme as Greta or Linus, most of us, to some degree, have an attachment to buying or having things. While it can be fun to buy and have things, a recent study indicates that things do little, if anything, to keep us happy in the long run. We in this country spend significantly more money on things now than we did some years ago, but the percentage of people who describe themselves as "moderately happy" is the same as it was then.

Instead of being driven to spend money on things, some people are driven to stockpile money without having any use for it. Relatively fewer people, like Felicia and Gary, are driven to avoid things or avoid money.

When we are coming from a Core State rather than a Driven State, our goal is not to give away all of our belongings, nor is it to own as much as we possibly can. We have a sense of well-being that is not dependent on buying and having things. Our enjoyment of things becomes an added benefit in our lives, rather than something we are driven by.

Driven By Control and Power

> Joel is manager of a marketing division for a large company. He likes many things about his position because most of the time he is his own boss—and the boss of the other people as well. When Joel says "jump," people jump. He likes that. Joel made a rule in his division that anyone who comes in late, even one minute, is fined $10. However, about once a week, Joel comes in late himself—just to show he is in charge.
>
> Several times a year Joel takes a seminar or reads books to improve his skills as a manager. He especially likes learning techniques he can use to get people to do what he wants. Last week Ned, one of Joel's subordinates, walked into Joel's office without an appointment with some ideas to market their company's product more effectively. While Joel was pleased with Ned's ideas he was annoyed by Ned's attitude. Ned seemed to lack proper respect for Joel's authority.
>
> Joel has always had trouble in the romance area of his life. He had been married for a short time to a very attractive, interesting woman. Trouble started almost immediately. He came home one day and noticed that she had moved some of the furniture around. Joel was annoyed. He very quickly realized that he had strong preferences for how things should be, and he didn't want to be with someone who challenged that. In addition, she sometimes made remarks about things he could do differently. This was intolerable to Joel.
>
> Joel never likes visiting his parents because it always makes him feel like a kid again. He remembers when he was a boy and his father made all of his decisions for him. His father punished him severely for doing things he didn't want Joel to do. If there is one thing Joel hates, it's when someone makes him do something.

> Doug, a social worker, is driven to *avoid* being in charge. When he had an idea about how things could be run more smoothly in his agency, he told one of his co-workers, so his co-

worker would take charge of it. When he works with clients he cares about them and wants to see them doing better, but he is uncomfortable with the idea of having an impact on their lives, so he just hopes they will get better on their own.

Most of us have times when we are annoyed by people and things we cannot control: traffic on the freeway, world politics, or the people around us, for example. Many of the arguments married couples have are about who's in control: who's in the driver's seat, who has the TV remote, who decides how money is spent. And then there are some people, like Joel, who have built their lives around having power and control. Being driven to *avoid* being in charge and having an impact, like Doug, is another way of being driven by control and power.

If we tend to judge people who seek power and control as bad people, this driver can be more difficult to observe in ourselves. If we find ourselves complaining or upset about *other* people seeking control or power, there is probably a part of *us* that wants control or power.

Freedom from Being Driven: A Secure Sense of Self and Well-Being

When we are coming from a Core State our goal is to take responsibility for the things that we have a choice about, and to be at peace with those things that are out of our domain of responsibility. Our inner peace and well-being is independent of power and control.

Darren is studying to become a schoolteacher. His life goals are very important to him, but he has a sense of well-being already, even before he has reached his goals. Darren's parents, both very successful lawyers, do not approve of Darren's chosen field because it is low-paying and lacks prestige. They are afraid their son will be a "nobody." However, Darren is unconcerned about that. He knows that following his own mission is more important to him than money or prestige. He is excited about entering a career where he will have the opportunity to make a positive difference in the lives of his classroom of children.

Although Darren works very intensely he also finds it easy to take time off for himself. He enjoys being with people and he also enjoys being alone. He has many friends who are attracted by his warm, accepting nature.

Darren turned a paper in to a professor and was given a poor grade. Initially he was disappointed, but then his disappointment quickly turned into curiosity about what his professor's perceptions were. He asked his professor for more detailed feedback, and found that he agreed with most of his professor's ideas. A few of the professor's suggestions about writing style did not fit with Darren's taste, but he was happy to utilize this input to give his professor more of what he wanted. His grade was much higher on his next assignment.

Darren recently began student teaching. He was a little unsure of how to proceed with the children, so he asked his supervising teacher to give him plenty of feedback and suggestions. One day, one of the students got mad at Darren and yelled, "I hate you! I want our real teacher back!" Darren had been noticing that the student looked frustrated, as if he was struggling to understand the lesson. Rather than getting defensive or assuming the child had bad motives, Darren listened to him and asked him questions so he could understand what the child wanted. The boy finally burst into tears and confided in him that something was bothering him at home and he had trouble thinking about school.

Darren's friend Bill disapproved of Darren's girlfriend, Stacy. Stacy did not have the glamorous movie star appearance Bill thought was important. "You can do better than Stacy," Bill said. Darren listened to what his friend had to say and realized that while Stacy wouldn't be right for Bill, he didn't share Bill's desire for a "movie star." He thanked Bill for his advice, and told him the qualities he found attractive in Stacy.

Melanie recently took her car into the shop for a repair. When she got her car back she noticed that the old problem was still there. While she was annoyed that the problem wasn't already handled and she needed to spend more time on it, she did not feel overwhelmed or outraged by it. She quickly went into a problem-solving mode. When she went back to the shop to gather information, rather than assuming that the mechanic was trying to take advantage of her, she was open to the possibility that the mechanic had made an honest mistake.

One evening Melanie's neighbors came over for dinner. Melanie's young children, Jason and Rebecca, began grabbing food off each other's plates, making each other unhappy. Melanie reminded them kindly and firmly that they were to touch the food on their *own* plates. She asked them if they would do that so they could stay sitting next to each other, or if they wanted her to sit between them this time. She did not feel embarrassed or become angry that they had misbehaved in front of the neighbor. She found a way to have a nice environment at the dinner table without needing to blame her children for misbehaving.

> When Melanie's husband spilled black ink all over her Oriental rug she felt angry and unhappy. She told her husband John how she felt, and soon moved into a state of acceptance. She gave the rug to the Salvation Army, asked her husband to get a new rug for her, and went on with her life.

Darren and Melanie have a basic sense of well-being and wholeness that is already there when they are faced with limitations and personal challenges. They have a secure sense of self and well-being and the inner freedom to make choices that work for them.

When we are in a Driven State, just telling ourselves to "have a secure sense of self and all-encompassing well-being" isn't likely to work. Just knowing intellectually that we are in a Driven State is not generally enough to facilitate change, because a part of us is still striving toward our Core States. If we don't have a way to get to a Core State we're likely to continue trying to get there using the methods we've always used—by going through our Intended Outcomes—even though that doesn't work.

Darren and Melanie's behavior doesn't arise out of *trying* to be perfect or *trying* to act mature. We all know the difference between trying to act loving—going through the motions—and having loving, kind behavior bubble up from inside of us because we are in a loving state. Darren naturally and automatically makes choices that are in alignment with his deepest values because he is coming from a Core State of being that isn't dependent on anything outside of himself. Melanie has the ability to be in a deeply calm and centered place when things around her are chaotic or upsetting because she has automatic access to those Core States inside herself. When she does feel angry or upset, having her Core States already present makes it natural for her to express her feelings without judging either herself or the other person and move on.

What If I Can't Tell What Is Driving Me?

Some things we're driven to do or have or be may not fit easily in the five general categories of drivers, or may seem to fit into several. For example, in our culture, it is very common to be driven to have the "right" appearance. Billions of dollars are spent each year on weight loss aids, cosmetics, plastic surgery, fashion clothing, and anti-aging products. Which driver generates all that effort? The answer is different for different people. Some people may be driven about their appearance in order to get love and approval from others. Others may be driven to maintain a certain image to be successful, and have a sense of achievement. For others, it's about power—some business people talk about wearing a "power suit." Some people "have to" dress a certain way to cheer themselves up. For others, having a closet full of expensive clothing means that they're rich.

Tanya was driven to compete with everyone around her, even strangers, to the point where it became destructive in her life. She told us:

> Competition was my life story. When I was young I competed with my brothers and sisters for my parents' attention. As an adult it got worse. I used to work for an ad agency, supposedly in a team with another person, but there was a lot of competition between us for salary and promotions, and it drove me crazy. I finally had to quit and find a job where I wasn't competing with anyone. I was being driven by an inner voice that was harsh and internally abusive. Even when I rode my bike, if someone passed me my inner voice said, "You're not good enough, how can you let this person pass you, you're a nobody."
>
> I did the Core Transformation Process with that voice and discovered that part wanted to be noticed, loved, and praised. More than that, it wanted love from me. Its Core State was being one with my spirit.
>
> Now I work with two other women and we have the same boss. One of the other women is the boss's favorite. In the past, I would have been very competitive and jealous, and tried to "win over" the boss, but now I don't have any desire to meddle with the situation. It hasn't been an issue.
>
> When I ride my bike and someone passes me, that harsh, critical voice is no longer there. It's like, "So what?"

Tanya was being driven to compete by a part of her that wanted attention, love and praise. Other "driven" behaviors may be more difficult to categorize, such as being driven to get revenge, being driven to drink or smoke, or being driven to talk. Fortunately, for this process it doesn't matter if we've correctly analyzed our behavior. The important thing is to notice the things we're driven to do or to have, so we can transform them.

—CHAPTER 29—

TRANSFORMING ILLNESS

Taking Advantage of Challenges

It often takes a crisis to break through our usual models of the world. A crisis is a gift, an opportunity, and perhaps a manifestation that life loves us, by beckoning us to go beyond the dance we presently perform.
—Leslie Lebeau

Serious illness can be one of the biggest crises we encounter in life. It is a threat to our vitality and sometimes to our physical existence. While none of us would consciously choose illness, this kind of crisis may be much more than it initially appears to be. The above quote is the conclusion that personal friend and author Leslie Lebeau came to after experiencing several major crises in her own life. Our illness may be an indication that "life loves us" enough to give us a major nudge. A health crisis, or any major crisis, may be the opportunity we need to go beyond the limits we've placed on ourselves. A crisis often makes it impossible to continue our old life or old routine as we've known it. This gives us the chance to allow a new life to emerge from a deeper level of inner health and well-being.

Many of us wait for a major life crisis to force us to experience transformative personal growth. Sometimes in ordinary life nothing challenges us to change at our deeper levels, at our core. We just develop a better facade, or a better act. It is as if we get better make-up, or a better costume, so that we look better on the outside. We may become very successful, but not necessarily very satisfied and fulfilled inside.

If this way of thinking—that a crisis is the way the universe gets our attention—has truth in it, then we may need some help deciphering the message. Not everyone automatically and naturally thrives on crisis. Two people who survived a plane crash were both impacted dramatically, but they responded very differently. One person realized that every moment was precious, lost weight and got "on track" with his life. The other decided he was a victim of circumstance in a dangerous world, became depressed and refused to leave his house.

The Core Transformation Process gives us a simple way to use an illness (or other crisis) as an opportunity to go beyond who we have been and discover the inner wholeness that can become the basis for our lives. It gives us a way to go deeper. It is tempting to move through life just getting better at the roles we play. We may successfully arrange our lives so that we don't need to face certain aspects of ourselves. We may avoid situations that would require us to be more—to grow and learn. Rather than helping us look better from the outside, the Core Transformation Process gives us a gentle yet powerful way to be different from the inside—to change at our core. This core change feels like returning home within ourselves, like a deep honoring within that we've always wanted without knowing we wanted it.

In this chapter we will be talking specifically about working with illness, but these principles can be applied to any life crisis.

Facets of An Illness

Our bodies have very sophisticated ways of keeping us healthy. Every day our immune system protects us from millions of viruses and bacteria. Many medical researchers now believe that our bodies produce cancer cells daily, and our immune systems "harvest" these cells before they develop into illness.

Despite our amazing natural abilities to stay healthy, sometimes we don't. Why? Research has linked many different factors to illness. These include our genetic background, our exposure to toxins, bacteria and viruses, our nutrition, whether we exercise, our connection to a social network of friends and family, and our mental and emotional well-being. It is rare that any one of these factors is 100 percent responsible for creating or preventing an illness. Usually when a major illness occurs, at least two or more of these factors have worked together to create it. We know that smoking cigarettes increases the chance of getting lung cancer, but not everyone who smokes gets lung cancer. We know that exercise can greatly reduce your chance of having heart disease, but some very fit athletes have heart disease.

Research has shown clear links between mental and emotional well-being and health. People are more likely to get cancer after the death of a loved one than at other times. We are more likely to get sick after the stress of any major life change—moving, changing jobs, or divorce, for example. Depending on how we respond to them mentally and emotionally, these stressful situations can affect our health. Even positive changes like marriage or a promotion can create stress because even positive changes require adjustments.

What does this mean? Let's say a woman has cancer. It may be that her family has a genetic predisposition to this type of cancer—her mother and one of her sisters had it. Perhaps her eating habits contributed to her disease—much of her life she ate a lot of fatty fried foods and very few vegetables. Perhaps she had little social support—she lived alone, had few friends and no pets. Finally, she experienced several life stresses before the onset of her illness. She lost her job of 20 years, and felt that the only thing she could count on in life was now gone.

Dr. Bernie Siegel has written about "exceptional patients" with "incurable" illnesses who get well even though their doctors have no effective medical treatment for them. This woman will probably increase her chances of being one of these exceptional patients if she lays the foundation for health in each of the areas that can contribute. This includes nutrition, exercise, rest, and creating a healthy, non-toxic environment, in addition to developing greater emotional and mental well-being. Because the Core Transformation Process has a major impact on our mental and emotional well-being it can positively impact our health to whatever extent these factors play a role in our illness.

What if My Illness is Caused by Physical Factors?

Some illnesses have very strong genetic or physical factors. However, even when an illness is influenced genetically or by exposure to a disease or toxin, this usually sets up only a *predisposition* for illness, not a certainty. This explains why some people recover from an illness that "runs in the family," or never get it in the first place, or why some people exposed to diseases or toxins are fine and others become ill.

We do not want to underestimate the importance of genetic, constitutional, and environmental factors in health and disease. Some people have a stronger physical constitution and are more physically able to remain healthy when those around them get ill. However, it is also important not to underestimate the power of our choices in the area of mental and emotional well-being. We are just beginning to learn how great our potential is to create a mental and emotional environment for healing.

The Core Transformation Process is not a substitute for seeking medical advice and treatment. If you have a major illness you will probably want to utilize all the medical resources available to you. We encourage you to seek medical advice and expertise to make sure you know what your choices are for physical levels of healing. The role of the mind and emotions in physical healing is well documented, and many doctors will support you in using all the avenues available to you for your healing. The Core Transformation Process can be a powerful tool for emotional healing, which can contribute considerably to healing physically.

Self-Healing vs. Self-Blame

The question often arises, "If I can cure myself with a psychological process, does that mean I am to blame for my illness? Does it mean that I got sick because I was somehow more messed up than other people who are healthy?"

Definitely not. If you have an illness, it may mean that you experienced more life challenges than another person. It may mean that your body had a different level of physical resilience. Or, it may mean that you are ready to seek a new level of well-being and wholeness for yourself. It may mean the universe is giving you a call to grow beyond where you are now, and you are ready to receive this call.

If you realize that you are blaming yourself, you'll learn more about working with parts that blame later in this chapter.

The Messages In An Illness

One of the most frequent messages in an illness is that we need to take better care of ourselves. Another is that we need to recognize and acknowledge parts of ourselves we have been excluding or shoving away. Another message is, "You are deeply OK as you are. You can slow down your fast-paced tempo, because you are already OK." Sometimes the message is, "You have gotten off of your path. It is time for you to become more true to yourself, and I—the illness—will stay here as a reminder until you do."

One way of thinking about illness is that it is the length our inner parts are willing to go on our behalf to get our attention. Creating an illness is no easy job for them, yet these inner parts are willing to go that far in their best efforts to get an important message across to us. To discover the messages in our own illness we can use the Core Transformation Process with each part involved.

Guidelines for Finding Parts

It is easiest to work with illness if we are receptive to the possibility that healing may happen right away, after working with only one part. At the same time we want to be completely ready and open to receive many parts. Sometimes working with one "set" or "cluster" of parts in one session is all that is needed before healing begins. When we do the Core Transformation Process with life-threatening or chronic illness there are usually multiple parts to work with. Even when healing begins right away, we will lay the foundation for continued health by using the Core Transformation Process over time. The following guidelines for finding parts that can support physical healing through Core Transformation are meant to be used over time, not all at once. Discover how many parts you are most comfortable working with in one sitting. Many people find that one or two at a time works well for ongoing work.

A Part That Created Illness

The most important parts for supporting healing are any that actively created the illness. When these parts are transformed they will support healing instead of illness. Illness often appears after a crisis or a particularly stressful time, when some part decided the illness was the best way it could think of to achieve a goal. Cynthia, who had migraine headaches, recalled a moment in her life when she was moving forward in her career. She was a workaholic and always felt she wasn't working quite hard enough. She felt stressed by the level of work always there to do, and never felt like she had done enough. Cynthia reached that critical moment when she felt there was no way out. She didn't want to continue the high-pressure course, but felt she had no alternative. Soon after that she began experiencing symptoms of migraines. These migraines were unpleasant, but kept her from working so hard and forced her to rest her body.

Physical illness can come as a wake-up call from parts of ourselves that we have set aside in some way. Bert was unhappy in his marriage. He considered divorce a failure, so it wasn't something he was willing to consider. At a very deep level he wasn't sure if any other woman would really want him. He felt he could never express his wants or feelings to his wife and be heard. Bert found himself always trying to appease his wife, who had strong ideas and opinions about things. Things came to a crisis point when he was offered a promotion at work. The promotion would have placed him in a management position and brought in more money, but Bert felt bad whenever he thought of moving into that role. He preferred his current job, computer programming. His wife insisted he take the promotion. Bert put his own feelings aside to do what he thought was really the right thing for his family. He took the promotion, and within a year was diagnosed as having a tumor. Bert set aside important parts of himself and in doing so laid the groundwork for physical illness. If we become physically ill it is likely that we, like Bert, have felt the need to stifle some part of ourselves.

We often are not aware of what crisis may be related to our illness. This is fine. In fact, if you think you know exactly what caused the disease, it is best to assume you may be wrong when you turn inside to work with your inner parts. Just ask the question, "Will the part of me that is responsible for my disease please emerge now." Be ready to receive any answer, and then notice what feelings, inner voices or images naturally emerge.

The Part That Maintains Illness

Sometimes one part of us creates a disease and another part or parts maintain it. For example, someone may become ill in response to an inner conflict. Then other parts may like the nurturing and care that others offer us when we are sick. These parts may want to continue the illness as a way to get nurturing and care from others. When we are working with health issues we can be ready to notice and receive these parts of ourselves that may help to maintain illness and prevent us from becoming healthy.

Off-Balance Parts

If I have an illness or disease and want to heal, it will be easier for my body to do that if all of my energy is available to support that process. It will serve me to notice all the other areas of my life that I can "clean up." For example, anything that results in my feeling stressed is something I can work with. If something enrages me, or makes me feel guilty or sad or resentful, these are parts I can work with and bring back into balance. Even if these areas of my life are not directly related to my illness, it is important to work with them because if I fly into rages easily, or feel intensely guilty or depressed, this drains energy that could be available for my healing. The more I am whole and balanced in all areas of my life, the more of my energy will be available for healing.

Acknowledging All Our Feelings

It is especially important to notice parts that want to stifle our feelings. If we have a strong reluctance to experience certain emotions, this could point to a useful inner part to work with. Ignoring emotions usually makes them more intense. The more we try to separate our feelings from ourselves, the more distorted they become. If I am annoyed by something one of my children or my husband does I can choose to acknowledge the annoyance to myself and tell them. This choice doesn't mean they did something wrong; it just means I don't like it. Another choice I have is to think, "Oh, it is a little thing and it shouldn't bother me, so I'll just forget it." If I think I shouldn't be bothered, I ignore signals coming from myself. The annoyed part tends to become more annoyed and may move into anger. I will hang on to the incident and remember it later. A little deal will become a big deal to some part of me.

The Core Transformation Process is not a magic wand that makes emotions go away. Feeling emotions such as anger is often an important part of healing. Illness often arises when we haven't accepted a part of ourselves:

"I *shouldn't* be angry."

"I *should* always be happy."

"I *shouldn't* feel jealous."

A "should" is a red flag for a part that needs attention and acceptance. The Core Transformation Process gives us a way to deeply accept and receive the parts with these feelings in a way that also transforms them. Some emotions will fade away. These are the "secondary emotions" such as envy, jealousy, revenge, guilt, and blind rage. As these fade away we can more cleanly and clearly express our primary emotions—anger, sadness, hurt, love, gratitude and joy.

Parts Concerned With Success and Failure

Sometimes after working with illness we feel we have failed if we are not healthy right away. This is an opportunity to work with a new part, the part of us that "feels like a failure." This part most likely manifests itself in other parts of our lives as well, so the illness is the current opportunity to notice this part, welcome and receive it, and reclaim the energy it contains.

Parts That Are Attached To Being Well

Parts that are attached to being well are often ignored. When someone has a life-threatening illness, there is often a quality of being attached to health in a way that does not serve becoming healthy. If the part *needs* to be healthy in order to feel OK, it may feel unworthy, or that something is deeply wrong as long as illness is present. This is an important part to work with, and one that can richly contribute to our well-being. To find this part, notice any feelings of intensely wanting to be well, or needing to be well. After you've worked with this part you will still want to be well. What will change is that at a deeper level you will experience access to deep states of OKness and well-being, and you will know you have access to these states whether or not your physical healing happens right away.

As I have worked with physical illness and healing in myself and others I have changed my goal from being physically well, to wholeness, inner peace, and well-being. These goals are always achievable, no matter what my physical condition, and this makes them better goals to seek. When we are emotionally and spiritually whole, when we have tapped into our own Core States and brought these through into practical daily living, we have created an environment in which the miracle of healing can happen more readily.

In working with others I have found parts of me that were "attached" to my client becoming healthy—these parts felt as if I would have failed if my client did not get well. When I find myself *needing* my clients to become well, I work with it in myself. This allows me to be there for them, ready to help them accept any result on the physical level. It is very important for us to be able to accept ourselves'—and our clients—fully, particularly in those moments when we or they are not well.

Parts That Want To Die

Parts that want to die often emerge, and people are sometimes frightened to discover this. There is no need to be afraid of them. We just ask, "And if you get that Intended Outcome, so you die, what do you want through dying, that is even more important?" The answer is usually something like "peace." Parts that want to die usually feel exhausted and helpless in the face of continuing turmoil. They desperately want to experience a deeply calm state right now, and think they need to die first to have that.

Again, they give us access to more of these deeply transforming states that are already there within us, waiting to be tapped.

Parts That Want To Blame

Parts that are concerned with blame— "I'm to blame for my illness," or, "I'm not to blame for my illness"—are very common. If we are ill, we may feel that we are somehow at fault. It is very easy to think, "I must have done something wrong," or "I should have done it differently." Blaming ourselves gets in the way of noticing the message within the illness and responding to it. The message an illness has to offer is actually quite wonderful. As we do the Core Transformation Process, we move toward appreciation for that message, and we realize that it is a blessing, not something to blame ourselves for.

Feeling a need to defend ourselves against blame is another position these parts can take. If we notice that we react defensively inside and tell ourselves and others, "I'm not responsible for this—there's nothing psychological about it," we can receive benefit from working with this part. Even if there is no psychological element to the illness, we can free up considerable energy by resolving our defensiveness. A woman spoke up at a seminar I offered and said angrily, "I think the physical components of illness are often ignored, and people are blamed for their illness. I have asthma, and that is a *physical* thing." She felt angry, and this may have been in response to well-meaning friends and relatives who did blame her for her illness.

If we find ourselves in the position of this woman, feeling angry and defensive about being blamed, we can gain most by working with this part of ourselves. This part that feels angry and defensive needs some honoring and attention from us. We can create the greatest opportunity for healing if we ignore whether or not our illness is *really* caused by physical or psychological factors. We don't *really* know. What we do know is that blaming ourselves or feeling the need to defend ourselves from blame is no fun and takes up a lot of energy we could be using to heal ourselves.

Parts That Doubt

You do not need to believe the Core Transformation Process will positively impact your health in order to have results. Several examples appear in this book of people who were not even working with health concerns, yet experienced a positive shift in their health. However, if you feel that doubt gets in the way of doing the process fully, work with the part of you that doubts. This is probably a younger part that can be reclaimed.

USEFUL QUESTIONS TO ASK

Here is a summary of questions that can guide you to inner parts that can help you heal.

√ What part created my illness?

√ What do I like about being ill?

√ When do I feel unbalanced?

√ Is there any part of me I am leaving out?

√ Is anything unacceptable to me?

√ Have I pushed aside any inner messages or feelings?

√ What are my "shoulds"?

√ Am I attached to succeeding?

√ Do I feel like blaming myself or someone else? Do I feel defensive about being "at fault?"

√ What part of me is most important to work with next to support my healing?

We have given you many ideas here. Please take one at a time. Begin with the aspects of yourself that are more obvious to you right now. Some people experience recovery after the first inner process, others after much inner work. Some do not recover from their illness, but find a new and profound sense of peace and vitality that enriches their lives. Many people recover from their illness long before they get through this list. After recovery, if you notice that you feel supported by continuing to discover parts within and working with them, please do. Continuing on this path will assist you in maintaining and increasing your inner resilience.

Chapter 26, "Finding More Parts to Transform," will also assist you in using the Core Transformation Process in an ongoing way. In Chapter 31, "How People Have Used Core Transformation," you will find several examples of people who worked with health concerns with the Core Transformation Process. We have received many other positive reports of the results of doing the Core Transformation Process with health issues, and expect that systematic research will be undertaken at some point.

—CHAPTER 30—

GENERALIZING THE CORE TRANSFORMATION PROCESS

The Whole Is Greater Than the Sum of Its Parts

Each separate being in the universe
returns to the common source.
Returning to the source is serenity.
—Lao-Tzu

Most of us have parts of ourselves that we stepped out of years ago. Sometimes these are parts that we did not want, or learned to be ashamed of. At other times these are parts that got hurt and left in order to protect themselves. Although sometimes temporarily stepping out of parts is a good way to get through a difficult situation, in the long run we all have an innate longing for wholeness.

One day, after I (Tamara) had worked with a woman named Rosa, doing the Core Transformation Process with two parts that were involved in a particular issue, an interesting thing happened. She saw in front of her a whole crowd of parts of herself. They told her they wanted to do the Core Transformation Process also!

Rather than doing the Core Transformation Process with them one at a time, which would have taken many hours, I invited them to go through the Core Transformation Process all at the same time. Because Rosa had already experienced Core Transformation, her unconscious mind already knew how to do the process. This made it possible to repeat it in a generalized, unconscious way with all these parts at once. After doing this she reported a major shift toward wholeness.

Since that time I have led other individuals and groups through this process in this way. When we are using the Core Transformation Process in this format we do not consciously identify specific issues that we are working on, so the results are typically experienced as a general shift toward wholeness or a greater sense of inner congruence. This generalization process can also be done every day as a meditation. We recommend doing the Core Transformation Process several times with a single part before attempting to generalize it.

The Generalized Core Transformation Process complements but does *not* replace the standard Core Transformation Process. Even when you do the Generalized Core Transformation Process regularly, there will be times when some part needs individual attention. We usually work with specific goals one part at a time, with the standard format. In addition, doing the Core Transformation Process one part at a time gives your unconscious mind more specific experiences with the process, which can then enhance your results with the generalized format.

DOING IT!

These are the steps for using the Core Transformation Process for yourself in a generalized way. For this to work well you will need to have already done the Core Transformation Process with two to five parts, to give yourself the conscious and unconscious grounding in how the process works.

GETTING READY

1. Find a comfortable place where you can sit or lie down. If you are doing the exercise on your own, read the exercise through once to learn the steps before doing the exercise. Whether you are doing this yourself or you have someone else reading it for you, we recommend that the instructions be read with a slow, soft tonality.

2. Close your eyes and let your whole body relax. As you sit or lie comfortably you can allow yourself to relax more and more. Any concerns you may have had about the past or the future can fade and disappear, as you become more and more aware of the present moment. Become aware of the darkness or patterns of light you see through your eyelids, the sounds around you, the feelings in your body. With each breath, a greater sense of ease and comfort can spread across your body. You can take all the time you need to become very comfortable and relaxed.

3. Make a system-wide announcement inside: "Any parts of me that would like to go through this process can make their presence known to me." This invitation will go to all of the parts you already know

exist within you. You can also invite parts of you to participate that are so separate from you, you aren't even aware yet of their existence. Take enough time to allow all of your inner parts to consider how the Core Transformation Process will benefit them. These parts may have been waiting for many years for the chance to fully have their Core State. These parts may make their presence known to you consciously through pictures, sounds, feelings, or all three. Parts that do not want to make their presence known to you consciously are also very welcome to participate.

DISCOVERING THE POSITIVE PURPOSE

4. Inwardly say, "I now invite all parts of me to notice what they want for me." Some parts may communicate this to you, others may keep it to themselves. This will be the first Intended Outcome.

5. Ask your unconscious mind to give you a signal letting you know when all participating parts have identified their positive intent or purpose. This signal may be a picture, sound, or feeling. Wait for the signal before going on. Since there may be many parts, and some may be slower than others, be patient. After a period of time it may be helpful to ask for a signal again.

DISCOVERING THE OUTCOME CHAIN

6. Next, inwardly say to all the participating parts of you, "I invite all parts of me to step into having your intended purpose fully taken care of, and notice what you want through having that that's even more important." Now invite all your parts to continue answering this question, until they arrive at their Core State. Some parts may go very quickly into their Core State on their own, and others may need you to repeat the question for them several times: "When you have that, fully and completely, what do you want, through having that, that's even more important?"

7. Ask your unconscious to give you a signal letting you know when all parts that are participating have stepped into and fully experience their Core State. Wait for the signal before going on.

8. Do you have a sense of what Core States your parts want for you? If so, what are they?

TAKING THE CORE STATE THROUGH THE OUTCOME CHAIN

9. Invite all parts to step even more fully into having their Core State and ask, "What is it like to just have your Core State as a way of being

in the world in an ongoing way? How are things different when you already have your Core State as a way of being?"

10. Invite all parts to now allow their Core State to transform all of their other Intended Outcomes. Ask them to, "Notice how already having your Core State as a way of being transforms each of your Intended Outcomes."

11. Ask your unconscious mind to give you a signal letting you know when all parts that are participating have allowed their Core State to transform all their other Intended Outcomes. Wait for the signal before going on.

GROWING UP THE PARTS

12. Invite all parts to identify their own age to themselves.

13. Now ask all parts, "Would you now like to benefit from all of the experiences, knowledge and wisdom that I have gained over the years? Would you like to manifest your Core State more fully by evolving to my current age?" Ask your unconscious to give you a signal when all parts have agreed to this.

14. Say to your parts, "Now, stepping fully into your Core States, begin moving forward through time, having your Core State already there through every experience. Allow your Core State to transform each of these experiences, even as you gain in skills, experience and wisdom, all the way through time until all parts are your current age."

BRINGING THE CORE STATES FULLY INTO YOUR BODY

15. If any parts are still outside of you, invite them into your body, with their Core State fully present. Allow all of these Core States to spread through every cell of your body, as they radiate through each other and through you.

TIMELINE GENERALIZATION

16. Allow your past to flow behind you and your future in front of you, in a pathway.

17. With your Core States flowing through you, let yourself float back over your past, going back to the moment of your conception.

18. Drop down into time, allowing your Core States to be fully present through your conception, through your birth, and through all your experiences, all the way up to the present. Your unconscious will do this for you.

19. When you have reached the present, watch yourself moving into the future with your Core States in every experience you will have. You can take all the time you want.

20. With your Core States fully present at this new level, you can cycle through your past, present and future again, to integrate these states even more.

21. When your Core States are fully integrated into your past, present and future, you can re-orient to the here and now.

....

—CHAPTER 31—

HOW PEOPLE HAVE USED CORE TRANSFORMATION

Learning From the Experience of Others

I could tell you my adventures—beginning from this morning," said Alice a little timidly; "but it's no use going back to yesterday, because I was a different person then."
—Alice in Wonderland

Reading about the transformative experiences of others can inspire us to make our own changes. These stories can give you a sense of the many areas of life in which the Core Transformation Process can make a powerful difference. We originally intended to group these stories under categories such as "career," "relationships," "money," "habits," etc., but we found that the changes people experience when they do Core Transformation are so pervasive that each person's experience falls under many categories. The effect is like the ripples that spread out around a pebble dropped in a still pool of water. In each heading we highlight several key areas of change.

Samantha: Career Change and Relationship

Most of us have had difficulty motivating ourselves at times. For Samantha, fear and frustration were preventing her from doing the things she needed to do to further her career. She experienced a dramatic shift as a result of repeated use of the Core Transformation Process:

One morning when I got up I was in a black hole of fear and frustration. I had been making a career change and things hadn't panned out. I was in an absolute panic that I wouldn't have enough money, that I would lose my house, my assets, and so forth. In fact for many months I had been paralyzed by my fear. I hadn't been doing the things I needed to be doing to make a successful career change.

But this time I had recently done the Aligned Self seminar, and instead of staying in the black hole of my fear, I did a quick version of the Core Transformation Process. That helped for awhile, and then the fear came back, so I did it again. I repeated the Core Transformation Process four times that morning, and each time I felt better and better. Then, at around noon, it fully shifted. Instead of feeling fear and frustration, I felt curiosity and excitement! Instead of saying to myself, "Oh, God, I'm going to lose everything," I was saying "Oh, wow! I'm excited about what's going to happen!" That day I took the first five steps I needed to take toward creating my new career. I called some people that I had been putting off calling for a long time.

Another issue that has shifted through doing the Core Transformation Process has to do with my relationship. I had been married for twenty-one years, and then divorced for three. I am now in a relationship that has been getting more and more intimate, and perhaps moving toward marriage. This has been very scary for me. At the same time that I was afraid of intimacy, I also had been feeling as if I had to be with him, as if there was no one else in the world for me. After doing the Core Transformation Process I no longer feel I *have* to be with him. If it is not him someone even better will come along. I can now relax into the relationship as it is. This is a huge shift for me!

He has two kids, and he has them every weekend. I've had the feeling that his kids don't like me, which made me very uneasy around them. Now when it feels like they may not like me, that's just fine. I have the freedom to be me around them.

I have also been using Core States in a different way. When I do yoga, it's as if I'm breathing in my Core States. When I'm preparing my salad, I'm mentally connecting my Core State with my vegetables, and then it's as if I'm eating my Core States! They're in the water I shower with, they're in the garden I grow. Doing this makes the world an extraordinarily friendly place!

Max: Meeting the Right Woman

Most of us want fulfilling, enjoyable relationships. Many of us focus on finding the right person to have a relationship with. While this can be important, another factor that is often overlooked is becoming internally ready for the relationships we want. Max used the Core Transformation Process a year and a half ago to get ready for the kind of relationship he wanted to have. Two months later, he met Katelyn:

> I was twenty-six years old, and I really wanted to find a woman and get married, but most of my relationships had been very short-term. I had been talking to some people about their experiences with relationships, and it sounded like it took most people about a year between finding someone and getting married. I wanted to be married before I was thirty, so I thought I'd better get started.
>
> There were a number of things that got in the way of finding a woman to be with. One was that I was perfectionist. I had such a long list of criteria that no one would ever fit. I had a very precise idea of what she would be like. I knew she would be brunette, and exotic-looking. I wanted someone shorter than me, but not too short. I wanted her to be athletic, to a certain degree. At the time, I could have given you a list a mile long. So, I worked with the part of me that was such a perfectionist.
>
> I'd had quite a few short relationships with women. In every relationship, at some point I got a strong feeling in my gut that said, "This is not right," and the relationship suddenly ended. One day I was totally into the relationship, and the next day I was gone. That feeling came up after being with a woman for as little as two weeks or as long as three months. So, I worked with the part of me that gave me that feeling in my gut.
>
> I knew that I would have to give up some things to have a long-lasting relationship. There was a part of me that didn't want to give up anything. I always did what I wanted to do when I wanted to do it, and that was nice. I could go out when I wanted, I could eat when I wanted, I could take any classes I wanted. That was very important to this part of me. I really enjoy sports, and at that time I spent most of my free time with sports. Obviously, if I was in a serious relationship, we wouldn't always be doing everything according to my schedule, and I wouldn't be able to spend such an enormous amount of time with my sports. So I worked with the part that didn't want to give up anything.
>
> After doing the Core Transformation Process my list of crite-

ria became shorter and more general. For example, I wanted her to be intelligent and have a sense of humor, but it no longer mattered to me that she fit my precise picture of how she should look.

I did the Core Transformation Process in October, and I met Katelyn in December of the same year. The way I describe meeting Katelyn was that I manifested it. I really wanted it, I thought about it, I talked about it all the time, and I made the internal changes I needed to make so that it could happen. We met a few days before Christmas. She was really animated and funny, and I knew right away that I wanted to get to know her. She left town for the Christmas holiday, and two days after she got back into town in January, I asked her out. In February I thought she might be the one. In March, I got clear that this could be a long-term relationship. In April, I really started realizing how much I loved her. Once I fully decided that she was the one for me, I asked her to marry me within the week. We became engaged in April.

The feeling that "this is not right" that I had with every other woman never came with Katelyn. The feeling that came instead was, "This is the right person!" It was 180-degrees different. I was ready to cut back on my sports, I was ready to give up a lot of things all of a sudden. For a time I stopped playing volleyball, and I just slowed down a lot so I could give more attention to her. I was really into the relationship in a new way.

Although my criteria had changed such that I no longer considered so many things to be essential, she matched most of my old criteria. I thought that was kind of interesting!

With Katelyn I was willing to deal with a lot of issues about being with a woman that I had always avoided dealing with before. For example, when Katelyn went out with some of her friends that she knew long before me, I felt jealous. I got an anxious feeling in my gut and wanted to know all the details about what they did. The jealousy issue was very difficult to work through. I thought that I had worked through it before, but it became very apparent that I hadn't. Now that I've worked through it, I still care about what she does, but I'm no longer anxious about it and I no longer need to know all the details. If we're out with some friends, I might get a little bit of the old feeling, just enough to tell me to check in with her. The response I have now seems appropriate to me.

With her, I became very non-judgmental. For example, with women before her, when we went out I was very concerned about how they looked—especially how they looked to other people. With Katelyn, I cared about who she was on the inside and how I felt about her. How she had done her hair, or how she looked to other people wasn't important. That was very different for me.

When I first met her I felt very confident with her. I knew that she was the one. When I met her, she was dating somebody else. I knew she needed to resolve that, and I didn't push it. I felt quite sure that she would choose me, without feeling arrogant about it. I had never had this kind of feeling before.

I was also very honest with her. The first time we went out I was really nervous. On our second date, I told her that I had been nervous the time before. I don't think I would have said that before doing this process. I just had a sense of being more real, of not needing to hide anything from her. I could be with Katelyn in a way that was very open, honest, and easy.

Instead of blaming each other for our problems, we each take responsibility for our issues and help each other with them. For example, when the jealousy issue came up for me, instead of blaming her for going out with her friends or accusing her of not caring about me, I dealt with it as my own issue. When I think that she has an issue to deal with, I don't point it out to her. She usually says what her issues are. This is a very different way of dealing with issues than I had been used to.

Looking back, the Core Transformation Process helped prepare me for this relationship, which is now one of the most important things in my life.

Mindy: Dissolving Irritation

Mindy used the Core Transformation Process with an issue that is, in a way, quite subtle. She didn't like some of her own behavior that was "a little bit mean." It is easy to notice things other people do that push our buttons, but it is usually much more difficult to notice the things we do that push theirs. How often do we hear people say, "This other person has been driving me up the wall!" How seldom do we hear people say, "I have been driving this other person up the wall!" Because Mindy was willing to notice this behavior in herself, she was able to use it as a doorway to a powerful, rich state of being:

I found the Aligned Self seminar incredibly valuable. I have much more alignment between who I am inside and how I go through the world. I am a lot more congruent than before.

Some of the behavioral changes are subtle, yet within myself I notice a definite difference. The way I move through the world is much easier on me.

I used to find certain people very irritating. It could be something as simple as a mannerism that would set me off. No matter how much I tried, sometimes they would get under my skin. Then I would say or do something that, while it wasn't overtly mean, was a subtle dig to get them back. If I ever apologized to the person they said, "Oh, that didn't bother me," but I knew inside myself that my action was a little bit mean and got mad at myself.

Since doing the Core Transformation Process, I very rarely do that. I have a new freedom inside to not be bugged by other people. When someone's behavior does bother me I am much more likely to talk to the person directly about what bothered me and what I want from them. And, even when I still do the old behavior I am much gentler with myself about it. I don't have to get mad at myself.

I work in a very busy clinic with a lot of very sick people. It's like being on the front lines of a war zone these days. We're really busy all the time, we're under-staffed most of the time, and it can generate a certain kind of tension. One woman who works there really used to bug me. She works part-time, she comes in late, she leaves early, she takes long lunches, and she basically abuses the system. I got really annoyed at her because I felt that she was doing less than her share. However, I never talked to her about this directly; instead, I sometimes found myself doing little things that pushed her buttons.

I was in the lab one day and she came in talking to someone else about a new person that she is dating. I sensed that she was slightly insecure about this relationship. So while we were sitting together looking at the microscope, I asked her about this person. Acting innocently, but with a very subtle sarcastic undertone, I said, "So, are you really nuts about this person? Do you really like this person a lot?" And she snapped back, "I really don't want to tell you about it." I replied, "Oh, that's fine, if you don't want to tell me about it, that's OK." I said it in a slightly mocking tone of voice, but not obviously enough that anyone could call me on it. That statement sounds OK on the surface but I knew I was really digging at her. I wasn't really saying it was OK, I was saying, "Fine, if you want to be insecure about it, don't tell me!" Even though she was the one who snapped at me, I knew that I had intentionally teased her; I had pushed her buttons. As I sat there looking through the microscope I thought, "I didn't need to do that." I got very angry with myself.

Later that day she came up to me and apologized. She said, "I'm sorry I snapped at you, I just feel really insecure about this relationship," and so forth. She did not recognize my part in provoking her. However, I knew what was really going on was that I was annoyed because she was not doing a good job, and instead of being direct with her, I teased her about her relationship.

At the workshop I did the Core Transformation Process with the part of me that made me dig at that co-worker. My experience doing the Core Transformation Process was phenomenal. We took the process to incredible depths. On the last day, the Parental Timeline Reimprinting was such an intensely freeing experience that there were tears streaming down my face. I called one of my Core States "done," which means being in harmony and balance within myself.

Now that co-worker doesn't bother me. When I see her coming back after taking an hour-and-a-half lunch break, I say to myself, "Oh, she's just done it again," and I go about my business. I have no need to even think about whether she is doing her share—it no longer concerns me. It's as if a thorn was taken out of my foot—there is no charge around it anymore.

I also have a much gentler response to myself at times when I mess up. I don't feel I have to be perfect. If someone is doing something I feel is inappropriate, rather than jab at them about something else, it's easier for me to be direct, and say, "What were you just doing? It looks to me like you were doing so and so."

And they might say, "I was doing this."

And I say, "Well, given that we've got thirty people waiting, I don't think that's appropriate to be doing right now." And then we can openly discuss what is most important to do. This is much more direct and honest than holding irritated feelings inside and then snipping. And even when I do push someone's buttons, I am much kinder to myself about it now.

Tracy: Releasing TMJ, and Relationships

People often report feeling more physically relaxed after doing the Core Transformation Process. In Tracy's case, this relaxation relieved her of TMJ, or Temporomandibular Joint Dysfunction Syndrome, a chronic problem caused by excess tension in muscles around the jaw:

I didn't intend to work on the TMJ during the workshop. I went specifically to find out why I was at a standstill with my writing and to see if I could improve my relationship with my son. I got both of those outcomes, and more!

I got TMJ about fifteen years ago when I went through a very difficult divorce. Through the years it has gotten worse. The feeling for me was like my jaw joint had slipped out of the socket. Every time I opened my mouth I would feel my jaw moving around instead of having a solid socket. That feeling was accompanied by a very loud crackling, popping sound. This occurred every time I ate, talked, or just opened my mouth to release the pressure on the muscle in my cheek. It was very annoying. At times it was painful. I could feel the stiffness in the muscles of my face, my jaw, and the cords down the back of my neck. It got to the point that my teeth clenched. I have several cracked teeth because of it. It was a pretty severe case.

It was really uncomfortable, so I sought every avenue I heard about to get relief. The first thing I did was go to the dentist, who gave me a retainer, and that didn't help much. Since then, I have had all kinds of people work with it—cranial adjusters, massage therapists, chiropractors—everybody who says they can help with TMJ. Nothing helped. I went to the dentist again about six months ago and when he looked at my jaw, he said, "God, that's bad! A chiropractor might be able to pop it back into place."

I said, "I've been to body workers of all kinds and they haven't been able to do much about it."

"Well," he said, "You might as well just accept it."

So I was basically resigned to thinking I'd have to live with this the rest of my life. When I did the Core Transformation Process in the workshop I was working with my writing block, but I had a very clever partner who was a body worker. Although he didn't know that I had TMJ, he noticed that the set of my jaw was stiff. As I did the process my Core State was calm centeredness. That was my word for it. My experience was like sitting in the center of the universe. I was totally calm, totally still. There was no inner dialogue. Everything was quiet. And my imagery was of outer space and the stars. I felt at one with the universe. I felt I was one with my body and also expanded beyond it. I felt like I filled half the room! It was an incredible experience in its own right.

I was able to achieve an inner state that I have read about in meditation books. They call it the still-point. All these meditation books tell you to meditate until you feel at one with the universe, all internal dialogue stops and you go into the silence. In this state, according to the books, you are totally open to the resources of the universe, "the all," or whatever you want to call it. Well, have you ever tried that? That's impossible for the average modern American! There is so much internal dialogue going on, that it has been impossible for me to go into the silence for more than a few seconds. Those conflicting parts were trying so hard to protect me, or whatever they were trying to do, that there was an incredible cacophony in there. Most people who try to meditate talk about how difficult it is to get that dialogue shut off. I call it infernal dialogue or foaming at the mind.

The people working with me in the exercise saw how much I was basking in that state, and they just let me stay there for about ten minutes. It was amazing to me that I could get to that point and stay there so long.

When I got to my Core State and had taken it back through the Outcome Chain, my partner had me take that Core State and put it into my jaw. I did what he said. I ran it up into my face and my jaw, without really expecting anything to happen. After I completed the process, I suddenly realized the TMJ was gone! I still can open my mouth wide without my jaw popping out. It's been three weeks since the workshop and it hasn't gone back out! For fifteen years I had been trying to get my jaw to heal and nothing helped at all, so I was quite shocked when, in a snap of the finger, the condition was no longer there. I'm really surprised.

Since the workshop I have been able to duplicate that state for myself in meditation. Several nights in my dreams I have felt the same Core State of calm wash over me like a wave.

The effects of the Core Transformation Process have spilled over into other areas of my life also. When I was little my mother thought I was shy, and at the same time, because I was so quiet she thought I was strong-willed and stubborn. She did not know how to talk with me or interact with me. When I was four she decided she would get me over my shyness by taking me to dancing school. Well, the problem was, she never asked me if I wanted to go. The dancing school incident seemed to be the first thing I thought I was being controlled over. It was such a core violation. I felt very disrespected. I wasn't asked. I was taken to dance school and expected to do something I didn't know how to do. Out of this dancing school experience I learned to distrust my mother and her control over me. The mistrust was reinforced over the years. She never asked me if I wanted to go to the doctor, she never asked if I wanted to get my hair cut, she just took me. Now she says the reason she never asked is that I would have said no. That was her assumption, so she just took me places and forced me into things rather than talking to me about them. So, I've had some major issues around control.

Several months before I took the Aligned Self seminar and did the Core Transformation Process, a grown son moved in with me. He looks and acts exactly like his father, my ex-husband, who had been a controlling influence on my life. Whenever my son told me I could or couldn't do something, or told me I had to do something, I got really angry. That surprised me. It was like somebody out of the past was trying to control me, and I was walking around angry all the time. If my son did any little thing I just screamed at him!

Now, since the seminar, we're really calm with each other. It's not at all the way it used to be. When he does the same kind of thing that used to make me angry I'm just amused. The calm centeredness is there and has shifted our relationship. And since my response is so different, now his behavior is beginning to shift too!

Barbara's Story: Working With Illness and Self-Consciousness

When we do the Core Transformation Process there are two kinds of results we typically get. One is the specific change we are going for. The other is a pervasive shift toward greater wholeness and well-being, which has a positive impact on many areas of life. For example, if I do the Core Transformation Process with a fear of public speaking, the first kind of result is to feel more confident with public speaking. The other kind of result is to have more well-being in general. This pervasive well-being usually results in other specific positive changes in my life that I didn't expect. I might discover I can express myself with my friends more easily or change an unwanted habit, or feel more motivated to do what I really want to do in my life. Occasionally these general benefits are pervasive, yet the original target limitation remains unchanged.

When we use the Core Transformation Process—especially when we repeat the process over time—we generally get both kinds of results: the specific change desired, and more well-being throughout our lives. Barbara is an example of a person who (after one Aligned Self seminar) hasn't yet reached the specific goal she started with, but is delighted with an overall inner result of "gaining a very solid sense of who I am." Barbara worked with a health issue using the Core Transformation Process. This story illustrates how even if we don't immediately get what we set out to get, the process is still very transformative from the beginning:

> I worked with a health issue at an Aligned Self seminar. I have multiple sclerosis. When I got the MS, I had worked my way up the ladder into a position with a major bank, where I had been for five years. There came a point where every day, when I went to work, I knew I shouldn't be there. I had a sense of not being in the right place, but didn't feel I could get out of it. I needed the security of the money, I needed the benefits. I didn't feel I had a choice in the matter. One day I was sitting at my desk and I looked up at the sky and said, "Help! I am at the end of my rope, I hate being here, I am frustrated, help me!" Within two weeks I had my first MS symptom. Both my legs started going numb, I couldn't walk, I had to be hospitalized. In a sense I got my answer, although it didn't come in the form that I expected. My MS prevented me from being at the bank, so I pursued the field of counseling. Now I have the sense that I am in the right field doing the right thing, but the price I paid to find out what I wanted to do with my life was my ability to walk.
>
> Although my health has not improved, I got a deep level of inner healing from doing the Core Transformation Process. I have a very solid sense of who I am. I have had glimpses of this before, but that particular process solidified it for me. I achieved a higher level of awareness of what I am here to do. It pulled me out of the small—but seemingly large—day-to-day problems that I sometimes have in my life. The Core State I experienced tied in spiritually for me to a larger connection with people, with love. I feel a lot calmer. I was quite fearful, and always struggled with a self-esteem issue. I tended to respond more to others than to myself. I had always had a goal to be more self-assured.
>
> What has evolved for me is a state of calm and peace that runs on an ongoing basis. Even as I face challenges, such as difficult client situations, that calm and peace is there. I was on a panel the other day speaking in front of a group of one hundred people. Speaking in front of people was always one of my fears. In this situation I felt extremely calm, I was very centered, I knew what I wanted to say and I said it, without having a written speech.
>
> I used to be self-conscious, nervous and unsure of myself. Because I was self-conscious, I sometimes said things that were silly or inappropriate. My attention was focused internally, questioning myself in my mind. Now, since I am not wasting that

> energy on those self-doubts, I can pay more attention. I'm in the moment with people now, so I'm more perceptive. How can you pay attention to other people if you're not there?
>
> That workshop was a springboard. Every fiber in my body knows why I am here. There is no question in my mind now that what I am doing and what I am learning is exactly what I am supposed to be doing and learning. I have a real sense of peace and calm about what I am doing in the world.

When someone makes the kind of changes Barbara made, yet isn't healthy, there are many possibilities. It may be that more parts need to be included for her to regain her health. (See Chapter 29, "Transforming Illness," for more about finding parts related to an illness.) There is also much we do not know. For any specific person we do not know *for sure* if it is possible for them to recover until they have done it. However, when someone desires to be well, we think self-healing is well worth pursuing. We also do not know the larger plan of which we are all a part. However, every move we make toward wholeness and well-being, such as Barbara made, is progress in and of itself.

When we do the Core Transformation Process it is important that we appreciate the progress we are making, as Barbara does, even if we do not immediately get the specific change we are going for. The progress we make now may provide the necessary foundation for the specific change we wanted to come at a later time. With health or any goal, when someone experiences incomplete results after doing the process once, we encourage them to continue using the process over time. This gives you the opportunity to discover how far this process will take you in your own healing—emotional and spiritual as well as physical. In the next example Heather shares how using the process repeatedly made a strong difference for her.

Heather: Staying Present & Recovering From Sexual Abuse

Heather had difficulty in relationships. She mentally "left" when another person was present. She recognized this pattern was unuseful, and even knew how it had started—she'd had very early experiences of being immobilized by polio, and then was molested sexually. "Spacing out" became her way of escaping from threat. Knowing what was wrong, and how it started, however, hadn't helped Heather become the person she wanted to be. After doing the Core Transformation Process Heather says she notices she can be more present in all her relationships. Heather did the Core Transformation Process three times, and found the repetition very helpful. When we have done the process once and notice that a piece of the old behavior, feeling or response is left, we can benefit even more if we repeat the process with the piece that is still there. Here is Heather's story:

I had a pattern that was interfering with my all of my relationships—with men, with my children, with everyone. This pattern stopped me from experiencing intimacy with another person. I called this pattern "defocusing." When I was with someone, I felt as if I split off. I couldn't stay present in communication. My thoughts went elsewhere, and I lost track of being with that person.

My children used to say to me, "Mom, you're spacing out!" Although I never noticed myself defocusing around my children, they did. I often could repeat back what they said, but their perception was that I was not listening to them. Although having my kids tell me I was spacing out was hurtful, this problem was the most painful when it interfered with intimacy in relationships with men. Because I couldn't stay present, I was unable to have a very good relationship. I couldn't be intimate with them. I have had a few failed relationships, including a divorce.

This difficulty goes back to my childhood. I had polio when I was four, and was temporarily paralyzed. This gave me an experience of being dis-empowered. My earliest memories are of sitting on the couch, unable to move. Then I was sexually molested when I was five. Although I had physically recovered from the polio, having experienced the complete dis-empowerment when I was paralyzed made the situation of molestation even more intense for me. I felt as though I couldn't do anything to take care of myself in that situation.

Later I was tormented verbally and emotionally by older boys. They shoved snakes and frogs in my face, they put me in a hole in the ground, they teased me about being a girl, that sort of thing. Since I already felt dis-empowered, their tormenting was excruciating. I was terrified that the older boys would overpower me. Although they never actually did anything terrible to me physically, it was very painful emotionally because I was constantly afraid that they would.

When I was sexually molested I responded to my fear by escaping the only way I could, by mentally leaving. After that, whenever something threatening happened, I just mentally left. That pattern finally became a habit. Eventually, I mentally left the scene whenever I was around other people, even if I wasn't in any danger. This response became so pervasive that I no longer even realized what I was doing—I just knew I had trouble staying focused on the present moment when I was with another person. It is very clear to me now that the part of me that was trying to escape those traumatic experiences had a very positive intention!

I went through the Core Transformation Process three times in a nine-month period. Each time I did the process I went to a deeper level. It's like peeling the layers of an onion down to the core. The abuse was so traumatic for me that it took some time to really get down to what happened, and heal that. Each time I did the process I got closer to "me" and I got a more intense Core State each time. By the third time I was aware of more abuse that had happened to me, and so I got to heal more.

The impact the Core Transformation Process had on my life is that now I can be present with whomever I'm with—I don't need to escape. I can get intimate without splitting off, going somewhere else. I can stay present and feel comfortable and safe, without a sense of intrusion. I have gotten back a sense of empowerment. This has affected all my friendships and my relationships with my children. My children notice that I am not spaced out as much anymore. Now that I have had the experience of being fully present with them, I notice when I am not present and can come back.

In my work, I have just returned to the area of sales. I feel the Core Transformation Process has made me a much more effective salesperson. I notice a big difference in my ability to remain with that other person, focusing on their communication with me.

I am beginning to get back together with my ex-husband. I don't know what will come of this, but right now we're hoping we can work things through. We love each other a lot. I enjoy being with him. I'm more able to be present and intimate with him. Although I don't know whether we will choose to stay together this time, my new ability to be present and intimate with him is making this relationship much more enjoyable for us both.

Marlin: Addiction

Marlin had been struggling with addictions for 20 years when he began working with an NLP therapist. Before beginning NLP therapy Marlin had been drinking a 12-pack of beer every day. Some NLP techniques helped him start to decrease his drinking, but the Core Transformation Process helped him resolve this issue more completely. At this point in time, Marlin has made a significant shift in his response to alcohol, and we expect him to maintain that shift. We consider this work with Marlin and others with similar problems to be preliminary work, since we haven't followed them over a number of years. However, our preliminary results suggest that using the Core Transformation Process over time is highly effective with serious limitations such as alcohol and drug abuse, multiple personality disorders, and physical and sexual abuse.

> I had reached a point in my life where I felt like if I didn't stop drinking I was going to die, 'cause I'd been doing it for 20 years. Plus I was just so totally unhappy, like I'd always been my whole life. But the main thing was I felt like I needed to get rid of the alcohol so I could clear up other areas in my life.
>
> There was one point after I went to a rehab center when I lasted for three months without drinking. That was two years ago. But it was just a hassle. I still wanted to drink, it was still a part of me. It was miserable because my mind was still consumed with drinking. Even though I wasn't drinking, I still felt like I wanted to. It just didn't last; I knew it wouldn't and I could sense that.
>
> When I started drinking again there were probably times when I went maybe one day, but never two days in a row without a drink. And before the rehab center, I'd say for ten years, there was never a period of time where I went three days in a row without a drink. And it didn't matter if I was deathly ill, or whatever, I drank.
>
> The third time I saw him (his NLP therapist), he took me through the Core Transformation Process, and after that it was like, I was finally becoming aware of who I really was. It's what I was always looking for. Stopping drinking is a major issue, but it went far beyond that to where I just have the inner peace, the joy. To me, miracle is a mild word to describe the difference in the way I feel now.
>
> I've had some really bad days where it would have been impossible before not to drink, but I just don't drink. I'm not saying I never will drink again—I don't know. But I do know I have this inner peace and that drinking is just not an issue anymore. It's like I don't even think about drinking anymore. Before it was my whole life, it consumed my life—wanting to do it, wanting to stop—where now it's almost like I never did it. It's hard to explain, because I'm still getting used to feeling this way. It's what I always wanted, and I believed it could happen—I just never found a way to make it happen until now. Every day gets a little better.
>
> I've always believed that the alcohol was not the problem. The problem was inside me and just taking away the alcohol would not solve my problems. With this process I'm being healed from the inside and these things that are destructive just sort of

drop off. It's not natural for a person to drink excessively. This is allowing me to be who I was meant to be, born to be, and the more me I become, the less destructive things I do to myself.

I even had two people at work say, "What's wrong with you? You're walking around here humming and smiling." I didn't even notice it but they did because I was always kind of a depressed person.

I did the Core Transformation Process every day for a while, and now I do it often but not every day. I'll deal with one issue and another one will come up and I just run the Core Transformation Process through it. It just keeps getting better. It feels fantastic. But it's a little strange because I'm trying to get used to feeling good.

I've spent probably thousands of dollars on positive mental attitude tapes, self-hypnosis tapes, any kind of tape or book that showed any type of promise or any type of hope. I got suckered by a lot of people but it was worth it to me to take a chance. If somebody said they could help me in a book or tape or whatever, I would get it. I've also—and this is nothing against the churches or God or anything—but I got involved in a charismatic movement and had numerous ministers lay hands on me to try to heal me. I even went through a four-hour session where these two elders of the church were "casting demons out of me." I've been to the rehab center. I've got a light and sound machine that was supposed to balance me and make me feel better. I bought a float tank. Dozens of things. Anything.

About ten years ago a psychiatrist diagnosed me as manic-depressive with suicidal tendencies and put me on anti-depressants. I felt better, I wasn't as depressed, but it was because I wasn't feeling anything, and I didn't stop drinking. Something inside said, this just isn't right, I don't want to live like a zombie the rest of my life. I've got a lot of people in my family who are on pills and I just didn't wish to end up that way the rest of my life.

I think of my unconscious mind as a friend now, instead of an enemy, and a friend who has some power. Like I said before, I always sensed that the healing was going to come from me being me, but I never knew how to do that. This somehow gets the job done. It's very natural. Oh, it was unnatural at first, because it was something I never did, but now it seems like the most natural thing in the world, and the sky's the limit. I'm excited. The excitement is so much different, where I'm very excited and very happy, but in a calm way, if that makes any sense. I've had to get used to it because I've been excited before, but it was like a draining type of excitement, a nervous excitement. This is an energizing type of exciting, and there is a peace to it, too. I am alive for the first time in my life, able to experience life. My whole viewpoint is different. There is a sort of flow to my life now. I'm not sure what's going to happen and I know there will be problems in the future, but I feel they're going to be taken care of in their own time, in their own way. Not that life's going to be perfect, but it's going to work out somehow. I don't know how, and I don't know what's going to happen, but I'll be able to handle it now, without fear. Fear is gone.

I feel a harmony with other people that I never felt before. Nothing's really changed with *them.* I still get shafted at work by people but I take it differently—they're not really doing anything to purposely hurt me. That's the way they are. And it doesn't bother me. It used to be when people hurt my feelings I would hate them and put myself down. Now I just ignore it.

My boss is a very nice man, and we're good friends, but when something goes wrong he takes a fatherly attitude and talks in a demeaning way to me. That always bothered me before, especially because I didn't have a very good relationship with my father and it's what my father did to me. It went right to hurt central and I would always put myself down very, very strongly. Since I started doing Core Transformation it's happened once and I just blew it off. That is the way it is, and he doesn't mean anything by it, really. And it doesn't put me down.

I have one beer in my refrigerator right now, and looking at it is like looking at a jar of mustard. I don't know why I don't just throw the beer away, but it's like I don't need to. It doesn't matter. Before if I had a beer in the refrigerator it would be in my stomach. That's another beautiful part of it. When I tried quitting at the treatment centers they told me I had to change my whole life. I couldn't be around people who drank, I couldn't be around alcohol. I couldn't do this, I couldn't do that. With how I feel now, I could have a case of beer sitting by my chair every night and it wouldn't matter.

I ran self-hate through the process, and anger came up as an objection. I did two or three processes where I was hating Dottie, my ex-fiancée. I wasn't *really* hating her. I loved her and hating her was the only way I could deal with her leaving. I cleaned that up. I also felt like I was obsessing about her. I still love her and I miss her, but it was making me dysfunctional, where I was consumed with nothing but thoughts of her. That's not good. So I took that through the process, and that helped immeasurably.

My kids are seeing the change in me, and they know more than anybody what it means for me not to drink. They have seen me try to stop drinking their whole life. It's had a powerful effect on them, especially my daughter. One day they had stopped by and my daughter kind of hung around while the other people were going out to the car, and she just hugged me, and she said, "I love you for not drinking." It hit me that it has hurt them all these years, that they've been watching me kill myself. She was so concerned about me. That felt good.

The changes Marlin has made in himself are rippling out into his family and work environment. Although Marlin found a rehab center ineffective for himself, the Core Transformation Process is very easily and naturally incorporated into networks and healing environments such as rehab centers and Twelve-Step Programs, which have provided a valuable place for thousands of people to take recovery from addiction seriously. The Core Transformation Process is in alignment with the deepest intentions of the Twelve-Step Programs. We know many Twelve-Step leaders who seek to incorporate the most effective ways to facilitate healing, and we expect that to happen when they use this process.

Martha: Assisting Others

Martha has taken many Aligned Self seminars, and uses the Core Transformation Process with herself in an ongoing way. She has also guided others through the process. Martha recently shared an experience she had doing the process with her elderly mother.

When we are guiding someone else through the process we do not need to know the details of what they want to work with. We can guide them through the process simply by reading the script and writing down their Intended Outcomes, if that is appropriate. The most important part of guiding someone else through the Core Transformation Process is to gently honor their parts, their timing, and *their* sense of what they want.

I want to thank you for the Core Transformation Process. I just used it with my mother who is in a nursing care center. For a long time she has been wanting to die. She asks my sisters and I "Why am I still alive?" She has been very angry that she hasn't died yet. We would tell her that we didn't know, maybe there was still some purpose to being alive, but she got very annoyed when we told her that.

> The other evening I guided her through the Core Transformation Process. We began with the part of her that wanted to die. She stopped talking for a while, but I kept asking for a new Intended Outcome. At times she would just smile or nod her head ever so gently. She never did tell me what her Intended Outcomes or Core State were, but I didn't need to know.
>
> Afterwards she looked so peaceful and radiant and beautiful. She just kept smiling and smiling. Two of my sisters were with me. As we kissed her good-bye she beamed and said, "We love you!" as if she were already joining with her loved ones beyond. My sisters and I were so all so moved by this experience that we had tears in our eyes as we left the room.
>
> Since then she hasn't complained to us about wanting to die the way she used to, and she looks peaceful with being here. I recently asked her if she wanted to die and she had this big smile and said, "Oh, whenever it happens is fine with me. It's up to God and *she'll* let me know!"

Lance: Recovering from Schizophrenia

An NLP Master Practitioner who is a therapist with a private practice wrote us about a young man with schizophrenia who has responded dramatically to the Core Transformation Process.

> When I started seeing Lance he was in his mid-twenties and hadn't felt "normal" since he was seven or eight years old. At about the age of 13 he started to deeply believe he was significantly different from other children. Most of his relationships were emotionally dry and quite stressful. He has always had an innate knack for working with electronics, computers and machinery, and is intellectually brilliant.
>
> Lance made it through high school, though he felt highly anxious and was beginning to have delusions of persecution and some kinesthetic and internal auditory hallucinations (little groups of people inside him controlling him and talking to him). He barely made it through his first year of college when he was overwhelmed with anxiety and could no longer function on many levels. He would forget to eat for days at a time, his emotions would swing from flat to extremely paranoid anxiety, and for over a year he believed that all the people around him were robots and he was the only flesh and blood person. When Lance was anxious (which was almost all the time) his legs and arms

would jerk and his face would twitch uncontrollably. Eventually he began to have grandiose and religious delusions and believed that devils were living in a deep place within him. He was hospitalized for six months and put on high levels of anti-psychotic and anti-anxiety medication.

When Lance was released from the mental hospital he went to live with his parents where he lived a hermit-like existence, avoiding other people as much as possible. He was unable to hold a job, and had no real motivation. The closest he came to motivation was anxiety.

When his parents called me to find out if I would work with Lance he was not seeing a therapist. For six years previously he had seen a psychiatrist who spent most of his time talking to Lance about taking care of his body, getting along with his family, and how to not feel angry. When that psychiatrist moved out of state, Lance began seeing another one who told him, after only two sessions, that his case was hopeless. He told Lance that he should continue on his medication and not expect any change. Since the psychiatrist did not think seeing Lance would help, he did not want to work with him.

After Lance and I had been working together for a few months with traditional NLP techniques, many of his symptoms had changed for the better. His physician had reduced his anti-psychotic medication from 15 mg. to 10 mg. daily, and stated this was unusual. He said the normal pattern was for medication to be increased over time, not decreased. Lance had also created some close friendships, gone on dates and enjoyed them, and his periods of anxiety were significantly reduced. His relationship with his parents improved, and he started college again. Though we had made significant progress, Lance still had a feeling of something wrong "deep inside of me in my guts and in my mind." He experienced this as having a black ball of evil inside of him.

I had recently started working with the Core Transformation Process and decided to try it with Lance. The "black ball of evil" sorted itself out into four parts: a part that wanted solitude; a part that wanted him to have control and be assertive; a part that wanted him to manage internal conflict better; and a part that wanted to hurt the other parts by talking to them. The Core States of these parts were peace of mind, ease-fullness-richness within, peace of mind (again), and peace through oneness.

Immediately after doing the process Lance said, "I feel a bit dizzy. Like I am looking at the world through new eyes. All the inner parts decided to work together, to help me and them feel better, and find new ways to get to where we want to go without anxiety." He had a much greater sense of connection to his parents after doing Parental Timeline Reimprinting.

When I saw Lance a week after doing the process he said, "I feel normal. The last time I remember feeling like this was when I was eight or nine years old. I feel calm inside. I'm having fun with things and I don't feel tired all the time. I haven't experienced any major anxiety at all in the past week. There were a few times when I'd feel it coming up and it would instantly disappear. A camping trip my dad and I were going on was canceled about two weeks ago because when I started to pack for it my anxiety level rose so high I couldn't do it. Two days ago I began packing for it with no problem. I felt great. I feel excited to be able to get away with my dad and know it will be fun. I'm feeling excitement! This is the first time I can remember feeling excited without feeling anxious since I was little."

During this session Lance's facial tics and leg and arm jerking, which had been frequent in all of our past sessions, were nearly gone. With a few brief exceptions he looked relaxed and calm. There are many areas of his life and behavior we will continue working on, but the shift he received in this one Core Transformation session was amazing. As we continue to work with specific areas of his life we will engage them from the Core Transformation Process.

Lance reported that in the week after our Core Transformation session he was in a situation with an attractive woman whom he vaguely knew. His usual pattern would be to fall into extreme anxiety until he could get away. When she prompted him to attempt a trick she had done, he failed. But instead of becoming anxious, with her and six other people watching, he clowned around. With no anxiety he joked with them and soon had everyone laughing, including himself. Lance was not someone who you could say "clowned around." He was usually very serious, and became anxious if any small pressure was put on him. It was only after he left the situation that it dawned on him that this was a new pattern.

Lance's doctor said that part of his need for medication has to do with his high stress response creating neurochemical imbalances. If we can handle the stress response there is a significant chance the neurochemistry will come back into balance. Lance, his physician and I have a goal of eliminating his dependency on medications in the near future.

> I have done the Core Transformation Process with numerous clients, and seen many positive changes, but Lance's shift is the most dramatic I've seen. The change has stayed stable, and has led me to a few conclusions about Lance. Not only is he not hopeless as his past psychiatrist stated, I predict he will be moving even further on and finding fulfillment in his life. I have seen him in a period of six months move from being schizophrenic to being more like someone with a high level of anxiety. The anxiety now seems to be rapidly coming under control.

This chapter is a small sample of the many personal stories we could share with you. We offer them to give you an idea of the range and the far-reaching nature of the results, and the way in which the results build by using the process over time. We hope it enriches your own ability to use the Core Transformation Process.

—CHAPTER 32—

CORE TRANSFORMATION AND SPIRITUALITY

Finding the God Within

We are not human beings having a spiritual experience.
We are spiritual beings having a human experience.
— Pierre Teilhard de Chardin

People who are on a spiritual path who learn the Core Transformation Process in the Aligned Self seminars are often struck with the similarity between what they experience fairly quickly in the seminar, and what they have been seeking through their spiritual path. They are deeply moved by getting access to their own deeper spirituality so surprisingly easily.

Most of us raised in a religious tradition primarily learned a set of beliefs and rules about spiritual reality. We were told what was true, rather than guided to discover deeper truths within ourselves. One of the intriguing effects of the Core Transformation Process is that it taps directly into spiritual states, without asking people to "have a spiritual experience." Rather than imposing a set of rules from the outside, the Core Transformation Process guides us in experiencing our own unique inner essence more fully. For me (Connirae), discovering that every part has a Core State that can be experienced as spiritual has been compelling evidence for a spiritual presence. The fact that each of our unconscious parts has an inner knowing of these Core States, each in its own unique fashion, has impressed me in a way that no theology ever has.

The Core Transformation Process results in less need for strongly-held beliefs and rules. Max, in the previous chapter, shared how his beliefs and expectations about the kind of woman he wanted to marry became much more flexible. He didn't have to think this through consciously and re-decide; it was just a natural consequence of doing the Core Transformation Process. When we live out of a Core State, many of our rigid beliefs just aren't meaningful to us any longer. Strong beliefs about spirituality or religion also tend to become gentler and less rigid as people gain the experience of universality that Core States offer. There is so much we do not know about the spiritual realm. Clinging to yet another strong belief system about what is real spiritually has pitfalls we are all too familiar with. Our history books and our daily news tell us of the tremendous damage done in the name of religious fervor.

Strong beliefs about spirituality can even get in the way of experiencing spiritual states. What our inner parts have to offer us is generally of a slightly different (or very different) quality than we have in mind when we try to "figure out" what spirituality should be. One man I worked with named Richard had trained in spiritual disciplines for years. He was convinced that all his parts should have "being in the light" as their Core State, since that was the state he sought in meditation. When he asked his unconscious parts what *they* wanted, he discovered important Core States like OKness and calm centeredness. These sounded less elevated and esoteric, but turned out to be much more solid and real experiences for him. These were the states he needed first, to move toward wholeness.

Laurel had been devoted to a spiritual teacher for many years, and spent time daily in meditation. When she came to what she saw as a block in her spiritual growth, she tried the Core Transformation Process:

> I worked with the part of me that is so devoted to my teacher that it's like being romantically in love. When I would speak to him I would be ga-ga for days, happy and blissed out, but not very grounded or functional, and I always came down from that high. I came to a point where that wasn't working for me anymore. I wanted my experience of spirit to be steadier and more within myself, not "out there" with a spiritual teacher. I also wanted to experience my spirituality as something that is as grounded in this world as in any other.
>
> My first Intended Outcome for this devoted part was "being happy." After that the Outcome Chain was, "complete calm," "to be with God," and then to "merge with my soul," which at first I thought was my Core State because it was so wonderful. But when I asked what that part wanted that was even more than that, the response was an experience that I call "just being." It's almost impossible to put it into words because it was a state of utter stillness, a kind of "is-ness."

> I have had quite a few of what I would call deep and profound spiritual experiences over the years, but this Core State of "just being" took me to a whole new place that was beyond phenomena. It just was. It feels like what many parts of me have been searching for, maybe for lifetimes. It's a sense of, "Oh, I don't have to do any of this other stuff, I can just go to that place of being." Now that may sound like "personal growth 101" but for me, to actually experience it and be there any time was a revelation. It's not a high that I go up to or come down from, it's a place of just being.
>
> Now when I feel myself starting to go outside myself looking for spirit or God, I go instead to that place of just being, which isn't inside or outside, it just is. I'm very grateful to have had this experience. For me, this process supports my study with my spiritual teacher, and I'm still devoted to that path, but it feels like I'm doing it from a more mature level, from a place that has more stillness and neutrality to it. And it's much easier for me to be in touch with spirit from that place of just being because I don't have to go anywhere, it's already always there.

Looking For God In All the Wrong Places

For thousands of years spiritual teachers and traditions have said, "God is everywhere," yet our human way of looking at things can make that reality difficult to embrace. How can God be within the evil in the world? Some things seem too awful to have God anywhere near them. It is easy to think that the way to find God is to create distance between ourselves and anything that smacks of "evil." Because of this, religious and spiritual people sometimes take the approach of separating from what they regard as evil, sinful or, in New Age terminology, "negativity." If we separate from parts within ourselves that we call evil, we have inner splits and conflicts. We try to act and feel in a balanced, whole, and loving way, even when some parts of ourselves don't want to. This approach results in feeling conflicted and feeling the need to control our negative thoughts, angers and desires, or shove them aside. Yet most of us have noticed that just shoving them aside doesn't work. We don't feel fully congruent in our "niceness."

Gloria was well-respected in her community. She was a devoutly religious woman who attended church regularly. Almost everyone who knew her had kind things to say about her. Yet Gloria was very troubled because she frequently became overwhelmed with fits of rage. In this state she would yell at her children viciously, and had even hit them several times.

Gloria was afraid she would seriously hurt her children, and afraid someone would find out. She was doing her best to develop spiritually, yet for her, the effort to be loving was at the expense of her angry feelings. She tried to squelch them until she was unable, and she just "lost it" to rage.

Many of us have done something like Gloria did. We have tried to force ourselves to be the wonderful person we want to be, only to find the "not nice" aspects of us still there, or maybe even a little magnified. However, what we think of as our "good" qualities and our "bad" qualities may be equally off-balance. If I am driven to act nice to people, even when I feel angry, that may be viewed by others as a "good" quality. But just because it is socially acceptable does not mean it is balanced. I am acting nice to take care of my relationship or image at the expense of my emotional balance and what is true for me. Any time I am driven to do or feel a certain way, even though I have to stifle other parts of myself, I am off-balance. This can include being driven to be right, successful, rich, intelligent, beautiful, brave, physically fit, kind, generous, or emotionally calm. Any of those things can be worthy goals; it is being attached to them that makes them off-balance.

When we go on a spiritual path we often seek "God" in the obvious places. We look to the parts of ourselves and others that *already* feel loving, compassionate and deeply peaceful. We try to feel these "good" feelings, and shove aside any parts of ourselves that don't fit. This creates a polarity between spiritual states and daily life—a split between our "nice" and "not-nice" parts. The spiritual states are wonderful in and of themselves, but are ungrounded and disconnected from the "unspiritual" parts of day-to-day living—the impatience, anger, irritation, jealousy, judgment and other negative behaviors, feelings and responses that are inevitable parts of being human and living. Parts we judge to be unacceptable and unspiritual are suppressed. The result of suppressing these parts is that they never come to resolution and never get access to the spiritual states, and the "spiritual" part remains disconnected to maintain its separateness from the "unspiritual" parts. This kind of search for our spiritual essence can actually diminish us. Every time we "disown" an emotion, desire, or other unwanted response as "not me—I'm beyond that!" we become a little bit smaller. We lose some of our vitality and our essence. We distance ourselves from universal truths. Attempting to suppress our own "dark side" actually leads to diminishing our spiritual growth.

With the Core Transformation Process we *start* with our worst flaws. We begin with what we dislike in ourselves, what seems least godlike, and then we find God within, even there. This integrates the spiritual with practical, daily living. Rather than experiencing spirituality as a separate thing we actually find spiritual states at the core of every limitation, every bad habit, every negative emotion and behavior we wish we didn't have. Rather than restricting a spiritual state to certain times of the day, certain days of the week, certain activities or certain rooms in a building, Core Transformation connects these spiritual states into specific real-life situations.

A profound self-acceptance gradually emerges out of transforming these limitations. The message embedded within the process is, "Every limitation, every response I have that I don't like, actually has God (good) within it." The process teaches the unconscious how to allow this spiritual core within every part to automatically transform us. Every annoying trait, every "unspiritual" action, thought or emotion actually becomes a direct doorway into experiencing our spiritual essence. We can understand and experience that our dark side is potentially a wonderfully enriching aspect of ourselves that can lead us to the very core of our beingness.

Three Spiritual Truths

A number of key truths are common to most major spiritual disciplines, and are spoken of in slightly different forms by different spiritual teachers. Three stand out to me. The first and most important is the message of oneness, which is discussed in Chapter 4, "The Five Core States," in some detail. This is one of the ways that Carl Jung experienced oneness: "At times I feel as if I am spread out over the landscape and inside things, and am myself living in every tree, in the splashing of the waves, in the clouds and the animals that come and go, in the procession of the seasons."

Another related spiritual truth—one that has been lost in many versions of organized religion—has to do with acceptance and compassion. It has to do with giving up judgment of ourselves and others, and coming to increasingly greater acceptance of ourselves and others, including our limitations. Whenever I judge either myself or someone else, I can feel myself becoming more tense physically. Holding onto judgment against something takes energy—it uses up some of our vitality. When we move to a place of acceptance, we relax on all levels—physically, emotionally, mentally and spiritually. We come into a greater wholeness and joy within and free up our energy for more useful things.

If we *force* ourselves to accept and not judge, that becomes another rule that makes us more rigid and tense. Any time we find ourselves judging ourselves or someone else it means we have discovered a place within ourselves where we have the potential for greater compassion.

A good beginning in becoming more accepting is always acknowledging what is, rather than trying to be something we are not. Total acceptance means acceptance of everything that goes on in ourselves and in the world—not in the sense of liking or condoning everything, and not in the sense that we become passive about changing the world for the better, but in the sense that we are attuned to the God within everything—even within what seems awful. We begin to have a knowing that it is all part of a larger plan that loves and embraces us. When an adult roughly grabs a young child out of the way of a speeding car, the child may feel very hurt and upset about the roughness, or about being stopped from going where he wanted to go. The child may not have any awareness that the adult just saved his life. In the same way, we may not have an awareness of just how life in the universe is unfolding, but we can have a consciousness that life is much bigger than we are and is unfolding perfectly. This is a fundamental acceptance of *what is.* When life grabs us roughly we know that it may have just saved our life. When we live from acceptance we tend to respond to the world with kindness and compassion.

The third spiritual truth has to do with surrender. I can think of my actions as arising out of my own personal will, preferences, and desires, or I can experience myself as surrendering to a larger purpose that I am a part of. In contrast to submission, which is giving up my own will, this kind of surrender is a congruent alignment of myself and my will with something much larger than me. My actions, my movement, my thoughts, all increasingly arise out of this alignment with the greater whole, rather than out of a separate personal willing. This kind of surrender is not passivity—waiting idly for the "spirit" to move me, but a dynamic sense of moving in concert with, of allowing myself to move naturally in that place of oneness.

Both "acceptance" and "surrender" are really natural extensions of the first truth, "oneness." Judgment presupposes separation between the judge and that which is judged. If in some deeper, spiritually true way I am really one with everything, then judgment makes no sense. When I experience myself as one with everything—a much larger experience than what I usually think of as myself—then I act out of this larger awareness. In a sense I have "surrendered" to that which is within me, which is everything, which is more truly me.

If we begin with a spiritual state we have already experienced and impose it on our off-balance parts, even though the experience is positive, it may have a slightly coerced quality to it. The Core State our inner part is seeking may be slightly different in quality and source. While the name and subtle feeling quality of the Core States we discover within vary infinitely, the common quality of experience tapped into is that of "oneness" or a "connection with all." It makes a difference that we reach these states through our flaws and our off-balance parts. This is what insures that our inner transformation is organic and real, and an uncovering of what is already within.

—CHAPTER 33—

INTEGRATING CORE TRANSFORMATION INTO OUR LIVES

Core States Can Go Everywhere With Us

When I'm preparing my salad, I'm mentally connecting my Core State with my vegetables, and then it's as if I'm eating my Core States! My Core States are in the water I shower with, they're in the garden I grow. Doing this makes the world an extraordinarily friendly place!
—Samantha

Those who get the most from the Core Transformation Process use it in an ongoing way. It can become a simple, loving, affirming process you do every day or several times a week for as long as you feel it is working for you. This can be a very enjoyable time of greater connection with the profound Core States within you.

The first level of change we experience from doing the Core Transformation Process comes from doing it thoroughly once. Most people get the specific change they wanted, plus other unexpected but welcome changes. Although not everyone gets a significant change their first time through the process, essentially everyone who sticks with it gets significant positive change in their lives. If you have done the process over time and the changes you want haven't yet occurred, you may find it useful to take the Aligned Self Seminar and have the assistance of someone skilled in the process. This can assist you in sorting out which parts to work with, deeply tuning in to your inner parts and Core States, and can provide you with an example of someone who has used the process deeply and effectively with themselves.

Doing the Core Transformation Process repeatedly over time brings deeper levels of change. If you want the fullest benefit from the Core Transformation Process in your life, we encourage you to use it as a personal practice that you do each day over a period of time. I (Connirae) have made an inner commitment to do the process at least once daily for periods of several months at a time. Once I became familiar with the process, it usually took only fifteen minutes. It is always very restful, and often opens my experience to profound inner states. As I followed through on my commitment, I found myself embracing and including more and more subtle layers of my self. The Core States I was reaching seemed to go through a progression. At the beginning I didn't go to the spiritual states that many of my clients discovered and exclaimed to me about. At the time I assumed that these people were just interpreting things spiritually because they had spiritual beliefs. However, as I worked with more of my own parts I soon discovered states that *I* couldn't describe in any way but spiritual. These spiritual states all had a quality of *oneness* to them. They left me with a deep sense of comfort and a way of understanding what spiritual leaders have described and written about for centuries. As I have continued, the Core States I reach continue to deepen, going to what I can only describe as ever greater levels of oneness. I have noticed a similar progression in others who have used the process over time.

It is very important not to try to jump ahead and force a spiritual state if your inner part wants something that sounds mundane to you. Really reclaiming each Core State that comes forward lays the foundation for truly experiencing the next level. You can also expect to go through some cycles. After tapping into a number of very spiritual parts, you may work with a part that wants something you think is more mundane. Cycling back through some of these basic Core States can set the stage for experiencing a new level. Fortunately we can trust our inner wisdom to always offer the Core State we most need at the time. Whatever our parts want is what we have separated ourselves from and need to reclaim.

We want to be clear that doing the Core Transformation Process will not make you into a perfect human being. However, if you do it repeatedly with yourself, it is almost certain to take you to greater levels of inner knowing and wisdom.

Doing It Daily

Doing the Core Transformation Process daily works best if you do it at the same time each day, so it becomes a habit—especially if you're going to be doing it for a few months at a time. Explore what works best for you. Perhaps you want to use the time in the morning as soon as you awaken. Some people like the evening, right before going to bed. Or, if you like to pause in the middle of the day, that might be the right time for you. If you already have a meditation time you may want to have the Core Transformation Process become part of your daily meditation. Some of our workshop participants who meditate regularly have commented to us that this work supports their meditation goals. While some of them could already go into a wonderful meditative state, it was as if some parts were left behind. When we do the Core Transformation Process regularly all parts of us can experience these powerfully transforming states.

Sometimes I have done the process with myself almost daily for periods of several months. After having done this repeatedly, I remember driving down the road one day, noticing I felt agitated about something. Before I had time to think about it very much consciously, I felt myself popping through a series of states to a wonderful place that was the Core State for the part that had felt agitated. Then I felt this Core State wash through the Intended Outcomes. It doesn't always happen this fast for me. Frequently I go back to working more explicitly with an inner part. When we do the process repeatedly we begin to experience life differently. Whatever happens to us, even if we feel off-balance, at an unconscious level we begin to sense the deeper-level Intended Outcomes and the Core State. We know they are there, even before we've arrived at them.

Lindsay's Story

The following is what one woman, Lindsay, had to say about using this process in her day-to-day life:

> I am so grateful to have learned the Core Transformation Process. It just got me through a very difficult week. I have been responsible for some very sensitive negotiations between my company and another company, with a major project at stake. For our company to go ahead, we needed the agreement of several key people in our organization. As we were negotiating a contract, several of the people in my company became very ego-involved from my point of view. While they raised some good concerns, they basically took the position that they wouldn't agree to the deal unless they got some concessions that I felt were designed mostly to serve them.
>
> I found myself crying myself to sleep one night after spending all day in meetings with these people. I was so frustrated, because I knew this deal could really help fulfill the mission of our company. I knew it would take a relatively small amount of company resources, benefit the individuals within our company, and provide a service. And, it looked like we were going to lose it.

So, I started doing the Core Transformation Process with all the parts I was aware of in me: the part that was frustrated, the part that was angry about possibly losing the deal, the part of me that felt hurt because of how one individual had treated me. In a matter of minutes my state changed completely. An enormous sense of relief and relaxation literally washed over me. I could feel it over my entire body. I didn't even always get to the Core State. Sometimes I couldn't get that far, so I just invited my unconscious mind to continue in a way that completely honored me.

It was a revelation to me that I didn't have to get through the whole process to make a difference. Even after doing part of it, I felt great and I could go to sleep. I had good dreams instead of nightmares. Through doing that, I came to an understanding of what I think is really important in this project. It was as if everything that wasn't important fell away, and what was important remained. Now I feel the clarity within me to either find an agreement that everyone who participates will feel good about, or to turn the deal down.

Before I learned this process I did not have a way to get to this level of clarity. I like that I can use it very practically in my life. It is such a comfort to know that when I have a difficult situation or an "unwanted" response, this gives me a way to acknowledge and utilize it in a positive way, instead of trying to ignore it, pushing it away or feeling guilty for even having it in the first place.

Climb Every Mountain

Core Transformation is a process, not an event. Each level we go to helps reveal the next one available. My experience with personal evolution is a little bit like climbing a large mountain. When I (Connirae) was nine years old I was allowed to go along on a climb up Pike's Peak. I was the youngest along, and ecstatic that I got to go. I still remember beginning the climb. I knew we couldn't see the very top, but was satisfied to climb toward the top that I could see. We all set out upward, toward the top of the first "hill." When we reached the top of that first hill, we felt exhilarated at our progress. Looking around we could now see the next, higher peak that was on the way to the top. Yet when we reached the top of that peak, there was still another and higher peak beyond that became visible. We "discovered" about eight peaks, all that led us toward the top of Pike's Peak.

As you arrive at each "peak" in yourself, give yourself full credit and appreciation for having reached that place, and notice how far you've come. It is arriving at one peak that allows the next one to become clearly visible. It is our inner progress that allows us to notice the next new step that is now possible for us. As far as we know, there isn't a "highest" peak on our inner journey.

Most of all, remember that this is a joyful, easy, uplifting process, designed to assist you in discovering your own light within what you thought was darkness.

—ABOUT THE AUTHORS—

Connirae Andreas

Connirae Andreas has gained international renown as an NLP trainer, with requests for appearances on all continents. Andreas is one of the most highly respected trainers and authors in the field of NLP today. She is a certified NLP Trainer through the Society of NLP; and the co-founder, trainer, and educational director of NLP Comprehensive, an organization specializing in international NLP training and product development.

Since 1978 Connirae has authored numerous articles, and through NLP Comprehensive, has produced over 75 video and audio tape products on NLP with her husband Steve Andreas. She has also co-authored several teaching manuals on NLP certification training.

Her other books, which have been translated into 12 languages, include *HEART OF THE MIND: Engaging Your Inner Power to Change with NLP* which is the definitive book on current NLP techniques, and *CHANGE YOUR MIND– And Keep the Change* (both co-authored with Steve Andreas).

Most recently Connirae has focused on teaching The Aligned Self seminar, which includes the Core Transformation Process, in several locations in the United States as well as in Europe.

Connirae lives in Boulder, Colorado with Steve Andreas and their three young sons.

Tamara Andreas

Tamara Andreas is a transformational seminar leader and trainer, and has a private practice. She has been specializing in the Aligned Self Seminars, which include the Core Transformation Process, giving workshops nation-wide.

When Tamara's sister, Connirae Andreas, first developed the Core Transformation Process, it was presented only at advanced NLP trainings. One of Tamara's contributions was to refine the teaching of the process and pioneer a new seminar format in which anyone could benefit from the process, regardless of their background. Because the demand for this seminar has increased across the country, this has become the primary focus of Tamara's work. She is now the primary Core Transformation seminar leader. Tamara's depth of skill combined with her sensitivity and compassion make her seminars an ideal place to experience the Core Transformation Process.

Tamara is the founder of NLP of Ohio, Inc., an NLP training organization. She offers NLP training at both the Practitioner and Master Practitioner levels. She has also offered presentations tailored for business groups, health professionals, and educators.

—RESOURCES—

To assist you in gaining full benefit from the Core Transformation Process in your own life, the following resources are available. Audiotapes include the richness of voice tone which can make it easier to experience the gentle impact of the process. Videotape goes a step farther toward offering a complete experience of being there. Of course trainings offer you the most complete support in using these processes in a deeply transforming way.

The following resources are all available through NLP Comprehensive.

CORE TRANSFORMATION RESOURCES

1. **Spirituality in NLP,** with Connirae Andreas
Connirae Andreas personally introduces you to the Core Transformation Process featured in this book. You will gain an understanding of how your limitations can be a doorway to spiritual experience. Includes a guided experience and demonstration of the Core State Exercise. (Audiotape, $12.95)

2. **The Core Transformation Process,** with Connirae Andreas
Includes a moving demonstration of the complete Core Transformation Process. (Videotape, 100 min., $95)

3. **Parental Timeline Reimprinting,** with Connirae Andreas
A demonstration of the Parental Timeline Reimprinting process with a woman whose father was an alchoholic. (Videotape, 43 min, $65)

ALIGNED SELF RESOURCES

The Core Transformation Process is drawn from the four-day personal development seminar called The Aligned Self Workshop.

1. **The Aligned Self,** with Connirae Andreas
An entire four-day workshop with Connirae Andreas, including a demonstration and discussion of the Core Transformation Process, Parental Timeline Reimprinting, and another breakthrough process called Aligning Perceptual Positions. (8-tape Audio set, $79.95)

2. **Aligning Perceptual Positions,** with Connirae Andreas
This process taps into the deep unconscious structure of our sense of ourselves in relationship with others. It can empower us in coming to a sense of wholeness and clarity within ourselves—what we want, think, and feel. At

the same time, it enables us to experience more compassion and connection with others. (Videotape, 77 min, $85)

CORE TRANSFORMATION AND ALIGNED SELF WORKSHOPS

In the workshop environment you have the loving guidance of the trainer and staff, plus the support of others attending the workshop, in unfolding your own inner essence. Call for dates and locations.

OTHER NLP RESOURCES

The field of NLP includes a vast array of processes that can assist us in our personal evolution, professional development, communication with others, and skill development. To introduce you to the field, we recommend the book *Heart of the Mind*, by Connirae and Steve Andreas.

NLP Comprehensive offers a wide range of audiotapes, videotapes and trainings that enable you to experience the benefits of this field.

TO ORDER AND FOR INFORMATION

NLP Comprehensive
4895 Riverbend Rd., Ste. A
Boulder, CO 80301-2640
1-800-233-1657

—BIBLIOGRAPHY—

Other Books on NLP

Andreas, Connirae and Andreas, Steve. *Heart of the Mind: Engaging Your Inner Power to Change with Neuro-Linguistic Programming.* Moab, Utah: Real People Press, 1989.

Andreas, Steve, and Andreas, Connirae. *Change Your Mind– And Keep the Change.* Moab, Utah: Real People Press, 1987.

Bandler, Richard, and Grinder, John. *Frogs into Princes: Neuro-Linguistic Programming.* Moab, Utah: Real People Press, 1979.

Bandler, Richard and Grinder, John. *Reframing: The Transformation of Meaning.* Moab, Utah: Real People Press, 1982.

Bandler, Richard. *Using Your Brain for a CHANGE.* Moab, Utah: Real People Press, 1987.

Cameron-Bandler, Leslie. *Solutions: Enhancing Love, Sex, and Relationships.* Moab, Utah: Real People Press, 1985.

Grinder, John, and Bandler, Richard. *Trance-Formations: The Structure of Hypnosis.* Moab, Utah: Real People Press, 1981.

Reference Bibliography

The following bibilograpy includes the books from which we drew quotes and other books that relate to our Core Selves.

Bly, Robert. *Iron John.* Reading, MA: Addison Wesley, 1990.

Carroll, Lewis. *Alice in Wonderland.* New York: Scholastic Inc., 1865.

Chopra, Deepak. *Unconditional Life.* New York: Bantam Books, 1991.

Covey, Stephen R. *The 7 Habits of Highly Effective People.* New York: Simon & Schuster, 1989.

Estes, Clarissa Pinkola, Ph.D. *Women Who Run With the Wolves.* New York: Ballantine Books, 1992.

Frankl, Viktor E. *Mans Search for Meaning.* New York: Simon & Schuster, 1959.

Gibran, Kahil. *The Prophet.* New York: Alfred A. Knopf, 1923.

Hanh, Thich Nhat. *Being Peace.* Berkeley, California: Parallax Press, 1987.

Hesse, Herman. *Damian.* P. London: Owen, 1958.

Houston, Jean. *The Search for the Beloved.* Los Angeles: Jeremy P. Tarcher, 1987.

Huang, Al. *Embrace Tiger, Return to Mountain.* Moab, Utah: Real People Press, 1973.

The I Ching: Or Book of Changes. The Richard Wilhem translation rendered into English by Cary F. Baynes. Princeton, New Jersey: Princeton University Press, 1950.

Jampolsky, Gerald G. *Love is the Answer: Creating Positive Relationships.* New York: Bantam Books, 1990.

Jampolsky, Gerald G. *Teach Only Love: The Seven Principles of Attitundinal Healing.* New York: Bantam Books, 1983.

John-Roger. *The Power Within You.* Mandeville Press, Los Angeles, 1976.

Jung, Carl. *Man and His Symbols.* New York: Bantam, 1964.

Jung, Carl. *Memories, Dreams and Reflections.* New York: Random-Vantage, 1989.

The Juniper Tree and Other Tales from Grimm. Selected by Lore Segal and Maurice Sendak, translated by Lore Segal, New York: Farrar, Straus and Giroux, 1973.

Juster, Norton. *The Phantom Tollbooth.* New York: Bullseye Books, Alfred A. Knopf, 1989.

May, Rollo. *The Art of Counseling.* New York: Gardner Press, 1989.
234

Millman, Dan. *Way of the Peaceful Warrior: A Book That Changes Lives.* Tiburon, California: HJ Kramer Inc., 1980.

Mitchell, Stephen, edited by. *The Enlightened Heart: An Anthology of Sacred Poetry.* New York: Harper & Row, 1989.

Mitchell, Stephen. *Tao Te Ching.* New York: Harper & Row, 1988.

Moyers, Bill. *Healing and the Mind.* New York: Doubleday, 1993.

Peace Pilgrim, *Peace Pilgrim: Her Life and Work In Her Own Words.* Santa Fe: An Ocean Tree Book, 1982.

Rinpoche, Sogyal. *The Tibetan Book of Living and Dying.* New York: Harper Collins, 1992.

Rumi, Jalauddin. *Open Secret: Versions of Rumi.* translated by John Moyne and Coleman Barks, Putney, Vermont: Threshold Books, 1984.

Rumi, Jalaluddin. *RUMI: We are Three.* translated by Coleman Barks, Athens, Georgia: Maypop Books, 1987.

Saint-Exupery, Antoine. *The Little Prince.* New York: Harcourt, Brace, Javanovich; 1943.

Satir, Virginia. *Making Contact.* Berkeley, California: Celestial Arts, 1976.

Satir, Virginia. *The New Peoplemaking.* Mountain View, California: Science and Behavior Books Inc., 1988.

Steinem, Gloria. *Revolution From Within.* Boston: Little, Brown and Co., 1992

Zukav, Gary. *The Seat of the Soul.* New York: Simon & Schuster, 1989.

—INDEX—